PSYCHOLOGY OF EMOTIONS, MOTIVATIONS AND ACTIONS

DEPRESSION IN THE ELDERLY

Psychology of Emotions, Motivations and Actions

Additional books in this series can be found on Nova's website under the Series tab.

Additional E-books in this series can be found on Nova's website under the E-books tab.

Aging Issues, Health and Financial Alternatives

Additional books in this series can be found on Nova's website under the Series tab.

Additional E-books in this series can be found on Nova's website under the E-books tab.

PSYCHOLOGY OF EMOTIONS, MOTIVATIONS AND ACTIONS

DEPRESSION IN THE ELDERLY

EMAAD ABDEL-RAHMAN
EDITOR

Nova Science Publishers, Inc.
New York

For permission to use material from this book please contact us:
Telephone 631-231-7269; Fax 631-231-8175
Web Site: http://www.novapublishers.com

Additional color graphics may be available in the e-book version of this book.

LIBRARY OF CONGRESS CATALOGING-IN-PUBLICATION DATA
Depression in the elderly / editor, Emaad Abdel-Rahman.
p. cm.
Includes index.
ISBN 978-1-61324-771-6 (hardcover)
1. Depression in old age. 2. Older people--Psychology. I. Abdel-Rahman, Emaad.
RC537.5.D476 2011
618.97'68527--dc23
2011048490

Published by Nova Science Publishers, Inc. † New York

CONTENTS

PREFACE

The world population is aging and the prevalence of age-related neurological diseases, such as stroke and neurodegenerative diseases, are continuously increasing. These diseases lead not only to impairment of motor function but also to the development of non-motor disorders, such as depression. In this book, the authors present current research in the study of depression in the elderly. Topics discussed include the links between geriatric depression and dementia; the physiological, psychological, social and environmental factors related to depression; depression in older adults with chronic kidney disease and physical activity and its anti-depressant effects for older people with depression.

Chapter 1 - Dementia and depression in later adult life share many pathophysiological, pathological, and clinical features. Late life depression defined as depression after age 65, is frequently associated with cognitive changes and memory impairments. On the other hand, dementia commonly presents with mood and behavioral changes particularly apathy and depressive symptoms. Neurodegeneration, impaired neuroprotection and increased inflammation are common pathological features of depression and dementia. Alterations in white matter (possibly due to vascular impairment), hippocampal atrophy, and abnormalities in hypothalamic-pituitary-adrenal axis and neurotransmitter disturbances are other common features of depression and dementia. This bidirectional relationship between dementia and depression in older adults makes the diagnosis of either condition challenging. Different types of dementias are associated with different degrees of depressive symptoms with different complexities. Depression itself, can lead to progression of reversible dementia to irreversible one. When diagnosing, several important points should be taken into account, including temporality of the symptoms (whether depression or dementia appeared first), using screening tools as well as excluding underlying medical illness such as thyroid disease and vitamin B12 deficiency. This review briefly discusses the clinical and pathophysiological similarities of and differences between these two conditions and explains the co-morbidity, together with diagnostic clues, in order to provide a better insight for understanding and differentiating these two disorders.

Chapter 2 - The mood disorders are characterized by alterations in the person´s general emotional state. Depression is one of the most common mood disorders experienced by elderly. Depression in elderly has different characteristics than in other life cycle stages. In the process of aging, physical changes can be confused with depressive symptoms. The physiological changes, psychological, social and environment factors are important for the development of depression. Likewise, depressive symptoms in old age have been associated with morbidity, physical dependence, cognitive impairment and dementia. The aim was to determine the prevalence of depression symptoms and its relationship with socio-demographic factors, cognitive function, co-morbidity and physical disabilities among elderly in a Mexican community setting.

The Inter-institutional Dementia Project in Jalisco (CONACYT 7994) was taken as the basis for this chapter. This is a cross-sectional study, multi-stage, random, and proportional with the participation of n=2,553 community-dwelling elders 60 and older. A battery of assessment was applied during an interview in which different areas were assessed: Depression (30-item GDS), cognitive function (MMSE), functional status (ADL, IADL), chronic medical conditions and vital risk factors (self-report). The questionnaire included also socio-demographic factors. Data obtained were validated and entered into a database. Crude Odds Ratio and confidence interval of 95% were calculated. Logistic regression models tested the relative contributions of demographic variables, diseases and impairments, and general conditions on depression.

It was found a prevalence of 30.9% depressive symptomatology. Mean age of participants was 71.6±8.7 years, mostly women (61.2%). Education level was low, mean was 3.6±3.8 years of education, illiterate 27.2%. 45.5% had no couple, widowed 32.3%, single 8.6%, and divorced 4.6%. Were mainly housewives (41.7%), and 79.2% not pensioners. Functional disability prevalence was 31.5% for IADL, 9.6% in ADL, and 14.3% had cognitive impairment. A mean of 1.5 for chronic diseases was reported. Depressive symptoms were associated in bivariate analysis with being female, cognitive impairment, ADL and IADL disability, co-morbidity, education and being married. Increased age was not related.

These results orient to the necessity of prevention and control of the depression in the primary care and to recognize it as a problem of public health. This study gives us the possibility not only to establish a diagnosis and treatment, but also to promote healthy lifestyles and prevention of depression in older people in order to remain active as long as possible and to improve their quality of life.

Chapter 3 - Older adults with chronic kidney disease (CKD) have a high incidence of clinical depression. This is of great importance as it is associated with increased morbidity and mortality, thereby adversely affecting these and other patient outcomes. Depression in older adults also negatively impacts functional status, quality of life and self-perception of health.

In this chapter, we review and synthesize recent evidence from the literature exploring the impact of depression in older adults with chronic kidney disease (CKD), especially the implications on physical and cognitive functioning, which are of great concern in the geriatric population. For the purposes of this review, CKD refers to predialysis patients with CKD stages 2 to 5, unless otherwise specified.

Optimal management of depressed older adults patients with CKD remains a challenge in the United States. Recent evidence on pharmacological management of depression including selection of drug therapies, non-pharmacological interventions such as psychotherapy, electroconvulsive therapy, physical activity and exercise that enhance the well being of these patients is also reviewed.

Chapter 4 - As individuals and as nations, we are growing older. The elderly, defined as those 65 years of age and above, are the fastest growing population group in America. According to the 2008 United States census bureau report, the number of elders grew from 29.6 million in 1990 to 36.8 million in 2008, representing a 20% incremental growth [1]. This aging of the population is mirrored by an increase in the number of patients with chronic kidney disease (CKD) [2]. Similar trends are noted in patients reaching end stage renal disease (ESRD); USRDS data indicate that the incident ESRD population is aging. In 1990, there were 21,479 incident ESRD patients aged 65 or older in the United States; this number steadily increased to 53,842 by 2006. In fact, older individuals comprise the most rapidly growing segment of the ESRD population in the wealthier countries [3]. In USA, the median age of incident dialysis patients is 64.4 years, and adjusted-incidence rate of ESRD in individuals older than 75 years has grown considerably when compared to subjects in the 20-44 or 45-64 age groups (11% vs. 2.4% vs. 6.1%, respectively) [4].

The course of CKD patients faces many challenges including medical and psychosocial challenges. While the medical factors arising as complications of CKD were vastly studied, we are now realizing the importance of the psychosocial factors associated with CKD. Hence, the impact of psychosocial factors on the outcome of CKD patients has been receiving more attention [5-8]. Depressive symptoms and depression are generally accepted to be the most common psychological problem encountered in CKD patients [9]. Depression is defined by the Diagnostic and Statistical Manual of Mental Disorders, 4th edition (DSM-IV), as having a loss of pleasure or interest for two weeks, accompanied by five or more psychological, somatic and behavioral symptoms [10]. Depression is one of the most common illnesses in the elderly. Under-recognition of depression in the elderly patients is a major concern, particularly given the evidence of its impact on morbidity and mortality.

Chapter 5 - Introduction: The world population is ageing and the prevalence of age-related neurological diseases, such as stroke and neurodegenerative diseases, continuously increases. These diseases lead not only to impairment of motor function but also to development of non-motor disorders, such as depression. Diagnosis of depression in the disorders that produce psychomotor impairment can be challenging and requires particular skills and experience to recognize and treat depression effectively. We investigated the prevalence of depression in patients with most common age-related neurological diseases and estimated the influence of depression on the health-related quality of life in these diseases.

Methods and patients: The prevalence of depression and its influence on the health-related quality of life was estimated in consecutively recruited patients with stroke or transient ischemic attacks (TIA) (n=151), Parkinson's disease (PD) (n=100) and Alzheimer dementia (AD) or vascular dementia (VD) (n= 98), which are the most prevalent neurological diseases of the elderly. Depression was diagnosed according to DSM-IV criteria and scored using the Beck Depression Inventory, the Geriatric Depression Scale and the Hospital Anxiety Depression Scale. The health-related quality of life (HrQoL) was evaluated using the EuroQol (EQ-5D and visual analogue scale). The neurological status was assessed by means of the validated severity scales: Barthel Index and modified Rankin Scale in patients with stroke/TIA, Unified Parkinson's disease Rating Scale (UPDRS) in patients with Parkinson's disease and Mini-Mental State Examination in patients with Alzheimer dementia or vascular dementia.

Results: The age was 72±11 (mean+/-SD) years in patients with stroke/TIA, 69±7 years in patients with Parkinson's disease and 77±8 years in patients with Alzheimer or vascular dementia. The prevalence of depression was 51% in stroke/TIA, 75% in Parkinson's disease and 86% in patients with Alzheimer or vascular dementia. In comparison to general population, HrQoL measured on the visual analogue scale was reduced by 23%, 35% and 54% in stroke/TIA, Parkinson's disease and patients with AD/VD, respectively. In the dimension "anxiety/depression" of the EQ-5D, 50% of patients with stroke/TIA, 86% of PD-patients and 81% of patients with AD/VD had moderate or severe problems. Depression showed significant association with reduced HrQoL in stroke/TIA, Parkinson's disease, Alzheimer and vascular dementia ($p<0.01$). Only 40% of patients with manifest depression received adequate antidepressant treatment.

Conclusions: The presence of age-related neurological diseases, such as cerebrovascular and neurodegenerative diseases, is associated with increased risk of depression in the elderly. Unfortunately, depression is often under-diagnosed in these patients being masked by motor impairment. Depression is a predictor of reduced HrQoL in elder individuals with neurological diseases. Therefore, they should be screened for presence of depressive symptoms and receive adequate antidepressant treatment.

Chapter 6 - Depression is not uncommon in the elderly. Psychotic depression, a major subtype of depression is more commonly seen in the elderly depressed patients than in younger patients with depression. Evidence indicates that psychotic depression in the elderly is associated with specific clinical, neurobiological and neuropsychological changes and has a worse prognosis than depression without psychosis in the elderly. In this chapter we review the epidemiology, clinical features, neurobiology, neuropsychology, assessment and treatments for this important psychiatric disorder in the elderly.

Chapter 7 - Depressive illness results in considerable functional disability and decreased quality of life. The prevalence of depression in older persons ranges from 5 to 30%. Older people often have depression concurrent with other illnesses, e.g., cardiovascular disease. Depression can also impact adversely on these disorders.

Current management of depression commonly involves drugs and psychotherapies, which whilst effective, have variable adherance rates. Non-pharmacological therapies offer potentially safer alternative management of depression in older people. Of the psychotherapies, cognitive behaviour therapy and reminiscence and life review have the best supporting evidence for older people. Few lifestyle change modalities have been sufficiently tested to recommend their use with older people. An exception is physical activity. Both endurance and resistance type physical activity has anti-depressant effects for older people with depression.

Older depressed people have much to gain from being physically active. Physical activity offers a therapy where negative events are minimal and benefits can accrue for both physical and mental health status. Physical activity may assist both in the prevention and management of depression in older people. As a health promotion intervention, it has the potential to reduce the risk of depression and to ameliorate co-morbid conditions. Using physical activity as an antidepressant can reduce the need for pharmacological intervention, minimizing iatrogenic and polypharmacy risk that is particularly prevalent for older people.

Chapter 8 - Severe, major depression is the most common differential diagnosis of dementia. Depression may be diagnosed before, concomitantly, or after the diagnosis of dementia. Generally, ~ 40% of people with dementia have coexistent depression. In most cases depression comes after some degree of cognitive decline and, mainly, functional dependence, in which case depression is said to be 'reactive' to the dementing process. However, depression might also come before dementia, suggesting it may be a prodrome of the dementia syndrome itself. Prevalence of depression seems to be highest during the mid stages of the dementing process. However, many dementia subtypes are intrinsically associated with (organic) depression, i.e., they probably share the same neuropathological processes that leads to both diseases. The coexistence of Vascular Dementia and Vascular Depression is the prototype in this last case, Depression, especially in its aphatic subtype, is more common in vascular dementia than in Alzheimer's Disease (AD). As AD progress through the Braak stages, it starts to involve not only cholinergic neurons, but also the serotoninergic and noradrenergic ones. This seems to be the case also for both Lewy-Body dementia (LBD) and Parkinson's dementia, where the initial cholinergic and dopaminergic deficits, respectively, evolves to compromise other neurotransmitter systems. Depression secondary to dementia may also be the consequence of limited functional independence, which often precedes the diagnosis of dementia. Partial functional dependence may rapidly evolve to full incapacity, further aggravating depression. In very late stages, however, regardless of the dementia subtype, depression is no longer a problem, since it needs some degree of cognitive function to be brought into consciousness. In the coexistence of depression and/or fluctuation of consciousness, visual hallucinations in LBD should not be mistaken for psychotic depression. In summary, depression often precedes and coexists with dementia. The peculiarities of this association are dementia-subtype–specific. In each case, the particularities of the dementia subtype should be taken in consideration in understanding and managing this common association.

In: Depression in the Elderly
Editor: Emaad Abdel-Rahman, pp. 1-25
ISBN 978-1-61324-771-6

Chapter 1

DEMENTIA AND GERIATRIC DEPRESSION: THE LINKS

Mahvash Shahidi*[1]*, Amirhossein Modabbernia*[2,3]*,
***Mohammad Mojtahed*[3] *and Ali Mojtahed*[3]**
[1]Department of Counseling, School of Psychology and
Training Sciences, Allameh Tabatabai University, Tehran, Iran
[2]Psychiatric research center, Roozbeh psychiatric hospital,
Tehran University of Medical Sciences, Tehran, Iran
[3]Deputy of research, Imam Khomeini hospital,
Tehran University of Medical Sciences, Tehran, Iran

ABSTRACT

Dementia and depression in later adult life share many pathophysiological, pathological, and clinical features. Late life depression defined as depression after age 65, is frequently associated with cognitive changes and memory impairments. On the other hand, dementia commonly presents with mood and behavioral changes particularly apathy and depressive symptoms. Neurodegeneration, impaired neuroprotection and increased inflammation are common pathological features of depression and dementia. Alterations in white matter (possibly due to vascular impairment), hippocampal atrophy, and abnormalities in hypothalamic-pituitary-adrenal axis and neurotransmitter disturbances are other common features of depression and dementia. This bidirectional relationship between dementia and depression in older adults makes the diagnosis of either condition challenging. Different types of dementias are associated with different degrees of depressive symptoms with different complexities. Depression itself, can lead to progression of reversible dementia to irreversible one. When diagnosing, several important points should be taken into account, including temporality of the symptoms (whether depression or dementia appeared first), using screening tools as well as excluding underlying medical illness such as thyroid disease and vitamin B12 deficiency. This review briefly discusses the clinical and pathophysiological similarities of and differences between these two conditions and explains the co-morbidity, together with diagnostic clues, in order to provide a better insight for understanding and differentiating these two disorders.

INTRODUCTION

Late life depression defined as depression after age 65 is an important problem of the elderly, with high burden [1-3]. Another important problem of this age is cognitive decline and dementia [4-9]. Apart from high prevalence of both conditions in the elderly, it seems that these two conditions share many pathophysiological and clinical features, and in addition they may contribute to the development and persistence of each other [10-23]. Forty percent of community-dwelling depressed subjects report memory disturbances, while the frequency is about 10-20% in normal adults [24]. Patients with dementia frequently suffer depressive symptoms which may complicate their diagnosis and treatment. Whether depression is a prodromal symptom of dementia, or a risk factor for subsequent development of dementia, have been addressed by many studies [16, 25-31]. Sometimes dementia and depression in the elderly may be indistinguishable for a clinician [7, 31-35]. This review will discuss the links between these two conditions and will address the similarities and differences regarding pathophysiology, symptomatology, and diagnosis.

EPIDEMIOLOGICAL LINKS BETWEEN DEPRESSION AND DEMENTIA

Depression and dementia frequently affect aged population and this seems to be a consistent finding across different nations. In a Greek study, on 536 patients aged 65 years and over, about 40% showed some evidences of cognitive impairment, while about one forth showed evidences of mild to moderate depression [4]. In a study on Lebanese nursing home residents, high prevalences of dementia (60%) and depression (58%) were observed [36]. These rates may differ with using different evaluation instruments. For example in a study by Schaub et al. [37], Geriatric Mental State (GMS) and DSM-III-R were used for diagnosis of depression and dementia in 516 subjects aged 70 or more. They found a 25.8% (16.5%), and 21.1% (13.8%) prevalence of depression and dementia using DSM-III-R (and GMS) respectively. In the Liverpool MRC-ALPHA Study on the 5222 subjects aged 65 or more and using the GMS-AGECAT package, about 5% and 10% of patients were diagnosed with dementia and depressive disorders respectively [2].

In 1989, Wragg and Jeste reviewed 30 studies about the prevalence of depressive symptoms in Alzheimer's disease (AD) [38]. They found 40% prevalence of depressive symptoms (mostly isolated symptoms) in these patients. Five years later, in a retrospective study of 478 patients with AD using DSM-III-R criteria, prevalence and incidence of major depression were reported to be less than 1.5%. The authors concluded that depression in dementia should be diagnosed by other criteria [39]. Starkstein and colleagues studied 670 patients with probable AD with the structured clinical interview (DSM-IV). Twenty-six percent of the patients had major depression, and 26% had minor depression [40]. Such discrepancy can be explained by differences in study design, sample selection, and using different instruments to diagnose depression in dementia. In addition some studies determined prevalence of symptoms while others investigated prevalence of depressive disorders. A recent study on prevalence of depression in early onset dementia (EOD) using Montgomery Asberg Depression rating scale (MADRS) found a 65.7% prevalence of depression in these patients [41]. In another study on 363 Swedish subjects aged 85 and over, prevalence of depression was 43% in people with dementia compared with 24% in people without dementia [42]. In a recent review of the English language literature, authors concluded that depression was significantly more prevalent in AD than normal population and that this higher prevalence could not be explained solely on the basis of psychological burden of the disease or disease self-awareness [43].

Prevalence of depression and its subtypes varies by dementia subtypes. Castilla-Puentes et al. [44] studied a large sample of 6440 demented patients aged 60 or older, among which there were 2947 patients with AD, 725 with vascular dementia (VaD), and 2768 with unspecified dementia. Forty-four percent of patients with VaD compared with 32% of patients with unspecified dementia and 18.5% of patients with AD had depressive disorder. Major depression, dysthymic disorder, and depression-not otherwise specified were more prevalent in VaD, whereas adjustment disorder with depressive symptoms was more prevalent in unspecified dementia. Using the Cornell Scale for Depression in Dementia (CSDD) in 306 patients with AD, Ownby et al. [45] found four categories of depression in these patients including asymptomatic, mild typical depression, severe typical depression, and sadness accompanied by prominent anxiety and irritability. In a population-based study of dementia, Newman and colleagues showed a prevalence of 3.2% for AD and 21.2% for VaD. Their study confirmed that depression is more prevalent in VaD compared to AD [46]. Parkinson's disease (PD) may also be accompanied by dementia. As shown in one study on more than 1500 patients with PD, one fourth of the patients had depression and this increased to about three fourth in patients with concomitant PD and dementia [47]. In a multicenter trial on PD and dementia, from the 538 patients 21% had a sub-threshold depression which was associated with female gender, younger age, and age at onset but not with PD severity, cognition or activities of daily living [48]. Horstmann et al. [49] studied 74 patients with frontotemproal dementia and 540 of their relatives and found that neither patients nor their family experienced depression more than general population. Some conditions like stressful life events may increase the risk of developing depression in dementia [50]. In addition, lack of exercise, less involvement in hobbies and taking choline esterase inhibitors are shown to be risk factors for depression in AD [51]. Dementia not only increases the risk of developing depression, but also increases the risk of hospitalization due to major depression [52].

The epidemiologic association of depression and dementia had been the subject of many studies. In a prospective study of 222 subjects, 124 of which had diagnosis of depression, 25% of subjects with depression and only 1% of subjects without depression had AD according to NINCDS-ADRDA criteria. Progression to dementia was associated with high scores on motivational symptoms of Beck depression inventory (BDI) which reflects high levels of apathy [53]. A Swedish twin study showed threefold increase in incident dementia in twins with prior history of depression compared with their non-depressed twins [16]. In a large study on more than 19103 individuals, depression increased the risk of progression to dementia with an OR of 2.38 [54]. Some studies showed the association of depression and dementia in a specific subgroup of the patients. For example, in two independent longitudinal studies held in Amsterdam, subjects with normal cognitive function were followed for detection of AD. Only depressed patients with higher level of education showed increased risk of progression to dementia [55]. In a study reporting two large prospective cohorts in China and the UK, subjects aged 65 years or more and without dementia were followed for up to four years. Incident dementia was related to the most severe depressive syndromes [18]. In a study by Fuhrer and colleagues, depressive symptoms increased the risk of subsequent dementia during an 8-year follow-up period. The risk for dementia was higher in depressed hypertensive men. Furthermore, elderly patients who developed VaD had more depressive symptoms than persons without dementia or with AD [56].

In patients with mild cognitive impairment (MCI) only persistence of depression to more than 2 years, or melancholic features might predict progression to AD [57]. Some studies have suggested that MCI that accompanies depression in the elderly might persist even after improvement of mood [58]. Similarly, in the individuals aged 80 or more, there is a tendency for progression to dementia in depressed subjects [59] . As shown in a prospective cohort study on more than 3500 patients with diabetes, depressed diabetic patients are also at increased risk of developing dementia compared with diabetic patients without depression [60]. In a review, Schweitzer et al. [61] discussed that patients with late onset depression (LOD) had more cognitive impairment as well as more deep white mater lesions. Jorm raised six hypotheses that might explain the association between depression and dementia (1) antidepressant treatments are a risk factor for dementia, (2) similar risk factors may be involved in causing both dementia and depression(3) depression may be a prodrome of dementia, (4) depression is an early reaction to cognitive decline, (5) depression lowers the threshold for presentation of dementia, and (6) depression causes dementia. A meta-analysis showed that depression was associated with an increased risk of incident dementia in both case-control studies and prospective cohort studies. So he concluded that hypotheses one and two had little support, and hypotheses three to six warranted further research [26]. Jorm updated the prior review in 2001 and concluded that most appropriate explanations for this association was that depression might be a prodrome of dementia, or brought forward the clinical picture of dementia, or damaged hippocampus by activating glucocorticoid cascade [25]. A meta-analysis by Mitchell on 37 cohort studies showed that severity of depression was a risk factor for progression of cognitive impairment, and none of the included studies had found an inverse association [24]. Whether or not patients with depression have increased risk of a specific type of dementia, remains inconclusive with some studies suggesting VaD, and others suggesting AD as the predominant type of dementia following depression [44, 46, 62-66].

Depression of AD (dAD) is a term defined by NIMH and includes depressive symptoms in patients with AD that may be resulted from a variety of causes, including neuro-degenerative course of AD, Vascular diseases, recurrence of major and minor depression, and emotional reaction to cognitive deficits [67].

Dementia is not only associated with depression in the demented patient, but also is related to depression in the caregiver. Waite et al. [68] showed that 43% of caregivers were depressed. Sansoni and colleagues showed a similar prevalence of 42% in Italian caregivers [69]. Professional caregivers might suffer less depression than non-professional ones [70]. The spouses of demented subjects are four times more likely to have depression than spouses of persons without dementia [71]. Several factors may contribute to the risk of depression in the caregivers of demented subjects. Gaugler et al. [72] studied caregiver burden in more than 1000 caregivers of demented subjects. Wives and daughters of demented patients were most prone to clinically persistent burden, whereas husbands were at more risk for being clinically depressed. Schulz and colleagues evaluated the relation between caregiver depression in 1222 demented subjects and their caregivers. Perceived patient suffering was an independent risk factor for caregiver depression and antidepressant use [73]. In a study with a large sample size, Covinsky et al. [74], investigated factors associated with depression in the caregivers of

5627 patients. Younger age, white and Hispanic ethnicity, lower level of education, dependence for activities of daily living, angry or aggressive behavior, low income, being wife, hours spent for caregiving, and functional dependence were associated with higher risk of depression. Other studies have demonstrated that being married, marital communication quality, perceived burden, having children and caring for a patient with comorbid dementia and cardiovascular diseases might be associated with increased risk of depression in the caregivers [75-77].

Diagnostic Links between Depression and Dementia

Diagnosis of depression in the elderly and differentiating it from dementia, and also diagnosing depression in a patient with a dementing disorder, both are challenging. Many studies tried to solve a part of this puzzle. Neurobehavioral disturbances affect up to 80% of patients with AD [78]; of these a so-called affective syndrome (including anxious, dysphoric, and irritable mood, and neurovegetative symptoms) affects about 25% to 30% of the patients [79]. Importantly, depression in the elderly may not present with typical symptoms of depression in younger adults, but rather presents with nonspecific feelings such as lack of pleasure (So-called masked depression). Kales et al. [80] showed that depression was correctly diagnosed in only 35% of the patients with concurrent depression and dementia and although these patients did not differ in baseline dementia stage or cognitive impairment as compared with demented patients (without depression), they were significantly more functionally impaired. Depression is a triad of mood disturbances, decreased vital sense and impaired self-attitude. In typical presentation, mood disturbances manifest as anhedonia and depressed mood, decreased vital sense manifests as neurovegetative symptoms, and impaired self-attitude shows itself by worthlessness, hopelessness and suicidal ideation. However in patients with AD, mood disturbances may present as recurrent, short lived mood alterations and are accompanied by agitated and anxious mood, and less prominently depressed mood. Lack of interest and social withdrawal are generally more obvious in depression of AD than typical depression. Vital sense impairment in depression of AD usually presents by inability to do activities of daily living, impaired sleep, and mild weight loss. Most common symptom in this category is apathy, which is manifested by loss of motivation. Impaired self-attitude including guilt feeling and suicidal ideation is less obvious in AD with depression. Low self-esteem and worthlessness are prominent symptoms in this category. Importantly, diurnal variation in symptoms, and presence of guilt feeling or suicidal thoughts (Although the latter is uncommon) are key clues to the diagnosis of depression in AD [79].

In a study on 580 patients in nursing home wards, point prevalence of depression was 19% and most prevalent symptoms were depressed mood, fatigue and irritability [81]. Such atypical presentation may become even more complex in the context of dementia. AD affects the reports on depressive symptoms. This may be resulted from neurodegenerative processes, altered perception of affective symptoms, or overlap of manifestations of AD and depression. In a study on AD patients with history of life-time major depression, these patients complained more about thought and concentration problems, and less about depressed mood or appetite problems than the non-demented subjects with lifetime history of major depression [82]. Kunik and coworkers studied 208 patients with dementia and showed that both psychotic symptoms and depression accounted for behavioral disturbances in these patients; depressive symptoms were associated with constant request for help, complaining and negativism [83]. In one study on 670 patients with probable AD, depression was associated with sad mood, more psychopathology, functional impairment, and social dysfunction [40]. Some researchers believe that psychiatric disturbances may occur in patients with impaired cognition who do not have essential symptoms of depression (dysphoria or depressed mood) [84]. One of the most common comorbidities of depression in AD is apathy. Apathy is seen in about 30% of patients with AD [67]. Most of these patients however, have comorbid depression. In a study on 150 patients with AD 7% had apathy, and 31% had depression. The authors concluded that apathy is a behavioral dimension independent of depression [85]. Both apathy and depression are predictors of functional and therapeutic outcomes of dementia irrespective of the cognitive status [86-88] and particular attention to their diagnosis and management is essential. Depression in AD is more likely to be associated with delusion, hallucination, poor cognitive function and pain [78, 88-90].

Distinguishing AD from depression with cognitive impairment is not a straightforward process. A prospective study on 111 non-demented subjects with cognitive impairment showed that higher age and severity of memory impairment may reliably distinguish preclinical AD from depression accompanied by cognitive impairment [91]. Although depressive symptoms may cause mild cognitive problems in preclinical AD, these effects may be masked by neurodegenerative course, when the diagnosis of dementia is established [92]. Vercelletto and colleagues found that although patients with mild to moderate dementia had no more depression than controls, they have negative symptoms more than controls which may be related to apathy and lack of motivation; in this regard apathy is also important in distinguishing depression from dementia [93]. On the other hand, LOD itself might also cause cognitive impairment [94]. Deficit in some cognitive tasks are in favor of progression of cognitive impairment to dementia. For example, eventhough cognitive decline may accompany depression, those patients with MCI that progresses to AD can be distinguished from depressed subjects by deficits in topographical recognition memory task [95]. In 1993, Lamberty reviewed neuropsychological tests used for differentiating depression from AD [96]. He concluded that distinguishing these two conditions is a straightforward process by using neuropsychological tests. However, more simple tests such as mini-mental state examination (MMSE) are not sensitive enough to detect the differences between depression with cognitive impairment and dementia. Patients with depression and concomitant cognitive deficits usually have problems on attentional and encoding tasks and have generally slowed mentation. Demented subjects usually suffer from more pervasive cognitive problems including deficits in memory, language, conceptual ability, etc. [96]. In one study from seven tasks of immediate and delayed free recall, randomized presentation, selective reminding, serial recall, and recognition after short and long delay, only recognition after short and long delay and delayed recall distinguished between depression and dementia [97]. In general, patients with AD have been shown to have poorer performance on tasks of language, praxis, gnosis [98], constructional praxis, word list recall [99], Clock tasks [100], nonverbal memory tasks [101], N-Back test, Wisconsin Card sorting test [102], Visuospatial associative learning task [103], cued recall (consisting of memory impairment screen-plus and visual association test) [104], odor identification test [105], Pocket smell test [106], and dual tasking [107] than patients with depression and cognitive impairment. Depressed patients may show poorer performance compared to AD patients in some tasks. For example in a study, although depressed patients and AD patients had similar scores on emotional stroop task, depressed patients had increased response time in color naming of words with negative emotions [108]. Another study which compared emotional memory for melodies between depression and AD found that, depressed patients cannot develop a positive affective bias of judgment for formerly heard melodies, while patients with AD can develop such bias [109].

ASSESSMENT INSTRUMENTS AND RATING SCALES

Assessment tools are of particular value in diagnosis and management of depression in patients with AD. Two important features of well-validated rating scales are providing cut-off scores for detection of depression and their ability to quantify the symptoms, thereby enabling the physician to assess the severity of depression [79]. Instruments which are used for rating depression in AD can be divided into four categories.

Self-rating scales including BDI and Geriatric depression scale (GDS) have been used to assess depression in patients with AD. For example Weintraub et al [110] showed that GDS had five dimensions in AD; using this scale, patients with AD reported more dissatisfaction with life and memory problems. Snow and colleagues showed that both demented and depressed individuals may underreport their depression compared with caregivers and physicians. Their findings showed that deficit awareness, rather than dementia itself may decrease the self-report accuracy [111]. In fact, patients with MMSE score of 15 or more may report their depression accurately and with acceptable sensitivity and specificity [112]. Generally spoken patients with mild to moderate dementia can provide reliable information regarding their depressive symptoms [87, 113].

Physician-rated instruments like MADRS and Hamilton depression rating scale (HDRS) are other options for the assessment of depression in patients with dementia. HDRS is primarily designed for evaluation of depressive symptoms in patients without cognitive problems and its use may not be appropriate in patients with dementia [79]. MADRS like CSDD is reliable in demented subjects with acceptable sensitivity and specificity [114, 115].

Specific rating instruments are developed to assess the depression in patients with dementia. CSDD is one of the most commonly studied and most commonly used of these instruments [116]. Muller-Thomsen and colleagues [114] evaluated detection of depression in AD using GDS, MADRS, CSDD, and Nurses Observation Scale for Geriatric Patients (NOSGER); in their study MADRS and CSDD provided most consistent findings with internal consistencies independent of AD stage. Both MADRS and CSDD correlated well with the Neuropsychiatric inventory (NPI) subscales and are capable of distinguishing depressed from non-depressed subjects with early onset dementia [115]. CSDD appears to be one of the best rating scales for detection of depression in dementia, even in other cultures [117-119]. CSDD has been also validated for use in patients with PD and dementia and in demented post-stroke patients [120, 121]. Different cut-off scores for CSDD have been reported; in a study using CSDD as a screening tool, a score of five or more showed a false negative rate of zero but was associated with high false positive results [118]. Generally, CSDD scores of 12 or more seems to warrant treatment for depression [79].

Generic neuropsychiatric instruments such as NPI [122] and Behavior pathology in Alzheimer's disease Rating Scale [123, 124] have related mood subscales that can be used to evaluate mood symptoms. However, most of these instruments are not sensitive for detection of depression in AD [79].

In a consensus statement on improving quality of mental health care in US nursing homes in 2003, some recommendations for screening and diagnosis of depression in patients with dementia were made. According to this statement, use of self-report scales such as GDS and BDI should be limited to demented patients with mild to moderate cognitive impairment, whereas Clinician-rated scales may be more suitable for patients with moderate to severe dementia [7].

In 2000, a workgroup developed criteria for diagnosing dAD [125-127]. These criteria were broader than the DSM-IV criteria for major depression. In 2005, an operationalized format was published which briefly contained following items:

Three or more of the following symptoms should have been present during the same two-week period and represent change from previous functioning: at least one of the symptoms should be either depressed mood or decreased interest and pleasure.

1) Clinically significant depressed mood
2) Decreased positive affect or pleasure in response to social contacts and usual activities
3) Social isolation or withdrawal
4) Disruption in appetite
5) Disruption in sleep
6) Psychomotor agitation or retardation
7) Irritability
8) Fatigue or loss of energy
9) Feeling hopelessness, worthlessness or excessive or inappropriate guilt
10) Recurrent thought of death, suicidal intention, plan or attempt.

In addition DSM-IV-TR criteria for AD should be met, the symptoms should cause significant distress or disruption of functioning, and should not occur exclusively during the course of delirium, and should be unrelated to drug abuse, medication, and other psychiatric disorders or medical conditions [128].

Neurobiological Links between Depression and Dementia

In addition to epidemiological and clinical similarities between depression and dementia, these two conditions share many neurobiological processes, which have been investigated extensively using neuroimaging, genetic, and biochemical studies.

Neuroimaging Studies

Neuroimaging studies have used several modalities including computed tomography (CT scan), Magnetic resonance imaging (MRI), Positron emission tomography (PET), and Single photon emission computed tomography (SPECT) to investigate structural or metabolic alterations in patients with dementia and/ or depression. Ventricular enlargement is one of the most consistent neuroimaging findings in dementia [61]. A meta-analysis of studies assessing ventricular enlargement in depressive disorders showed similar finding in depressed subjects [129]. Some studies showed that cortical atrophy and ventricular enlargement in LOD are similar to that of dementia, and are different from that of EOD (defined as depression before age of 60) [130]. Cortical thinning might be associated with increased risk of dementia in patients with depression [131]. Several studies have reported temporal lobe atrophy in AD, whereas studies in patients with LOD, have reached contradictory results. However in a study, Greenwald and colleagues showed correlation of medial temporal atrophy with cognitive impairment in patients with LOD [132]. Steffens et al. [133] showed that small left hippocampal volume might be a marker for dementia in depressed subjects who had not yet met the criteria for a clinical dementia. Medial temporal lobe thickness may be a good discriminatory factor between AD, and dementias of other types or psychiatric conditions [134]. In several MRI studies, deep white mater hyperintensities (DWMH) have been associated with depression and periventricular hyperintensities (PVH) have been associated with AD. DWMH correlates with cognitive impairment in depressed subjects and may herald progression to VaD [61]. A study on old depressed patients showed that change in white matter hyperintensity volume was associated with incident dementia, especially non-AD dementias. The authors also found a trend for association of change in subcortical gray matter with development of dementia [135]. In a recent study, it was shown that larger volumes of white matter hyperinetnsities in the parietal lobe might be associated with depression in demented subjects [136].

Functional neuroimaging (including PET and SPECT) have increased our knowledge of the ongoing processes in the brain of patients with dementia and depression. With the help of functional neuroimaging, abnormalities of the serotoninergic system have found to be of great importance in both depression and dementia. The hypothesis that serotonin (5HT) might be a link between dementia and depression, has been tested in some studies. Higher levels of cortical 5HT1A receptors, have been found in depressed patients with dementia with Levy body or PD [137]. Meltzer reviewed studies on the serotoninergic system in both depression and dementia and concluded that dysfunction of serotoninergic system existed in both conditions, but he also stated that effects of many factors such as age, gender, medications, etc. required more clarification [138].

Disturbances in regional blood flow and metabolism of several parts of the brain have been shown in neuroimaging studies of dementia and depression. In a study Hanada and colleagues showed that, regional blood flow in lateral parietal and temporal, bilateral precuneus, and bilateral posterior cingulate gyrus significantly decreased in AD patients compared with patients with major depression. Regional blood flow of lateral frontal, bilateral medial frontal, and left thalamus were significantly lower in patients with major depression compared with patients with AD [139]. Authors concluded that perfusion SPECT was a promising tool for distinguishing AD from major depressive disorder. Ebmeier and colleagues studied regional blood flow and white matter intensities in patients with dementia and patients with depression using perfusion SPECT and MRI. Patients with dementia showed reduced perfusion mostly in left parietotemporal cortex. Interestingly, patients with LOD showed perfusion values intermediate between that of patients with EOD and patients with dementia. No difference in white matter intensity was found between patients. No difference was found in temporal width between EOD and LOD, but significant difference was observed between patients with dementia and depressed patients. Decrease in perfusion was related to PVH and scores of MMSE were correlated with white matter hyperintensities in depressed patients and temporal perfusion in patients with dementia [140, 141].

Following a systematic review on the role of dorsal raphe nucleus and 5HT in AD and depression, Michelsen and colleagues hypothesized a link between disturbances in regional blood flow and changes of serotoninergic system in patients with AD which might be responsible for increased risk of depression in these patients [142]. Many cerebral blood vessels are surrounded by serotoninergic fibers and 5HT can cause vasoconstriction [143]. In AD, loss of serotoninergic neurons may occur due to damage to dorsal raphe nucleus and this may cause disturbances in regional blood flow. Disturbed regional blood flow is associated with depression [144]; in fact antidepressant treatment can normalize blood flow in some regions of the brain of depressed subjects [144, 145].

Other modalities like magnetoencephalography (MEG) or FDG-PET have been used to evaluate AD and depression. Using MEG, Maetsu et al. [146] showed reduced activity in the temporal lobe of the patients with AD compared to both depressed patients and healthy control subjects. Using FDG-PET, Lee and colleagues found that frontal lobe dysfunction (mainly right frontal gyrus) in MCI might cause depressive symptoms [147]. As mentioned above, apathy and depression are independent syndromes with distinct constructs; at the biological level, it was shown that patients with apathy had significant hypometabolism in left orbitofrontal areas compared to healthy controls whereas depressed patients had hypometabolism in dorsolateral prefrontal areas [148].

Biochemical and Pathological Studies

Studies on several neurotransmitters, neurotrophic factors, inflammatory and endocrine pathways have increased our knowledge of pathophysiological mechanisms of dementia and depression.

Studies of neurotransmitters have mainly focused on 5HT. Reduction of 5HT receptor binding sites in frontal and temporal regions, amygdala, dorsal raphe nucleus, and hippocampus has been reported in both depression and AD [149-160]. While 5-HT1A binding in the hippocampus is related to cognitive decline [161, 162], 5-HT2 binding in the cortical areas is related to the formation of neurofibrillary tangles [156]. Interestingly, Serotonin through its 5HT4 receptor, can prevent formation of neurotoxic Aβ [163, 164]. In this line, antidepressants can inhibit Aβ production [165].

Depression and dementia may show similar disturbances in inflammatory pathways [10, 166]. It is proposed that the progression to dementia in depressed subjects could result from the activation inflammatory cells in brain and blood and secretion of pro-inflammatory cytokines [167]. Production of IL-1β, IL-6, TNF-α, and IL-12 seems to be increased in both AD and depression [10, 168-171]. Leonard et al. 172, 173] proposed that inflammatory changes might result in apoptosis and decrease in synthesis of neurotrophic factors and kyneurenic acid, leading to neuronal destruction which may predispose patients with chronic depression to dementia.

Disturbances in the hypothalamic-pituitary-adrenal (HPA) axis have been shown in dementia and depression [11, 174-176]. Studies have shown that both depressed and demented patients had higher cortisol values and impaired negative feedback of glucocorticoids on the HPA axis [177-181]. Decrease in cognitive function, reduced hippocampal neurogenesis, retraction of hippocampal dendrites, susceptibility to neuronal toxins (such as Aβ), and increased hippocampal apoptosis are all associated with elevated glucocorticoids levels [180, 182-189]. A glucocorticoid antagonist (Mifepristone) has been shown to improve the symptoms of both AD and depression [185, 186]. Disturbances in 5HT together with high cortisol levels may contribute to neuronal damage in both depression and dementia, and permit formation of neurofibrillary tangles [11].

Neurotrophic factors play a key role both in depression and dementia. Disturbances in brain-derived neurotrophic factor (BDNF), nerve growth factor (NGF), transforming growth factor beta (TGFβ), and vascular endothelial growth factor (VEGF) have been shown in serum and cerebrospinal fluid (CSF) of animal models and human subjects with dementia and depression [185, 190-197]. Interestingly, pharmacological treatments such as antidepressant treatments, mood stabilizers, statins, and aspirin may exert their effect on depression and dementia through changes in these growth factors [185, 198, 199]. Tsai hypothesized that the link between depression and AD, might be explained by disturbances in BDNF [198]. In this line, Borroni et al. [200, 201] showed that BDNF gene variations could increase the risk of AD-related depression.In addition, reduced levels of NGF and BDNF have been shown in AD patients with history of major depression compared with patients with AD and without such history [202]. Interactions between BDNF, serotoninergic system, neuronal inflammation, and HPA might be important in causing neurodegeneration, cognitive, and mood problems and subsequent dementia and depression [10, 11, 185, 203, 204].

Genetic Studies

Most genetic studies have focused on deviation in serotoninergic system, neurotrophic factors, Apolipoprotein E gene (APOE), and inflammatory pathways. In a study on 158 patients with AD, Holmes and coworkers found significant association between 5HT receptor variation (namely 5HT2A, and 5HT2C) and depression in these patients [205]. In another study Liu and colleagues, found no association between C267T polymorphism of 5HT6 receptor and depression in AD [206]. Another genetic component which might be related to both AD and depression is 5HT transporter-linked polymorphic region (5HTTLPR) [11]. 5HTTLPR polymorphism is associated with reduced hippocampal volumes, cognitive decline, depressive states and increased risk of developing AD [207-216].

BDNF gene polymorphism is associated with impaired cognitive and hippocampal function, and depression [217-220]. A well-studied polymorphism of BDNF gene (Val66Met) seems to be associated with both mood and memory disturbances and might be responsible for depression in patients with AD [200, 201].

Kim et al. [221] followed 518 old subjects over 2.5 years to determine the rate of dementia and showed synergistic interaction of APOE ε4 genotype and depression on incident dementia. Geda and colleagues obtained similar results in a study on 850 cognitively normal adults [222]. Delano –Wood and colleagues, tested APOE ε4 genotype in 323 patients with AD and showed that women with this genotype were four times more depressed than women without this genotype [223]. However, these results were not replicated in a recent study on 264 patients with AD and with or without depression [200]. The hypothesis that APOE ε4 genotype might be associated with incident dementia was not proved in a study on

161 old depressed subjects [135]. Regarding inflammatory mechanisms, genetic studies showed increased expression of pro-inflammatory cytokines in human and animal studies of depression and dementia [10, 167, 185, 224-228].

CONCLUSION

Dementia and depression seems to share many epidemiological, clinical and pathophysiological features. Depression (particularly LOD) may increase the risk of incident dementia. On the other hand, both demented patients and their caregivers are more likely to get depressed. Pathophysiologically, depression and dementia are associated with disturbances in serotoninergic transmission, altered neurotrophic factors levels, increased pro-inflammatory cytokines, structural brain changes (particularly temporal lobe and hippocampus), and changes in HPA axis. Although distinguishing between dementia and depression, and diagnosing depression in patients with dementia are challenging, criteria for diagnosing dAD, neuropsychological tests, rating scales (such as CSDD), and neuroimaging studies may help in differentiating these two conditions.

REFERENCES

[1] Alexopoulos GS, Borson S, Cuthbert BN, *et al.* Assessment of late life depression. *Biological Psychiatry*. 2002 52: 164-174.

[2] Saunders PA, Copeland JR, Dewey ME, *et al.* The prevalence of dementia, depression and neurosis in later life: the Liverpool MRC-ALPHA Study. *Int. J. Epidemiol.* 1993 22: 838-847.

[3] Thomas AJ, O'Brien JT. Mood disorders in the elderly. *Psychiatry*. 2006 5: 127-130.

[4] Argyriadou S, Melissopoulou H, Krania E, Karagiannidou A, Vlachonicolis I, Lionis C. Dementia and depression: two frequent disorders of the aged in primary health care in Greece. *Fam. Pract.* 2001 18: 87-91.

[5] Komahashi T, Ohmori K, Nakano T, *et al.* Epidemiological survey of dementia and depression among the aged living in the community in Japan. *Jpn J. Psychiatry Neurol.* 1994 48: 517-526.

[6] Reisberg B, Prichep L, Mosconi L, *et al.* The pre-mild cognitive impairment, subjective cognitive impairment stage of Alzheimer's disease. *Alzheimers Dement.* 2008 4: S98-S108.

[7] Consensus statement on improving the quality of mental health care in U.S. nursing homes: management of depression and behavioral symptoms associated with dementia. *J. Am. Geriatr. Soc.* 2003 51: 1287-1298.

[8] Esser SR, Vitaliano PP. Depression, dementia, and social supports. *Int. J. Aging Hum. Dev.* 1988 26: 289-301.

[9] Johnson JC. Depression and dementia in the elderly: a primary care perspective. *Compr. Ther.* 1996 22: 280-285.

[10] Wuwongse S, Chang RC, Law AC. The putative neurodegenerative links between depression and Alzheimer's disease. *Prog. Neurobiol.* 2010 91: 362-375.

[11] Sierksma AS, van den Hove DL, Steinbusch HW, Prickaerts J. Major depression, cognitive dysfunction and Alzheimer's disease: is there a link? *Eur. J. Pharmacol.* 2010 626: 72-82.

[12] Hugo FN, Hilgert JB, Corso S, *et al.* Association of chronic stress, depression symptoms and cortisol with low saliva flow in a sample of south-Brazilians aged 50 years and older. *Gerodontology*. 2008 25: 18-25.

[13] Boland RJ. Depression in Alzheimer's disease and other dementias. *Curr. Psychiatry Rep.* 2000 2: 427-433.

[14] Zalsman G, Aizenberg D, Sigler M, Nahshony E, Karp L, Weizman A. Increased risk for dementia in elderly psychiatric inpatients with late-onset major depression. *J. Nerv. Ment. Dis.* 2000 188: 242-243.

[15] Butters MA, Young JB, Lopez O, *et al.* Pathways linking late-life depression to persistent cognitive impairment and dementia. *Dialogues Clin. Neurosci.* 2008 10: 345-357.

[16] Brommelhoff JA, Gatz M, Johansson B, McArdle JJ, Fratiglioni L, Pedersen NL. Depression as a risk factor or prodromal feature for dementia? Findings in a population-based sample of Swedish twins. *Psychol. Aging*. 2009 24: 373-384.

[17] Chen R, Hu Z, Wei L, Qin X, Copeland JR. Is the relationship between syndromes of depression and dementia temporal? The MRC-ALPHA and Hefei-China studies. *Psychol. Med.* 2009 39: 425-430.

[18] Chen R, Hu Z, Wei L, Qin X, McCracken C, Copeland JR. Severity of depression and risk for subsequent dementia: cohort studies in China and the UK. *Br. J. Psychiatry*. 2008 193: 373-377.

[19] Christensen H, Griffiths K, Mackinnon A, Jacomb P. A quantitative review of cognitive deficits in depression and Alzheimer-type dementia. *J. Int. Neuropsychol. Soc.* 1997 3: 631-651.

[20] Dierckx E, Engelborghs S, De Raedt R, *et al.* Differentiation between dementia and depression among older persons: can the difference between actual and premorbid intelligence be useful? *J. Geriatr. Psychiatry Neurol.* 2008 21: 242-249.

[21] Edwards N. Differentiating the three D's: delirium, dementia, and depression. *Medsurg. Nurs.* 2003 12: 347-357; quiz 358.

[22] Have G, Kolbeinsson H, Petursson H. Dementia and depression in old age: psychophysiological aspects. *Acta Psychiatr. Scand.* 1991 83: 329-333.

[23] Meyers BS. Depression and dementia: comorbidities, identification, and treatment. *J. Geriatr. Psychiatry Neurol.* 1998 11: 201-205.

[24] Mitchell AJ. Depression as a risk factor for later dementia: a robust relationship? *Age Ageing*. 2005 34: 207-209.

[25] Jorm AF. History of depression as a risk factor for dementia: an updated review. *Aust. N. Z. J. Psychiatry*. 2001 35: 776-781.

[26] Jorm AF. Is depression a risk factor for dementia or cognitive decline? A review. *Gerontology*. 2000 46: 219-227.

[27] Potter GG, Steffens DC. Contribution of depression to cognitive impairment and dementia in older adults. *Neurologist*. 2007 13: 105-117.

[28] Raskind MA. The clinical interface of depression and dementia. *J. Clin. Psychiatry*. 1998 59 Suppl 10: 9-12.

[29] Steffens DC, Plassman BL, Helms MJ, Welsh-Bohmer KA, Saunders AM, Breitner JC. A twin study of late-onset depression and apolipoprotein E epsilon 4 as risk factors for Alzheimer's disease. *Biol. Psychiatry*. 1997 41: 851-856.

[30] Tsuno N, Homma A. What is the association between depression and Alzheimer's disease? *Expert Rev. Neurother*. 2009 9: 1667-1676.

[31] Wright SL, Persad C. Distinguishing between depression and dementia in older persons: neuropsychological and neuropathological correlates. *J. Geriatr. Psychiatry Neurol*. 2007 20: 189-198.

[32] Addonizio G, Shamoian CA. Depression, dementia, and pseudodementia. *Compr. Ther.* 1987 13: 8-11.

[33] Chaves ML, Izquierdo I. Differential diagnosis between dementia and depression: a study of efficiency increment. *Acta Neurol. Scand.* 1992 85: 378-382.

[34] Cummings JL. Dementia and depression: an evolving enigma. *J. Neuropsychiatry Clin. Neurosci*. 1989 1: 236-242.

[35] Yesavage J. Differential diagnosis between depression and dementia. *Am. J. Med.* 1993 94: 23S-28S.

[36] Chahine LM, Bijlsma A, Hospers AP, Chemali Z. Dementia and depression among nursing home residents in Lebanon: a pilot study. *Int. J. Geriatr Psychiatry*. 2007 22: 283-285.

[37] Schaub RT, Linden M, Copeland JR. A comparison of GMS-A/AGECAT, DSM-III-R for dementia and depression, including subthreshold depression (SD)--results from the Berlin Aging Study (BASE). *Int. J. Geriatr Psychiatry*. 2003 18: 109-117.

[38] Wragg RE, Jeste DV. Overview of depression and psychosis in Alzheimer's disease. *Am. J. Psychiatry*. 1989 146: 577-587.

[39] Weiner MF, Edland SD, Luszczynska H. Prevalence and incidence of major depression in Alzheimer's disease. *Am. J. Psychiatry*. 1994 151: 1006-1009.

[40] Starkstein SE, Jorge R, Mizrahi R, Robinson RG. The construct of minor and major depression in Alzheimer's disease. *Am. J. Psychiatry*. 2005 162: 2086-2093.

[41] Rosness TA, Barca ML, Engedal K. Occurrence of depression and its correlates in early onset dementia patients. *Int. J. Geriatr. Psychiatry*. 2010 25: 704-711.

[42] Bergdahl E, Allard P, Gustafson Y. Depression among the very old with dementia. *Int. Psychogeriatr*. 2010: 1-8.

[43] Even C, Weintraub D. Case for and against specificity of depression in Alzheimer's disease. *Psychiatry Clin. Neurosci*. 2010 64: 358-366.

[44] Castilla-Puentes RC, Habeych ME. Subtypes of depression among patients with Alzheimer's disease and other dementias. *Alzheimers Dement*. 2010 6: 63-69.

[45] Ownby RL, Acevedo A, Harwood DG, Barker WW, Duara R. Patterns of depression in Spanish- and English-speaking patients with Alzheimer's disease. *J. Geriatr Psychiatry Neurol*. 2008 21: 47-55.

[46] Newman SC. The prevalence of depression in Alzheimer's disease and vascular dementia in a population sample. *J. Affect Disord*. 1999 52: 169-176.

[47] Riedel O, Klotsche J, Spottke A, *et al.* Frequency of dementia, depression, and other neuropsychiatric symptoms in 1,449 outpatients with Parkinson's disease. *J. Neurol.* 2010 257: 1073-1082.

[48] Ehrt U, Bronnick K, De Deyn PP, *et al.* Subthreshold depression in patients with Parkinson's disease and dementia--clinical and demographic correlates. *Int. J. Geriatr Psychiatry*. 2007 22: 980-985.
[49] Horstmann V, Grasbeck A. Occurrence of depression in families with frontotemporal dementia: a family history study. *Neuroepidemiology*. 2009 33: 124-130.
[50] Waite A, Bebbington P, Skelton-Robinson M, Orrell M. Life events, depression and social support in dementia. *Br. J. Clin. Psychol.* 2004 43: 313-324.
[51] Regan C, Katona C, Walker Z, Livingston G. Relationship of exercise and other risk factors to depression of Alzheimer's disease: the LASER-AD study. *Int. J. Geriatr Psychiatry*. 2005 20: 261-268.
[52] Nilsson FM, Kessing LV, Sorensen TM, Andersen PK, Bolwig TG. Enduring increased risk of developing depression and mania in patients with dementia. *J. Neurol. Neurosurg. Psychiatry*. 2002 73: 40-44.
[53] Bartolini M, Coccia M, Luzzi S, Provinciali L, Ceravolo MG. Motivational symptoms of depression mask preclinical Alzheimer's disease in elderly subjects. *Dement Geriatr. Cogn. Disord.* 2005 19: 31-36.
[54] Buntinx F, Kester A, Bergers J, Knottnerus JA. Is depression in elderly people followed by dementia? A retrospective cohort study based in general practice. *Age Ageing*. 1996 25: 231-233.
[55] Geerlings MI, Schoevers RA, Beekman AT, *et al.* Depression and risk of cognitive decline and Alzheimer's disease. Results of two prospective community-based studies in The Netherlands. *Br. J. Psychiatry*. 2000 176: 568-575.
[56] Fuhrer R, Dufouil C, Dartigues JF. Exploring sex differences in the relationship between depressive symptoms and dementia incidence: prospective results from the PAQUID Study. *J. Am. Geriatr. Soc.* 2003 51: 1055-1063.
[57] Houde M, Bergman H, Whitehead V, Chertkow H. A predictive depression pattern in mild cognitive impairment. *Int. J. Geriatr. Psychiatry*. 2008 23: 1028-1033.
[58] Lee JS, Potter GG, Wagner HR, Welsh-Bohmer KA, Steffens DC. Persistent mild cognitive impairment in geriatric depression. *Int Psychogeriatr.* 2007 19: 125-135.
[59] Peters R, Pinto E, Beckett N, *et al.* Association of depression with subsequent mortality, cardiovascular morbidity and incident dementia in people aged 80 and over and suffering from hypertension. Data from the Hypertension in the Very Elderly Trial (HYVET). *Age Ageing*. 2010 39: 439-445.
[60] Katon WJ, Lin EH, Williams LH, *et al.* Comorbid depression is associated with an increased risk of dementia diagnosis in patients with diabetes: a prospective cohort study. *J. Gen. Intern. Med.* 2010 25: 423-429.
[61] Schweitzer I, Tuckwell V, O'Brien J, Ames D. Is late onset depression a prodrome to dementia? *Int. J. Geriatr Psychiatry*. 2002 17: 997-1005.
[62] Ballard C, Bannister C, Solis M, Oyebode F, Wilcock G. The prevalence, associations and symptoms of depression amongst dementia sufferers. *J. Affect Disord.* 1996 36: 135-144.
[63] Ballard C, Neill D, O'Brien J, McKeith IG, Ince P, Perry R. Anxiety, depression and psychosis in vascular dementia: prevalence and associations. *J. Affect Disord.* 2000 59: 97-106.
[64] Brodaty H, Luscombe G. Depression in persons with dementia. *Int. Psychogeriatr.* 1996 8: 609-622.

[65] Copeland JR, Davidson IA, Dewey ME, *et al.* Alzheimer's disease, other dementias, depression and pseudodementia: prevalence, incidence and three-year outcome in Liverpool. *Br. J. Psychiatry*. 1992 161: 230-239.

[66] Linka E, Bartko G, Agardi T, Kemeny K. Dementia and depression in elderly medical inpatients. *Int. Psychogeriatr*. 2000 12: 67-75.

[67] Lee HB, Lyketsos CG. Depression in Alzheimer's disease: heterogeneity and related issues. *Biol. Psychiatry*. 2003 54: 353-362.

[68] Waite A, Bebbington P, Skelton-Robinson M, Orrell M. Social factors and depression in carers of people with dementia. *Int. J. Geriatr Psychiatry*. 2004 19: 582-587.

[69] Sansoni J, Vellone E, Piras G. Anxiety and depression in community-dwelling, Italian Alzheimer's disease caregivers. *Int. J. Nurs Pract*. 2004 10: 93-100.

[70] Margallo-Lana M, Reichelt K, Hayes P, *et al.* Longitudinal comparison of depression, coping, and turnover among NHS and private sector staff caring for people with dementia. *BMJ*. 2001 322: 769-770.

[71] Joling KJ, van Hout HP, Schellevis FG, *et al.* Incidence of depression and anxiety in the spouses of patients with dementia: a naturalistic cohort study of recorded morbidity with a 6-year follow-up. *Am. J. Geriatr Psychiatry*. 2010 18: 146-153.

[72] Gaugler JE, Mittelman MS, Hepburn K, Newcomer R. Clinically significant changes in burden and depression among dementia caregivers following nursing home admission. *BMC Med*. 2010 8: 85.

[73] Schulz R, McGinnis KA, Zhang S, *et al.* Dementia patient suffering and caregiver depression. *Alzheimer Dis. Assoc. Disord*. 2008 22: 170-176.

[74] Covinsky KE, Newcomer R, Fox P, *et al.* Patient and caregiver characteristics associated with depression in caregivers of patients with dementia. *J. Gen. Intern. Med*. 2003 18: 1006-1014.

[75] Braun M, Mura K, Peter-Wight M, Hornung R, Scholz U. Toward a better understanding of psychological well-being in dementia caregivers: the link between marital communication and depression. *Fam. Process*. 2010 49: 185-203.

[76] Rosness TA, Mjorud M, Engedal K. Quality of life and depression in carers of patients with early onset dementia. *Aging Ment Health*. 2011: 1-8.

[77] McConaghy R, Caltabiano ML. Caring for a person with dementia: exploring relationships between perceived burden, depression, coping and well-being. *Nurs. Health Sci*. 2005 7: 81-91.

[78] Lyketsos CG, Olin J. Depression in Alzheimer's disease: overview and treatment. *Biol. Psychiatry*. 2002 52: 243-252.

[79] Lyketsos CG, Lee HB. Diagnosis and treatment of depression in Alzheimer's disease. A practical update for the clinician. *Dement Geriatr. Cogn. Disord*. 2004 17: 55-64.

[80] Kales HC, Chen P, Blow FC, Welsh DE, Mellow AM. Rates of clinical depression diagnosis, functional impairment, and nursing home placement in coexisting dementia and depression. *Am. J. Geriatr. Psychiatry*. 2005 13: 441-449.

[81] Verkaik R, Francke AL, van Meijel B, Ribbe MW, Bensing JM. Comorbid depression in dementia on psychogeriatric nursing home wards: which symptoms are prominent? *Am. J. Geriatr. Psychiatry*. 2009 17: 565-573.

[82] Heun R, Kockler M, Ptok U. Lifetime symptoms of depression in Alzheimer's disease. *Eur. Psychiatry*. 2003 18: 63-69.

[83] Kunik ME, Snow-Turek AL, Iqbal N, *et al.* Contribution of psychosis and depression to behavioral disturbances in geropsychiatric inpatients with dementia. *J. Gerontol. A. Biol. Sci. Med. Sci.* 1999 54: M157-161.
[84] Potvin O, Hudon C, Grenier S, Preville M. Non-essential symptoms of depression and cognitive impairment no dementia (CIND) in community-dwelling elders without dysphoria or anhedonia. *Int. Psychogeriatr.* 2010 22: 1344-1352.
[85] Starkstein SE, Ingram L, Garau ML, Mizrahi R. On the overlap between apathy and depression in dementia. *J. Neurol. Neurosurg. Psychiatry.* 2005 76: 1070-1074.
[86] Benoit M, Andrieu S, Lechowski L, Gillette-Guyonnet S, Robert PH, Vellas B. Apathy and depression in Alzheimer's disease are associated with functional deficit and psychotropic prescription. *Int. J. Geriatr. Psychiatry.* 2008 23: 409-414.
[87] Espiritu DA, Rashid H, Mast BT, Fitzgerald J, Steinberg J, Lichtenberg PA. Depression, cognitive impairment and function in Alzheimer's disease. *Int. J. Geriatr. Psychiatry.* 2001 16: 1098-1103.
[88] Bartels SJ, Horn SD, Smout RJ, *et al.* Agitation and depression in frail nursing home elderly patients with dementia: treatment characteristics and service use. *Am. J. Geriatr. Psychiatry.* 2003 11: 231-238.
[89] Bassiony MM, Warren A, Rosenblatt A, *et al.* The relationship between delusions and depression in Alzheimer's disease. *Int. J. Geriatr. Psychiatry.* 2002 17: 549-556.
[90] Nakaaki S, Murata Y, Sato J, *et al.* Association between apathy/depression and executive function in patients with Alzheimer's disease. *Int. Psychogeriatr.* 2008 20: 964-975.
[91] Visser PJ, Verhey FR, Ponds RW, Kester A, Jolles J. Distinction between preclinical Alzheimer's disease and depression. *J. Am. Geriatr. Soc.* 2000 48: 479-484.
[92] Berger AK, Fratiglioni L, Winblad B, Backman L. Alzheimer's disease and depression: preclinical comorbidity effects on cognitive functioning. *Cortex.* 2005 41: 603-612.
[93] Vercelletto M, Martinez F, Lanier S, Magne C, Jaulin P, Bourin M. Negative symptoms, depression and Alzheimer's disease. *Int. J. Geriatr. Psychiatry.* 2002 17: 383-387.
[94] Bhalla RK, Butters MA, Becker JT, *et al.* Patterns of mild cognitive impairment after treatment of depression in the elderly. *Am. J. Geriatr. Psychiatry.* 2009 17: 308-316.
[95] Ritter E, Despres O, Monsch AU, Manning L. Topographical recognition memory sensitive to amnestic mild cognitive impairment but not to depression. *Int. J. Geriatr. Psychiatry.* 2006 21: 924-929.
[96] Lamberty GJ, Bieliauskas LA. Distinguishing between depression and dementia in the elderly: a review of neuropsychological findings. *Arch. Clin. Neuropsychol.* 1993 8: 149-170.
[97] Lachner G, Satzger W, Engel RR. Verbal memory tests in the differential diagnosis of depression and dementia: discriminative power of seven test variations. *Arch. Clin. Neuropsychol.* 1994 9: 1-13.
[98] Crowe SF, Hoogenraad K. Differentiation of dementia of the Alzheimer's type from depression with cognitive impairment on the basis of a cortical versus subcortical pattern of cognitive deficit. *Arch. Clin. Neuropsychol.* 2000 15: 9-19.
[99] Kunig G, Jager M, Stief V, Kaldune A, Urbaniok F, Endrass J. The impact of the CERAD-NP on diagnosis of cognitive deficiencies in late onset depression and Alzheimer's disease. *Int. J. Geriatr. Psychiatry.* 2006 21: 911-916.

[100] Bodner T, Delazer M, Kemmler G, Gurka P, Marksteiner J, Fleischhacker WW. Clock drawing, clock reading, clock setting, and judgment of clock faces in elderly people with dementia and depression. *J. Am. Geriatr. Soc.* 2004 52: 1146-1150.

[101] Contador I, Fernandez-Calvo B, Cacho J, Ramos F, Lopez-Rolon A. Nonverbal memory tasks in early differential diagnosis of Alzheimer's disease and unipolar depression. *Appl. Neuropsychol.* 2010 17: 251-261.

[102] Borkowska A, Drozdz W, Jurkowski P, Rybakowski JK. The Wisconsin Card Sorting Test and the N-back test in mild cognitive impairment and elderly depression. *World J. Biol. Psychiatry.* 2009 10: 870-876.

[103] Swainson R, Hodges JR, Galton CJ, *et al.* Early detection and differential diagnosis of Alzheimer's disease and depression with neuropsychological tasks. *Dement Geriatr. Cogn. Disord.* 2001 12: 265-280.

[104] Dierckx E, Engelborghs S, De Raedt R, De Deyn PP, Ponjaert-Kristoffersen I. Differentiation between mild cognitive impairment, Alzheimer's disease and depression by means of cued recall. *Psychol. Med.* 2007 37: 747-755.

[105] Pentzek M, Grass-Kapanke B, Ihl R. Odor identification in Alzheimer's disease and depression. *Aging Clin. Exp. Res.* 2007 19: 255-258.

[106] Duff K, McCaffrey RJ, Solomon GS. The Pocket Smell Test: successfully discriminating probable Alzheimer's dementia from vascular dementia and major depression. *J. Neuropsychiatry Clin. Neurosci.* 2002 14: 197-201.

[107] Kaschel R, Logie RH, Kazen M, Della Sala S. Alzheimer's disease, but not ageing or depression, affects dual-tasking. *J. Neurol.* 2009 256: 1860-1868.

[108] Dudley R, O'Brien J, Barnett N, McGuckin L, Britton P. Distinguishing depression from dementia in later life: a pilot study employing the Emotional Stroop task. *Int. J. Geriatr. Psychiatry.* 2002 17: 48-53.

[109] Quoniam N, Ergis AM, Fossati P, *et al.* Implicit and explicit emotional memory for melodies in Alzheimer's disease and depression. *Ann. N. Y. Acad. Sci.* 2003 999: 381-384.

[110] Weintraub D, Xie S, Karlawish J, Siderowf A. Differences in depression symptoms in patients with Alzheimer's and Parkinson's diseases: evidence from the 15-item Geriatric Depression Scale (GDS-15). *Int. J. Geriatr. Psychiatry.* 2007 22: 1025-1030.

[111] Snow AL, Kunik ME, Molinari VA, *et al.* Accuracy of self-reported depression in persons with dementia. *J. Am. Geriatr. Soc.* 2005 53: 389-396.

[112] McGivney SA, Mulvihill M, Taylor B. Validating the GDS depression screen in the nursing home. *J. Am. Geriatr. Soc.* 1994 42: 490-492.

[113] Arlt S, Hornung J, Eichenlaub M, Jahn H, Bullinger M, Petersen C. The patient with dementia, the caregiver and the doctor: cognition, depression and quality of life from three perspectives. *Int. J. Geriatr. Psychiatry.* 2008 23: 604-610.

[114] Muller-Thomsen T, Arlt S, Mann U, Mass R, Ganzer S. Detecting depression in Alzheimer's disease: evaluation of four different scales. *Arch Clin Neuropsychol.* 2005 20: 271-276.

[115] Leontjevas R, van Hooren S, Mulders A. The Montgomery-Asberg Depression Rating Scale and the Cornell Scale for Depression in Dementia: a validation study with patients exhibiting early-onset dementia. *Am. J. Geriatr. Psychiatry.* 2009 17: 56-64.

[116] Alexopoulos GS, Abrams RC, Young RC, Shamoian CA. Cornell Scale for Depression in Dementia. *Biol. Psychiatry.* 1988 23: 271-284.

[117] Lam CK, Lim PP, Low BL, Ng LL, Chiam PC, Sahadevan S. Depression in dementia: a comparative and validation study of four brief scales in the elderly Chinese. *Int. J. Geriatr. Psychiatry*. 2004 19: 422-428.
[118] Schreiner AS, Hayakawa H, Morimoto T, Kakuma T. Screening for late life depression: cut-off scores for the Geriatric Depression Scale and the Cornell Scale for Depression in Dementia among Japanese subjects. *Int. J. Geriatr. Psychiatry*. 2003 18: 498-505.
[119] Ownby RL, Harwood DG, Acevedo A, Barker W, Duara R. Factor structure of the Cornell Scale for Depression in Dementia for Anglo and Hispanic patients with dementia. *Am. J. Geriatr. Psychiatry*. 2001 9: 217-224.
[120] Schreiner AS, Morimoto T. Factor structure of the Cornell Scale for Depression in Dementia among Japanese poststroke patients. *Int. J. Geriatr. Psychiatry*. 2002 17: 715-722.
[121] Williams JR, Marsh L. Validity of the Cornell scale for depression in dementia in Parkinson's disease with and without cognitive impairment. *Mov. Disord*. 2009 24: 433-437.
[122] Cummings JL. The Neuropsychiatric Inventory: assessing psychopathology in dementia patients. *Neurology*. 1997 48: S10-16.
[123] Auer SR, Monteiro IM, Reisberg B. The Empirical Behavioral Pathology in Alzheimer's Disease (E-BEHAVE-AD) Rating Scale. *Int. Psychogeriatr*. 1996 8: 247-266.
[124] Reisberg B, Borenstein J, Salob SP, Ferris SH, Franssen E, Georgotas A. Behavioral symptoms in Alzheimer's disease: phenomenology and treatment. *J. Clin. Psychiatry*. 1987 48 Suppl: 9-15.
[125] Olin JT, Katz IR, Meyers BS, Schneider LS, Lebowitz BD. Provisional diagnostic criteria for depression of Alzheimer disease: rationale and background. *Am. J. Geriatr. Psychiatry*. 2002 10: 129-141.
[126] Olin JT, Schneider LS, Katz IR, *et al.* Provisional diagnostic criteria for depression of Alzheimer's disease: description and review. *Expert Rev Neurother*. 2003 3: 99-106.
[127] Olin JT, Schneider LS, Katz IR, *et al.* Provisional diagnostic criteria for depression of Alzheimer disease. *Am. J. Geriatr Psychiatry*. 2002 10: 125-128.
[128] Rosenberg PB, Onyike CU, Katz IR, *et al.* Clinical application of operationalized criteria for 'Depression of Alzheimer's Disease'. *Int. J. Geriatr. Psychiatry*. 2005 20: 119-127.
[129] Elkis H, Friedman L, Wise A, Meltzer HY. Meta-analyses of studies of ventricular enlargement and cortical sulcal prominence in mood disorders. Comparisons with controls or patients with schizophrenia. *Arch. Gen. Psychiatry*. 1995 52: 735-746.
[130] Alexopoulos GS, Young RC, Shindledecker RD. Brain computed tomography findings in geriatric depression and primary degenerative dementia. *Biol. Psychiatry*. 1992 31: 591-599.
[131] Pomara N, Sidtis J. Does cortical thinning in persons at increased risk for major depression also increase their risk for Alzheimer's disease? *Proc. Natl. Acad. Sci. USA*. 2009 106: E82; author reply E83.
[132] Greenwald BS, Kramer-Ginsberg E, Bogerts B, *et al.* Qualitative magnetic resonance imaging findings in geriatric depression. Possible link between later-onset depression and Alzheimer's disease? *Psychol. Med*. 1997 27: 421-431.

[133] Steffens DC, Payne ME, Greenberg DL, *et al.* Hippocampal volume and incident dementia in geriatric depression. *Am. J. Geriatr. Psychiatry*. 2002 10: 62-71.

[134] Denihan A, Wilson G, Cunningham C, Coakley D, Lawlor BA. CT measurement of medial temporal lobe atrophy in Alzheimer's disease, vascular dementia, depression and paraphrenia. *Int. J. Geriatr. Psychiatry*. 2000 15: 306-312.

[135] Steffens DC, Potter GG, McQuoid DR, *et al.* Longitudinal magnetic resonance imaging vascular changes, apolipoprotein E genotype, and development of dementia in the neurocognitive outcomes of depression in the elderly study. *Am. J. Geriatr. Psychiatry*. 2007 15: 839-849.

[136] Starkstein SE, Mizrahi R, Capizzano AA, Acion L, Brockman S, Power BD. Neuroimaging correlates of apathy and depression in Alzheimer's disease. *J. Neuro psychiatry Clin. Neurosci*. 2009 21: 259-265.

[137] Sharp SI, Ballard CG, Ziabreva I, *et al.* Cortical serotonin 1A receptor levels are associated with depression in patients with dementia with Lewy bodies and Parkinson's disease dementia. *Dement Geriatr. Cogn. Disord.* 2008 26: 330-338.

[138] Meltzer CC, Smith G, DeKosky ST, *et al.* Serotonin in aging, late-life depression, and Alzheimer's disease: the emerging role of functional imaging. *Neuropsycho pharma cology*. 1998 18: 407-430.

[139] Hanada K, Hosono M, Kudo T, *et al.* Regional cerebral blood flow in the assessment of major depression and Alzheimer's disease in the early elderly. *Nucl. Med. Commun.* 2006 27: 535-541.

[140] Ebmeier KP, Prentice N, Ryman A, *et al.* Temporal lobe abnormalities in dementia and depression: a study using high resolution single photon emission tomography and magnetic resonance imaging. *J. Neurol. Neurosurg. Psychiatry*. 1997 63: 597-604.

[141] Ebmeier KP, Glabus MF, Prentice N, Ryman A, Goodwin GM. A voxel-based analysis of cerebral perfusion in dementia and depression of old age. *Neuroimage*. 1998 7: 199-208.

[142] Michelsen KA, Prickaerts J, Steinbusch HW. The dorsal raphe nucleus and serotonin: implications for neuroplasticity linked to major depression and Alzheimer's disease. *Prog. Brain Res*. 2008 172: 233-264.

[143] Chan-Palay V. Serotonin axons in the supra- and subependymal plexuses and in the leptomeninges; their roles in local alterations of cerebrospinal fluid and vasomotor activity. *Brain Res*. 1976 102: 103-130.

[144] Mayberg HS. Modulating dysfunctional limbic-cortical circuits in depression: towards development of brain-based algorithms for diagnosis and optimised treatment. *Br. Med. Bull*. 2003 65: 193-207.

[145] Zobel A, Joe A, Freymann N, *et al.* Changes in regional cerebral blood flow by therapeutic vagus nerve stimulation in depression: an exploratory approach. *Psychiatry Res*. 2005 139: 165-179.

[146] Maestu F, Fernandez A, Simos PG, *et al.* Profiles of brain magnetic activity during a memory task in patients with Alzheimer's disease and in non-demented elderly subjects, with or without depression. *J. Neurol. Neurosurg. Psychiatry*. 2004 75: 1160-1162.

[147] Lee HS, Choo IH, Lee DY, *et al.* Frontal Dysfunction Underlies Depression in Mild Cognitive Impairment: A FDG-PET Study. *Psychiatry Investig*. 2010 7: 208-214.

[148] Holthoff VA, Beuthien-Baumann B, Kalbe E, *et al.* Regional cerebral metabolism in early Alzheimer's disease with clinically significant apathy or depression. *Biol. Psychiatry*. 2005 57: 412-421.
[149] Francis PT, Pangalos MN, Stephens PH, *et al.* Antemortem measurements of neurotransmission: possible implications for pharmacotherapy of Alzheimer's disease and depression. *J. Neurol. Neurosurg. Psychiatry*. 1993 56: 80-84.
[150] Bowen DM, Allen SJ, Benton JS, *et al.* Biochemical assessment of serotonergic and cholinergic dysfunction and cerebral atrophy in Alzheimer's disease. *J. Neurochem*. 1983 41: 266-272.
[151] Bowen DM, Najlerahim A, Procter AW, Francis PT, Murphy E. Circumscribed changes of the cerebral cortex in neuropsychiatric disorders of later life. *Proc. Natl. Acad. Sci. USA*. 1989 86: 9504-9508.
[152] Gross-Isseroff R, Salama D, Israeli M, Biegon A. Autoradiographic analysis of age-dependent changes in serotonin 5-HT2 receptors of the human brain postmortem. *Brain Res*. 1990 519: 223-227.
[153] Middlemiss DN, Palmer AM, Edel N, Bowen DM. Binding of the novel serotonin agonist 8-hydroxy-2-(di-n-propylamino) tetralin in normal and Alzheimer brain. *J. Neurochem*. 1986 46: 993-996.
[154] Ouchi Y, Yoshikawa E, Futatsubashi M, Yagi S, Ueki T, Nakamura K. Altered brain serotonin transporter and associated glucose metabolism in Alzheimer disease. *J. Nucl. Med*. 2009 50: 1260-1266.
[155] Palmer AM, Francis PT, Benton JS, *et al.* Presynaptic serotonergic dysfunction in patients with Alzheimer's disease. *J. Neurochem*. 1987 48: 8-15.
[156] Perry EK, Perry RH, Candy JM, *et al.* Cortical serotonin-S2 receptor binding abnormalities in patients with Alzheimer's disease: comparisons with Parkinson's disease. *Neurosci. Lett*. 1984 51: 353-357.
[157] Reynolds GP, Arnold L, Rossor MN, Iversen LL, Mountjoy CQ, Roth M. Reduced binding of [3H]ketanserin to cortical 5-ht2 receptors in senile dementia of the Alzheimer type. *Neurosci. Lett*. 1984 44: 47-51.
[158] Tejani-Butt SM, Yang J, Pawlyk AC. Altered serotonin transporter sites in Alzheimer's disease raphe and hippocampus. *Neuroreport*. 1995 6: 1207-1210.
[159] Thomas AJ, Hendriksen M, Piggott M, *et al.* A study of the serotonin transporter in the prefrontal cortex in late-life depression and Alzheimer's disease with and without depression. *Neuropathol. Appl. Neurobiol*. 2006 32: 296-303.
[160] Truchot L, Costes N, Zimmer L, *et al.* A distinct [18F]MPPF PET profile in amnestic mild cognitive impairment compared to mild Alzheimer's disease. *Neuroimage*. 2008 40: 1251-1256.
[161] Chen CP, Alder JT, Bowen DM, *et al.* Presynaptic serotonergic markers in community-acquired cases of Alzheimer's disease: correlations with depression and neuroleptic medication. *J. Neurochem*. 1996 66: 1592-1598.
[162] Kepe V, Barrio JR, Huang SC, *et al.* Serotonin 1A receptors in the living brain of Alzheimer's disease patients. *Proc. Natl. Acad. Sci. USA*. 2006 103: 702-707.
[163] Nitsch RM, Deng M, Growdon JH, Wurtman RJ. Serotonin 5-HT2a and 5-HT2c receptors stimulate amyloid precursor protein ectodomain secretion. *J. Biol. Chem*. 1996 271: 4188-4194.

[164] Lezoualc'h F, Robert SJ. The serotonin 5-HT4 receptor and the amyloid precursor protein processing. *Exp. Gerontol.* 2003 38: 159-166.

[165] Pakaski M, Bjelik A, Hugyecz M, Kasa P, Janka Z, Kalman J. Imipramine and citalopram facilitate amyloid precursor protein secretion in vitro. *Neurochem Int.* 2005 47: 190-195.

[166] Maes M, Yirmyia R, Noraberg J, *et al.* The inflammatory and neurodegenerative (IandND) hypothesis of depression: leads for future research and new drug developments in depression. *Metab. Brain Dis.* 2009 24: 27-53.

[167] Leonard BE. Inflammation, depression and dementia: are they connected? *Neurochem. Res.* 2007 32: 1749-1756.

[168] Bremmer MA, Beekman AT, Deeg DJ, *et al.* Inflammatory markers in late-life depression: results from a population-based study. *J. Affect Disord.* 2008 106: 249-255.

[169] Vukic V, Callaghan D, Walker D, *et al.* Expression of inflammatory genes induced by beta-amyloid peptides in human brain endothelial cells and in Alzheimer's brain is mediated by the JNK-AP1 signaling pathway. *Neurobiol. Dis.* 2009 34: 95-106.

[170] Sutcigil L, Oktenli C, Musabak U, *et al.* Pro- and anti-inflammatory cytokine balance in major depression: effect of sertraline therapy. *Clin. Dev. Immunol.* 2007 2007: 76396.

[171] Pace TW, Miller AH. Cytokines and glucocorticoid receptor signaling. Relevance to major depression. *Ann. N. Y. Acad. Sci.* 2009 1179: 86-105.

[172] Leonard BE, Myint A. Inflammation and depression: is there a causal connection with dementia? *Neurotox Res.* 2006 10: 149-160.

[173] Leonard BE, Myint A. Changes in the immune system in depression and dementia: causal or coincidental effects? *Dialogues Clin. Neurosci.* 2006 8: 163-174.

[174] Gottfries CG, Balldin J, Blennow K, *et al.* Hypothalamic dysfunction in dementia. *J. Neural. Transm. Suppl.* 1994 43: 203-209.

[175] Sotiropoulos I, Cerqueira JJ, Catania C, Takashima A, Sousa N, Almeida OF. Stress and glucocorticoid footprints in the brain-the path from depression to Alzheimer's disease. *Neurosci. Biobehav. Rev.* 2008 32: 1161-1173.

[176] Yu S, Holsboer F, Almeida OFX. Neuronal actions of glucocorticoids: Focus on depression. *The Journal of Steroid Biochemistry and Molecular Biology.* 2008 108: 300-309.

[177] Krishnan KR, Heyman A, Ritchie JC, Utley CM, Dawson DV, Rogers H. Depression in early-onset Alzheimer's disease: clinical and neuroendocrine correlates. *Biol. Psychiatry.* 1988 24: 937-940.

[178] Krishnan KRR, Gadde KM, Kim Y-D. PSYCHONEUROENDOCRINOLOGY AND BRAIN IMAGING IN DEPRESSION. *Psychiatric Clinics of North America.* 1998 21: 465-472.

[179] Hoogendijk WJ, Meynen G, Endert E, Hofman MA, Swaab DF. Increased cerebrospinal fluid cortisol level in Alzheimer's disease is not related to depression. *Neurobiol. Aging.* 2006 27: 780 e781-780 e782.

[180] Raadsheer FC, van Heerikhuize JJ, Lucassen PJ, Hoogendijk WJ, Tilders FJ, Swaab DF. Corticotropin-releasing hormone mRNA levels in the paraventricular nucleus of patients with Alzheimer's disease and depression. *Am. J. Psychiatry.* 1995 152: 1372-1376.

[181] Balldin J, Gottfries CG, Karlsson I, Lindstedt G, Langstrom G, Walinder J. Dexamethasone suppression test and serum prolactin in dementia disorders. *Br. J. Psychiatry*. 1983 143: 277-281.
[182] Sheline YI, Mittler BL, Mintun MA. The hippocampus and depression. *European Psychiatry*. 2002 17: 300-305.
[183] Belanoff JK, Gross K, Yager A, Schatzberg AF. Corticosteroids and cognition. *Journal of Psychiatric Research*. 35: 127-145.
[184] O'Brien JT, Ames D, Schweitzer I, Colman P, Desmond P, Tress B. Clinical and magnetic resonance imaging correlates of hypothalamic-pituitary-adrenal axis function in depression and Alzheimer's disease. *Br. J. Psychiatry*. 1996 168: 679-687.
[185] Caraci F, Copani A, Nicoletti F, Drago F. Depression and Alzheimer's disease: neurobiological links and common pharmacological targets. *Eur. J. Pharmacol.* 2010 626: 64-71.
[186] Pomara N, Greenberg WM, Branford MD, Doraiswamy PM. Therapeutic implications of HPA axis abnormalities in Alzheimer's disease: review and update. *Psychopharmacol. Bull.* 2003 37: 120-134.
[187] Spijker AT, van Rossum EF. Glucocorticoid receptor polymorphisms in major depression. Focus on glucocorticoid sensitivity and neurocognitive functioning. *Ann. N. Y. Acad. Sci.* 2009 1179: 199-215.
[188] Swaab DF, Fliers E, Hoogendijk WJG, Veltman DJ, Zhou JN. Interaction of prefrontal cortical and hypothalamic systems in the pathogenesis of depression. In: H.B.M. Uylings GGvEJPCdBMGPFCMAP, ed. *Progress in Brain Research*: Elsevier, 2000: 369-396.
[189] Lucassen PJ, Müller MB, Holsboer F, *et al.* Hippocampal Apoptosis in Major Depression Is a Minor Event and Absent from Subareas at Risk for Glucocorticoid Overexposure. *The American Journal of Pathology*. 2001 158: 453-468.
[190] Duman RS, Monteggia LM. A Neurotrophic Model for Stress-Related Mood Disorders. *Biological Psychiatry*. 2006 59: 1116-1127.
[191] Isingrini E, Desmidt T, Belzung C, Camus V. Endothelial dysfunction: A potential therapeutic target for geriatric depression and brain amyloid deposition in Alzheimer's disease? *Curr. Opin. Investig Drugs*. 2009 10: 46-55.
[192] Ziegenhorn AA, Schulte-Herbrüggen O, Danker-Hopfe H, *et al.* Serum neurotrophins--A study on the time course and influencing factors in a large old age sample. *Neurobiology of Aging*. 2007 28: 1436-1445.
[193] Thakker-Varia S, Alder J. Neuropeptides in depression: Role of VGF. *Behavioural Brain Research*. 2009 197: 262-278.
[194] Knapman A, Heinzmann JM, Hellweg R, Holsboer F, Landgraf R, Touma C. Increased stress reactivity is associated with cognitive deficits and decreased hippocampal brain-derived neurotrophic factor in a mouse model of affective disorders. *Journal of Psychiatric Research*. 2010 44: 566-575.
[195] Karege F, Vaudan G, Schwald M, Perroud N, La Harpe R. Neurotrophin levels in postmortem brains of suicide victims and the effects of antemortem diagnosis and psychotropic drugs. *Molecular Brain Research*. 2005 136: 29-37.
[196] Murer MG, Boissiere F, Yan Q, *et al.* An immunohistochemical study of the distribution of brain-derived neurotrophic factor in the adult human brain, with particular reference to Alzheimer's disease. *Neuroscience*. 1999 88: 1015-1032.

[197] Murer MG, Yan Q, Raisman-Vozari R. Brain-derived neurotrophic factor in the control human brain, and in Alzheimer's disease and Parkinson's disease. *Progress in Neurobiology*. 2001 63: 71-124.

[198] Tsai S-J. Statins may enhance the proteolytic cleavage of proBDNF: Implications for the treatment of depression. *Medical Hypotheses*. 2007 68: 1296-1299.

[199] Duman RS. A role for CREB and BDNF in the actions of antidepressants. *Biological Psychiatry*. 1996 39: 558-559.

[200] Borroni B, Archetti S, Costanzi C, *et al.* Role of BDNF Val66Met functional polymorphism in Alzheimer's disease-related depression. *Neurobiol Aging*. 2009 30: 1406 1412.

[201] Borroni B, Grassi M, Archetti S, *et al.* BDNF genetic variations increase the risk of Alzheimer's disease-related depression. *J. Alzheimers Dis*. 2009 18: 867-875.

[202] Rapp MA, Haroutunian V, Heinz A. FC05-03 Altered levels of neurotrophic factors in alzheimer's disease patients with a lifetimne history of depression. *European Psychiatry*. 2009 24: S315-S315.

[203] Shalev I, Lerer E, Israel S, *et al.* BDNF Val66Met polymorphism is associated with HPA axis reactivity to psychological stress characterized by genotype and gender interactions. *Psychoneuroendocrinology*. 2009 34: 382-388.

[204] Mattson MP, Maudsley S, Martin B. BDNF and 5-HT: a dynamic duo in age-related neuronal plasticity and neurodegenerative disorders. *Trends in Neurosciences*. 2004 27: 589-594.

[205] Holmes C, Arranz M, Collier D, Powell J, Lovestone S. Depression in Alzheimer's disease: the effect of serotonin receptor gene variation. *Am. J. Med. Genet. B. Neuropsychiatr Genet*. 2003 119B: 40-43.

[206] Liu HC, Hong CJ, Liu CY, *et al.* Association analysis of the 5-HT6 receptor polymorphism C267T with depression in patients with Alzheimer's disease. *Psychiatry Clin. Neurosci*. 2001 55: 427-429.

[207] Lesch KP, Bengel D, Heils A, *et al.* Association of anxiety-related traits with a polymorphism in the serotonin transporter gene regulatory region. *Science*. 1996 274: 1527-1531.

[208] Li T, Holmes C, Sham PC, *et al.* Allelic functional variation of serotonin transporter expression is a susceptibility factor for late onset Alzheimer's disease. *Neuroreport*. 1997 8: 683-686.

[209] Mossner R, Daniel S, Albert D, *et al.* Serotonin transporter function is modulated by brain-derived neurotrophic factor (BDNF) but not nerve growth factor (NGF). *Neurochem. Int*. 2000 36: 197-202.

[210] O'Hara R, Schroder CM, Mahadevan R, *et al.* Serotonin transporter polymorphism, memory and hippocampal volume in the elderly: association and interaction with cortisol. *Mol. Psychiatry*. 2007 12: 544-555.

[211] Oliveira JR, Carvalho DR, Pontual D, *et al.* Analysis of the serotonin transporter polymorphism (5-HTTLPR) in Brazilian patients affected by dysthymia, major depression and bipolar disorder. *Mol. Psychiatry*. 2000 5: 348-349.

[212] Otte C, McCaffery J, Ali S, Whooley MA. Association of a serotonin transporter polymorphism (5-HTTLPR) with depression, perceived stress, and norepinephrine in patients with coronary disease: the Heart and Soul Study. *Am. J. Psychiatry*. 2007 164: 1379-1384.

[213] Quaranta D, Bizzarro A, Marra C, *et al.* Psychotic symptoms in Alzheimer's disease and 5-HTTLPR polymorphism of the serotonin transporter gene: evidence for an association. *J. Alzheimers Dis.* 2009 16: 173-180.
[214] Stober G, Heils A, Lesch KP. Serotonin transporter gene polymorphism and affective disorder. *Lancet.* 1996 347: 1340-1341.
[215] Tsai SJ, Hong CJ, Liu TY, Cheng CY, Liu HC. Association study for a functional serotonin transporter gene polymorphism and late-onset Alzheimer's disease for Chinese patients. *Neuropsychobiology.* 2001 44: 27-30.
[216] Wankerl M, Wust S, Otte C. Current developments and controversies: does the serotonin transporter gene-linked polymorphic region (5-HTTLPR) modulate the association between stress and depression? *Curr. Opin. Psychiatry.* 2010 23: 582-587.
[217] Egan MF, Kojima M, Callicott JH, *et al.* The BDNF val66met Polymorphism Affects Activity-Dependent Secretion of BDNF and Human Memory and Hippocampal Function. *Cell.* 2003 112: 257-269.
[218] Grünblatt E, Hupp E, Bambula M, *et al.* Association study of BDNF and CNTF polymorphism to depression in non-demented subjects of the "VITA" study. *Journal of Affective Disorders.* 2006 96: 111-116.
[219] Hayashi M, Mistunaga F, Ohira K, Shimizu K. Changes in BDNF-immunoreactive structures in the hippocampal formation of the aged macaque monkey. *Brain Research.* 2001 918: 191-196.
[220] Schüle C, Zill P, Baghai TC, *et al.* Brain-derived neurotrophic factor Val66Met polymorphism and dexamethasone/CRH test results in depressed patients. *Psychoneuroendocrinology.* 2006 31: 1019-1025.
[221] Kim JM, Stewart R, Kim SY, *et al.* Synergistic associations of depression and apolipoprotein E genotype with incidence of dementia. *Int. J. Geriatr. Psychiatry.* 2010.
[222] Geda YE, Knopman DS, Mrazek DA, *et al.* Depression, apolipoprotein E genotype, and the incidence of mild cognitive impairment: a prospective cohort study. *Arch. Neurol.* 2006 63: 435-440.
[223] Delano-Wood L, Houston WS, Emond JA, *et al.* APOE genotype predicts depression in women with Alzheimer's disease: a retrospective study. *Int. J. Geriatr. Psychiatry.* 2008 23: 632-636.
[224] Beal MF. PL-2-1 Oxidative mechanisms, inflammation, and Alzheimer's disease pathogenesis. *Neurobiology of Aging.* 2004 25: S24-S24.
[225] Bonotis K, Krikki E, Holeva V, Aggouridaki C, Costa V, Baloyannis S. Systemic immune aberrations in Alzheimer's disease patients. *Journal of Neuroimmunology.* 2008 193: 183-187.
[226] Dobos N, Korf J, Luiten PG, Eisel UL. Neuroinflammation in Alzheimer's disease and major depression. *Biol. Psychiatry.* 2010 67: 503-504.
[227] Eikelenboom P, Veerhuis R. The importance of inflammatory mechanisms for the development of Alzheimer's disease. *Experimental. Gerontology.* 1999 34: 453-461.
[228] Payao SLM, Barbosa FAF, de Labio RW, *et al.* P1-297: Interleukin-6 gene promoter polymorphism in Alzheimer's disease patients. *Alzheimer's and Dementia.* 2006 2: S183-S184.

In: Depression in the Elderly
Editor: Emaad Abdel-Rahman, pp. 27-48

ISBN 978-1-61324-771-6

Chapter 2

DEPRESSIVE SYMPTOMS AMONG COMMUNITY-DWELLING MEXICAN ELDERLY

E. D. Arias-Merino[1], G. G. Ortiz[2], N. M. Mendoza Ruvalcaba[1], M. J. Arias-Merino[1], I. E. Velázquez-Brizuela[2], R. M. Meda-Lara[1] and A. E. Morales-Sánchez[1]

[1]Universidad de Guadalajara, Centro Universitario de Ciencias de la Salud, Departamento de Salud Pública. Gerontología. Guadalajara, Jalisco, México
[2]Centro de Investigación Biomédica de Occidente, IMSS. Guadalajara, Jalisco, México

ABSTRACT

The mood disorders are characterized by alterations in the person´s general emotional state. Depression is one of the most common mood disorders experienced by elderly. Depression in elderly has different characteristics than in other life cycle stages. In the process of aging, physical changes can be confused with depressive symptoms. The physiological changes, psychological, social and environment factors are important for the development of depression. Likewise, depressive symptoms in old age have been associated with morbidity, physical dependence, cognitive impairment and dementia. The aim was to determine the prevalence of depression symptoms and its relationship with socio-demographic factors, cognitive function, co-morbidity and physical disabilities among elderly in a Mexican community setting.

The Inter-institutional Dementia Project in Jalisco (CONACYT 7994) was taken as the basis for this chapter. This is a cross-sectional study, multi-stage, random, and proportional with the participation of n=2,553 community-dwelling elders 60 and older. A battery of assessment was applied during an interview in which different areas were assessed: Depression (30-item GDS), cognitive function (MMSE), functional status (ADL, IADL), chronic medical conditions and vital risk factors (self-report). The questionnaire included also socio-demographic factors. Data obtained were validated and entered into a database. Crude Odds Ratio and confidence interval of 95% were calculated. Logistic regression models tested the relative contributions of demographic variables, diseases and impairments, and general conditions on depression.

It was found a prevalence of 30.9% depressive symptomatology. Mean age of participants was 71.6±8.7 years, mostly women (61.2%). Education level was low, mean was 3.6±3.8 years of education, illiterate 27.2%. 45.5% had no couple, widowed 32.3%, single 8.6%, and divorced 4.6%. Were mainly housewives (41.7%), and 79.2% not pensioners. Functional disability prevalence was 31.5% for IADL, 9.6% in ADL, and 14.3% had cognitive impairment. A mean of 1.5 for chronic diseases was reported. Depressive symptoms were associated in bivariate analysis with being female, cognitive impairment, ADL and IADL disability, co-morbidity, education and being married. Increased age was not related.

These results orient to the necessity of prevention and control of the depression in the primary care and to recognize it as a problem of public health. This study gives us the possibility not only to establish a diagnosis and treatment, but also to promote healthy lifestyles and prevention of depression in older people in order to remain active as long as possible and to improve their quality of life.

Introduction

The mood disorders are characterized by alterations in person's general emotional state. Depression is one of the most common mood disorder experienced by elderly.

The Diagnostic and Statistical Manual of Mental Disorders DSM-IV defines depression as characterized by a state of deep sadness and loss of interest or pleasure, which lasts for at least two weeks and is present most of the day (American Psychiatric Association, 2002). Consistently, World Health Organization defines depression as a common mental disorder that presents with depressed mood, loss of interest or pleasure, feelings of guilt or low self-worth, disturbed sleep or appetite, low energy, and poor concentration. These problems can become chronic or recurrent and lead to substantial impairments in an individual's ability to take care of his or her everyday responsibilities (WHO, 2011).

Prevalence in Elderly

The WHO considers depression as the most common mental disorder, affecting about 340 million people worldwide. Major depression is a public health problem due to its high morbidity, as 5% of the world population has a depressive disorder. It is the most common psychiatric disorder among the elderly which can manifest as major or as a minor depression characterized by a collection of depressive symptoms.

Like many disorders in most studies, prevalence rates for depression vary considerably depending on the sample studied (community-based, community centers, hospitalized, or nursing home) and methods used (diagnostic criteria: clinical or screening).

In a review it was found a variation range of 1% - 4% for major depression and 11% - 16% for depressive symptomatology (Blazer, 2003). In a study carried on in Utah with non-demented individuals aged 65 to 100 years, the prevalence of major depression determined by DSM-IV criteria was 4.4% in women and 2.7% in men (Stefens, Skoog, Norton, Hart, Tchanz, et al., 2000).

The results are higher when studying the prevalence of depressive symptomatology. In a population study, 27% of older people reported depressive symptoms, 19% were diagnosed as suffering mild dysphoria, 4% symptomatic depression, 2% dysthymia, 1.2% a mixed depressive and anxiety syndrome, and 0.8% major depression. (Blazer, Hughes, and George, 1987).

In a study conducted in a Brazilian community persons aged 75 years were screened for depression and mental disorders using the General Health Questionnaire (GHQ-12) and Geriatric Depression Scale (GDS), the prevalence of depressive episode was 19.2%, with no effect of gender or age, 9.0% of the elderly presented dysthymia (Costa, Barreto, Uchoa, Firmo, Lima-Costa, et al., 2007).

There have been found differences in depressive symptomatology in urban and rural areas in Kentucky, where urban elderly population reported higher prevalence (54.3%) than rural population (21.9%) (Schulman, Gairola, Kuder and McCulloch (2002), while in the rural area of Malaysia a depression prevalence of 7.6% (measured with GDS-30) was reported in people 60 years and older, the prevalence is higher in people with chronic diseases (9.0%) compared with people without chronic diseases (5.6%) (Mohd Sidik, Mohd Zulkefli and Mustaqim, 2003).

Also there has been studied the difference in depressive symptoms among older people of different races over time, and it was found that is higher in black people with a range from 17.3% to 23.6% compared to the white, 8.8% to 12.2%. in women a higher prevalence than men was found (Skarupski, Mendes de Leon, Bienias, Barnes, Everson-Rose, et al, 2005).

In community centers, a study conducted in Brasilia reported that 31% of elderly suffered depressive symptomatology (measured by GDS-15), and 4% severe depression, all of them aged between 60 and 64 years old (Oliveira, Gomes and Oliveira, 2006), in community centers in Guadalajara Mexico it was found a prevalence of 27.6% among women (Flores Saiffe, and Mendoza Ruvalcaba, 2009).

A special aspect is the prevalence of depression in institutionalized settings, where prevalence increases, in a study conducted in nursing homes in Guadalajara (México), it was found that 64.3% showed depressive symptoms (measured by GDS-30), men 49.6% and women 71.6%, besides it was found an association between cognitive impairment and depressive symptomatology (OR= 3.55, 95% CI= 2.23 – 5.67) (Arias-Merino, Orozco-Mares, and Garabito-Esparza, 2003).

Depression in Elderly

Depression in older adults differs in both subtle and obvious ways from depression earlier in the lifespan. Presentation, etiology, risk and protective factors, and potential outcomes all reflect aspects of the older adult's position in the lifespan. The knowledge of the ways in which age may alter factors associated with the onset and maintenance of depression is essential for effective treatment of depressed older adults (Alexopoulos, 2005).

A key distinction in discussions of mental disorder in older adults is between those individuals who have already experienced mental illness earlier in life and those whose first encounter with mental illness occurs in old age. The distinction portends differences in etiology and prognosis, but also differences in the lived experience of having a mental illness (Alexopoulos, 2005; Butters, Becker, Nebes, Zmuda, and Mulsant, 2000; Christensen, Jorm, Mackinnon, Korten, and Jacomb, 1999).

The search for specific genes associated with depression in older adults has encompassed both genes studied in the non-geriatric population and genes that might relate to distinctive aspects of late life depression (Chow, Hamagam and, Nesselroade, 2007). Genetic studies in the non-geriatric population have, most of them, focused on the short variant of an insertion/deletion polymorphism located in the promoter region of the serotonin transporter gene (5-HTTLPR). In one of the few extensions of this work to older adults, a significant effect for the A/A genotype of the 5-HTR2A gene promoter polymorphism was found and also depressed mood for older males but not for older females was found. In this study, the 5-HTT serotonin transporter gene was not associated with depressed mood (Gallo, Anthony and Muthén, 1994; Hickie, Scott, Naismith, Ward and Turner, 2001; Jansson, Gatz, Berg, Johansson, and Malmberg, 2002).

Non-genetic biological risk factors for depression are particularly important in old age, mainly because of age-related changes that make these factors more common in older adults. These biological risks include endocrine, inflammatory or immune, cardiovascular, and neuroanatomical factors. Furthermore, biological status may interact with efficacy of treatment (Gallo, Rabins, Lyketsos, Tien, and Anthony, 1997; Gallo, Cooper-Patrick, and Lesikar, 1998).

Not all neurobiological risks have later life origins. For example, earlier-in-life depression may predispose an individual to late-life depression through stress-related hormones leading to reduced secretion of neurotropic factors and decreased neurogenesis (Gallo, Anthony, and Muthén, 1994). Further, depression that appears earlier in life may be a risk factor for vascular disease, which in turn can increase risk of late life depression. This association suggests that these two disorders may share a common pathological process, for example, the serotonin transporter promoter polymorphism 5-HTTLPR associated with depression is also associated with higher platelet factor 4 and beta-thromboglobulin levels, leading to increased platelet activation (Jansson, Gatz, Berg, Johansson, and Malmberg, 2003).

It is well known that late- life depression frequently occurs in the context of medical illness. Although virtually any serious or chronic condition can produce a depressive reaction, the conditions believed to be most strongly associated with depression include cardiac and cerebrovascular disease and neurological conditions, discussed in more detail below. Depression may also be caused by infections or malignancies. Diabetes has been investigated as a risk factor for depression, although recent research suggests that depression may actually be a risk factor for the development of diabetes (Kockler, and Heun, 2002; Tiemeier, 2003).

Depression in older adults may present with some differences than in younger adults. For example, older adults are less likely to endorse cognitive-affective symptoms of depression, including dysphoria and worthlessness/guilt, than are younger adults (Gallo, Anthony, and Muthén, 1994). Sleep disturbance, fatigue, psychomotor retardation, loss of interest in living, and hopelessness about the future may be more prevalent in late-life depression than in depression in younger or middle-aged adults (Gallo, Anthony, and Muthén, 1994; Gallo, Rabins, Lyketsos, Tien, and Anthony; 1997; Gallo, Cooper-Patrick, and Lesikar, 1998). Subjective complaints of poor memory and concentration are also common among depressed older adults. Slower cognitive processing speed and executive dysfunction are frequent findings from objective testing. Overall there do not appear to be substantial differences by gender or ethnicity. Some evidence suggests that older African Americans are less likely to report dysphoria than European-Americans and more likely to report thoughts of death

(Gallo, Cooper-Patrick and Lesikar, 1998). With respect to somatic symptoms, depressed older women report more appetite disturbance than men, whereas older men report more agitation (Gallo, Cooper-Patrick and Lesikar, 1998; Hickie, Scott, Naismith, Ward and Turner, 2001).

Several geriatric-specific variants of depression have been proposed. One variant, reflecting the predominant age differences in presentation, has been called *depression without sadness* or *depletion syndrome*. Another variant is the "depression-executive dysfunction syndrome" (Kockler and Heun, 2002; Tiemeier; 2003). As the name indicates, cognitive performance in this syndrome is typically impaired on measures of verbal fluency, naming, and initiation/perseveration. The syndrome also includes psychomotor retardation and anhedonia but less severe vegetative symptoms, agitation, and guilt than other types of depression.

Depression in the elderly is often associated with anxiety, almost half of depressed older adults have symptoms of anxiety, half of patients with depression have symptoms of anxiety, both are not always presented clearly or simply both disorders are presented together. So that in some older adults with depression may be found some of the features listed for anxiety, and vice versa.

A 70 percent of depressive disorders show anxiety of different grades and types, and an even higher percentage of older adults with anxiety disorders, eventually also present depressive symptoms of varying degrees. The relationship that may arise between anxiety and depression in the elderly, is not fixed and unchanging, in contrast, it shows oscillations along its course, so that over time it is possible the predominance of one or another symptom.

Anxiety is not a prerequisite for the diagnosis of major depression, as listed in DSM-IV (First, Frances and Pincus, 2001) or ICD-10 (WHO, 1994), where the mood and anxiety disorders are recognized as separate and distinct entities. There are guidelines indicating that anxiety is one of the most prevalent symptoms of clinical depression, and that the evaluation and treatment of severe anxiety are of vital importance in the successful treatment of depression.

- Principio del formulario
- Final del formulario

On the other hand, anxiety and depression are common in hospitalized older adults, where the prevalence is high especially in women, with no relation to the severity of the disease and it is associated with the patient's subjective perception of greater severity and less improvement (Abuli Picart, Comas Casanovas, Suner Soler, and Grau Martín, 2003; Hansen, Fink, Frydenberg, Oxho, Søndergaard, et al., 2001).

In 50 percent of older adults with depression, the neuropsychological evaluation shows cognitive impairment that may be so intense that it causes a pseudodementia, in which a specific core of cognitive deficits have been identified in to varying degrees in all depressed patients, characterized by poor concentration, poor attention and memory impairment (Steffens, et al., 2000).

And while the most frequent complaint of older adults with depression is the recurrent forgotten memory disturbances these are not the primary feature for differential diagnosis between dementia and pseudodementia by depression.

There are specific points that neuropsychological assessment provides for differentiation. The truth is that depressive states produce diffuse cognitive impairments that affect the visual explicit learning, and a lower affectation in verbal learning and performances (Lopez-Pousa, S., Villalta, J., and Llinas, 1996; Bermejo, 2000).

Early detection of depression, early identification and differential diagnosis between normal aging and changes associated with dementing processes are of great importance for the development of prevention and care interventions that seek to prevent or delay deterioration and disability, which would be more likely in the first symptoms of depression (Vinkers, Gussekloo, Stek, Westendorp, and Van der Mast, 2004).

RISK FACTORS FOR DEPRESSION IN ELDERLY

Among the most common causes of depression can be mentioned: death of spouse and loved ones, loss of employment, discrimination, solitude, isolation, and others but life events should not be considered as the only causes for depression (Kraaij, Arensman, and Spinhoven, 2002). Likewise, depressive symptoms in old age have been associated with morbidity, physical dependence, cognitive impairment and dementia. Also, the institutionalization and hospitalization are increasingly frequent causes of depression.

Risk factors for depression include many of the things that people experience as they get old and not the age itself. There may be present biological factors (genetic and neuro-endocrine factors), psychiatric disorders, family history of depression, personality traits, psychosocial factors and disease.

Lenze, Rogers, Martire, et al., (2001) mention that depression and anxiety disorders are associated with excess disability. They found in a review 16 cross-sectional community studies a significant association between depression and disability in ADLs and IADLs in multivariate analyses, controlling for age, gender, education, income, cognition, physical performance measure, and medical conditions.

In the elderly depression coexists with other medical conditions and disabilities, and may be caused by diseases such as diabetes mellitus, stroke, cardiovascular disease, malnutrition, electrolyte imbalances, anemia, Alzheimer's, Parkinson's and arthritis, among others.

They are also considered as risk factors drug use or combination of drugs (antihypertensive drugs, analgesics, hormones, sedatives, medicines used to treat cancer, among others), social isolation, prolonged economic difficulties, recent bereavement, presence severe or chronic pain, immobility, impaired body image, fear of death, previous history of depression, family history of major depression, previous suicide attempts and substance abuse. (Cyr, 2007; Twedell, 2007;Vázquez-Barquero, 2008).

In Mexico, the elderly present a significant risk for depression due in part to the frequency of chronic degenerative diseases. Lozano, Frenk-Mora, and González-Block (1996) analyzed that in Mexico diseases in the elderly are located in two disease groups: a) those traditionally with high frequency at this age, such as ischemic heart problems, diabetes and cerebrovascular disease, and b) disabling disease, dementia, falls and arthritis. Diabetes Mellitus type 2, continues today in the leading causes of morbidity and mortality in the country followed ischemic heart disease and cerebral vascular disease. Also significant vision disorders, especially cataracts and glaucoma is reported (Rodríguez-Abrego, Escobedo de la Peña, Zurita, and Ramírez, 2007).

Advanced age as a risk for depression is often taken as a hypothesis. However, controversy exists taking into account the approach of the studies (mainly from cross-sectional and longitudinal). The prevalence of depression is lower in rural areas, and rural residents tend to be older than urban residents. The prevalence of depression is higher in women, however, the number of women increases with age. Depressive symptoms have been associated with social isolation or with less contact with members of their social networks. (Blazer, Burchett, Service, and George, 1991). In an exploratory epidemiological study there was found that age does not constitute a substantial risk for depressive symptoms.

On the other hand, there is evidence that untreated depression in the elderly, has severe complications that worsen the prognosis (Cole, Bellavance, and Mansour, 1999) and double the risk of death (Saz and Dewey, 2001). Several studies indicate that depression is associated with an increased risk of death in some elderly patients with disease. In populations where these findings have been reported include the presence of major depression in older hospitalized patients. Unsurprisingly, the fact is that depression affects more and more older adults and the highest rate of suicide by age occur in people over 70 years (Blazer, 2001).

In addition, the elderly may suicide with less previous attempts (Andraca, 1998) and, interestingly, tend to see a doctor before taking it out (Torres and Vázquez, 2002). Knowing that depression is little diagnosed in the elderly is even less done, with grades of 32-50% underdiagnosis and undertreatment of 37-50% (Cole, Bellavance, and Mansour, 1999; García Solano, 2001). And, despite the existence of clear criteria and a consensus on the management of depression in older adults (Charney, Reynolds, Lewis, Lebowitz, Sunderland, et al., 2003), the diagnosis is not easy, due to its usual atypical presentation and cultural vision of old age as something sad (Herrera Tejedor, 2000).

Other studies show that living alone is associated with depression, and within these, men are the most affected. Institutionalization in nursing homes is associated with factors that favor the appearance of depressive symptoms and can lead to an increased prevalence of this disorder, this is due to the feelings of abandonment, economic hardship, social network and family isolation, changes in lifestyle, stress increase, adaptation to rules that can determine and limit privacy, autonomy, lead to feelings of worthlessness and loss of freedom.

In the elderly, social support networks are important as they may be determining the state of health of the people, lack of support, especially among relatives and poor social support networks accentuate the risk of various psychological disorders such as depression (Pando Moreno, Aranda Beltrán, and Salazar Estrada, 1998). It is well known that the biggest complaint manifested by elderly is the loss of old social roles, and the most widespread disease in this age is depression, which causes are the separation or loss of property, real or fantasized, considered as necessary to satisfy a desire (Salvarezza, 1993).

Depression Assessment

The instruments for assessing depression in older people have shown a boom in recent years. Depression can be diagnosed clinically or through the identification of their symptoms, this is an important distinction, because generally studies that focus on symptoms of depression report much higher prevalence than studies using diagnostic procedures, due to sensibility and specificity of the test. The clinical diagnosis is defined by the DSM-IV and by the ICD-10 (International Classification of Diseases of World Health Organization).

According to the DSM-IV, a person who suffers from Major Depressive Disorder:

A. Must either have (1) a depressed mood or (2) a loss of interest or pleasure in daily activities consistently for at least a two-week period. This mood must represent a change from the person's normal mood; social, occupational, educational or other important functioning must also be negatively impaired by the change in mood. This disorder is characterized by the presence of five (or more) of the following symptoms:

(Symptoms that are clearly due to a general medical condition, or mood-incongruent delusions or hallucinations must not be included).

1) Depressed mood most of the day, nearly every day, as indicated by either subjective report (e.g., feels sad or empty) or observation made by others (e.g., appears tearful).
2) Markedly diminished interest or pleasure in all, or almost all, activities most of the day, nearly every day (as indicated by either subjective account or observation made by others).
3) Significant weight loss when not dieting or weight gain (e.g., a change of more than 5% of body weight in a month), or decrease or increase in appetite nearly every day.
4) Insomnia or hypersomnia nearly every day.
5) Psychomotor agitation or retardation nearly every day (observable by others, not merely subjective feelings of restlessness or being slowed down).
6) Fatigue or loss of energy nearly every day.
7) Feelings of worthlessness or excessive or inappropriate guilt (which may be delusional) nearly every day (not merely self-reproach or guilt about being sick).
8) Diminished ability to think or concentrate, or indecisiveness, nearly every day (either by subjective account or as observed by others).
9) Recurrent thoughts of death (not just fear of dying), recurrent suicidal ideation without a specific plan, or a suicide attempt or a specific plan for committing suicide.

B. The symptoms do not meet criteria for a Mixed Episode.
C. The symptoms cause clinically significant distress or impairment in the social, occupational, or other important areas of functioning.
D. The symptoms are not due to the direct physiological effects of a substance (e.g., a drug of abuse, a medication) or a general medical condition (e.g., hypothyroidism).
E. The symptoms are not better accounted for by Bereavement, i.e., after the loss of a loved one, the symptoms persist for longer than 2 months or are characterized by marked functional impairment, morbid preoccupation with worthlessness, suicidal ideation, psychotic symptoms, or psychomotor retardation.

Diagnostic criteria for Dysthymic Disorder are also provided by the DSM-IV, they include:

A. Depressed mood most of the day, for more days than not, as indicated either by subjective account or observation by others, for at least 2 years.
B. Presence, while depressed, of two (or more) of the following:

1) poor appetite or overeating
2) insomnia or hypersomnia
3) low energy or fatigue
4) low self-esteem
5) poor concentration or difficulty making decisions
6) feelings of hopelessness

C. During the 2-year period of the disturbance, the person has never been without the symptoms in Criteria A and B for more than 2 months at a time.
D. No Major Depressive Episode has been present during the first 2 years of the disturbance (1 year for children and adolescents); i.e., the disturbance is not better accounted for by chronic Major Depressive Disorder, or Major Depressive Disorder, In Partial Remission.

Note: There may have been a previous Major Depressive Episode provided there was a full remission (no significant signs or symptoms for 2 months) before development of the Dysthymic Disorder. In addition, after the initial 2 years (1 year in children or adolescents) of Dysthymic Disorder, there may be superimposed episodes of Major Depressive Disorder, in which case both diagnoses may be given when the criteria are met for a Major Depressive Episode.

E. There has never been a Manic Episode, a Mixed Episode, or a Hypomanic Episode, and criteria have never been met for Cyclothymic Disorder.
F. The disturbance does not occur exclusively during the course of a chronic Psychotic Disorder, such as Schizophrenia or Delusional Disorder.
G. The symptoms are not due to the direct physiological effects of a substance (e.g., a drug of abuse, a medication) or a general medical condition (e.g., hypothyroidism).
H. The symptoms cause clinically significant distress or impairment in social, occupational, or other important areas of functioning.

On the other hand, the IDC-10 proposes diagnostic criteria for depression using an agreed list of ten depressive symptoms (key symptoms):

1) Persistent sadness or low mood; and/or
2) Loss of interests or pleasure
3) Fatigue or low energy

At least one of these, most days, most of the time for at least 2 weeks, if any of above present, associated symptoms must be asked:

1) Disturbed sleep
2) Poor concentration or indecisiveness
3) Low self-confidence
4) Poor or increased appetite
5) Suicidal thoughts or acts
6) Agitation or slowing of movements
7) Guilt or self-blame

These 10 symptoms help to define the degree of depression (not depressed, mild, moderate, and severe) and the management is based on the particular degree.

In addition to the clinical criteria, there are several instruments designed for assessing depression, and although some of them were not created specifically for elderly, are widely used.

- The Beck Depression Inventory, BDI (Beck, Ward, Mendelson, Mock, and Erbaugh, 1961): is a self-report questionnaire composed by 21 multiple choice items and, designed for individuals aged 13 and over, their items are related to symptoms of depression such as hopelessness and irritability, physical symptoms such as fatigue, weight loss, and lack of interest in sex, as well as cognitions such as guilt or feelings of being punished. There are three versions of the BDI, the latest revised and published in 1996. The BDI is widely used by health care professionals and researchers in a variety of settings.
- The Hamilton Rating Scale for Depression (Hamilton, 1960): Is a test measuring the severity of depressive symptoms in individuals (both children and adults), often those who have already been diagnosed as having a depressive disorder. It must be applied by an interviewer who provides ratings on the different items, based also in information obtained from family, friends and patient record. There are two versions, 17-item and 21-item, both include symptoms like guilt, suicide, insomnia, agitation, anxiety, physical symptoms, among others.
- Zung Self-rating Depression Scale, SDS (Zung, 1965): is a self-administrated screening tool, a general gauge of depression and mood that rate the four common characteristics old depression: pervasive effect, physiological equivalents, other disturbances, and psychomotor activities. Composed by 20 items scored on a scale of 1 through 4, allows to set levels of depression (normal, mild, moderate, severe), recommended for persons 18 and older.
- The Hopkins Symptom Checklist (Derogatis, Lipman, Rickels, Uhlenhuth, and Covi, 1974): is a self-report symptom inventory, designed to identify common psychiatric symptoms, scored on five underlying symptom dimensions: somatization, obsessive-compulsive, interpersonal sensitivity, anxiety and depression.
- Affect Scale Balance: is a 10-item rating scale, containing five statements reflecting positive feelings (interest, pride, satisfaction, on the top, that things are going on the right way) and five statements reflecting negative feelings (loneliness, unhappiness, boredom, upset, concern), which is administrated to determine overall psychological well-being at a given point time.

- The CES-D Scale (Sawyer, 1997): is a short self-report scale, designed for use in epidemiologic studies to measure current level of depressive symptomatology in the general population, with emphasis on the affective component and depressed mood. The items of the scale are symptoms associated with depression.
- Geriatric Depression Scale, GDS (Yesavage, 1983): It was developed as a basic screening measure for depression in older adults, composed by 30 dichotomic self-report items. Is commonly used as a routine part of a comprehensive geriatric assessment. A short version of the GDS contains 15 questions; both (GDS-30 and GDS-15) have shown well established reliability and validity. This scale is useful for establishing levels of depression (severe – mild – no depression) and can be used with healthy, medically ill and mild to moderately cognitively impaired older adults.

It is important to emphasize that these tools assess only the presence of depressive symptoms. Therefore, we must be cautious in the use of these scales for clinical diagnosis purposes.

In summay, besides to the high prevalence of depression and the socio-demographic trend characterized with a gradual increase in the older population, depression in older adults acquires a special character. Thus, this requires a greater study in the elderly population, since most research has focused on older adults living in nursing homes.

Given the consequences that this mood disorder can bring to individuals, their families and society in general, such as comorbidity, disability, hospitalization, institutionalization, risk of suicide and even death, it is necessary to establish in our context the prevalence of depression among elderly community-dwelling, as well as factors related to it.

METHOD

Based on the Inter-Institutional Project to Study Dementias in Jalisco, an interview was performed in the State of Jalisco, Mexico, on elderly persons 60 years and older, from January 1st to December 31st, 2005 (Arias Merino et al., 2006). Total population of Jalisco in 2005 was 6,814,808, of which 8.9 % were elderly, according to the National Institute of Statistics and Geography (INEGI, 2005).

A cross-sectional study was designed for persons 60 years of age and older community-dwelling in Jalisco, a state in western Mexico. A total of 2,639 elderly persons were included in a multi-stage, proportional, and randomized sample that included the Metropolitan Area of Guadalajara and 6 municipalities of the State of Jalisco, which were chosen for the following reasons: first, due to the higher concentration of elderly population and second, because this is representative of the socio-economic regions presented by this state.

Maps and lists of potential populations were provided by the INEGI. To carry the survey out in the geographical area, study areas were defined through the National Geostatistics Structure; this system allows relating statistical information to the corresponding geographical space, it divides the national territory in areas of easy identification in the field and it is appropriate for information capture activities. Basic Geostatistical Areas (*AGEB*) were used, which constitute the fundamental unit that adjusts to the municipal and state borders of the country's political-administrative division, as much as possible (INEGI, 2000).

The *AGEB* of the 7 study populations were chosen randomly, and the same was done regarding blocks and homes until finding the study subject. Persons 60 years of age and older who had been living at least one year in the State of Jalisco at the time of the interview were invited to participate in the study if they wanted to do so. If the person was unable to provide information, we asked for the participation of a suitable informant (spouse, son/daughter, or primary caretaker) to carry out the interview, 280 informants mainly son/daughter were used. Of those selected for interview (n=2639), 68 persons were excluded due to insufficient overall, and an additional 18 due to lack of information, resulting in an analysis sample of 2,553 persons. Non-response rate was 10%. (n=261).

A comprehensive interview was applied to examine different items: socio-demographic characteristics, basic and instrumental activities of daily living (ADL and IADL, respectively), cognitive function, depression, and health self-reporting. Although disability is generally treated as a continuous construct, we focus on establishing the disability status.

Depressive symptomatology was assessed using the Spanish version of the Geriatric Depression Scale (GDS) of 30 items (Yesavage, 1983), a cutoff point of 10/11 was considered for depression and non-depression. In our study, an analysis of internal reliability, the GDS showed a Cronbach alpha of 0.89, no significant differences by gender and geographic distribution.

Functional disability was measured in terms of limitations in activities of daily living (ADL), such as bathing, transferring, dressing, toileting, continence, and feeding, using the Katz Index (Katz et al., 1963); not being able to perform at least one of the tasks unassisted was considered a dependence in ADL and a cutoff point was assigned of 5/6 dependent/independent on a dichotomous scale. We assessed the limitations in instrumental activities of daily living (IADL), which included preparing meals, cleaning, laundry, managing finances, managing own medication, ability to use the telephone, going shopping, and the use of transportation) using the Lawton Scale (Lawton, 1969). Since the activities assessed by the Lawton Scale are tasks mainly associated with the female role, the Menendez and San Jose proposal (1995) has been taken into consideration, in regard to the fact that when applying this tool to males the cutoff point be lowered 3 points, considering the mainly female activities, which the males of our culture generally do not perform throughout their lives, regardless of if they are able to do so or not; these activities are: preparing meals, doing laundry, and cleaning the house. Given this consideration, the total score ranged from 0-8 points for women and 0-5 points for men (higher score indicates higher independence). We considered the cutoff point of 7 / 8 for women and 4 / 5 for men (dependence / independence) to convert the variable into a dichotomous variable.

Cognitive impairment was measured using the Spanish version of the Mini-Mental State Examination (Folstein, 1975); a modification of the original was used; in the execution of the series of seven (sequential subtraction of 7 of 100) participants were invited to execute a series of 3s (sequential subtraction of 3 of 30); the MMSE score was calculated using the sum of correct answers (0-30 points), the cutoff point was 19/20 to eliminate the bias of education and culture (Escobar et al. 1986; Teresi et al. 1995; Ramirez, Teresi, Holmes, Gurland and Lantigua, 2006).

Participants were also asked if they had or not a disease diagnosed by the doctor, health conditions included were hypertension, diabetes, cardiovascular disease, cerebrovascular disease, epilepsy, Parkinson´s disease, cancer and cholesterol.

Procedure

The age variable was categorized, for this study, in both five-year groups and as a dichotomous variable (60-74, 75 years and more). In the marital status, the category "lives alone" includes: single, widower, and divorced; while "married" includes: those who live with a partner (married and common law partner). Educational level was categorized by years of education using the following intervals: 0, 1-4, 5-6, more than 7, and as dichotomous variable in 0-4 and 5 years or more. The self-report of disease was entered for each disease event that was diagnosed by the doctor, and that as dichotomous variable was categorized as disease yes/no, where the presence of at least one condition qualified for "disease yes". Occupation (main life occupation) was re-codified by type of effort needed to perform it: physical, mental, and combined (OPS, 2004.); housewife was included as a single category. Occupations included in this physical effort category were: farmer, factory worker, and elementary occupations; mental effort: white-collar worker; and combined effort: craftsman/shopkeeper, and other. Variables were converted into dichotomous for the calculation of the OR: housewife–non-housewife, physical-no physical effort, mental–non-mental effort, combined–uncombined.

Statistical Analysis

Data obtained were validated and entered into a database for analysis.

For describing the socio-demographic characteristics of the sample we used categorical variables, then, we determine the prevalence of depression, cognitive impairment, and disability in IADL/ADL in the sample, as well as a confidence interval of 95% (CI 95%) using standard descriptive methods. Crude Odds Ratio and confidence interval of 95% were calculated by crosstabs. Logistic regression models tested the relative contributions of variables demographics (gender and age), diseases and impairments (cognitive impairment, depression, number of diseases), and conditions (education and marital status) on depression, all variables entered were dichotomized. The models estimated the effects of four sequentially entered blocks of variables: 1) demographics, 2) demographics plus diseases and impairments, 3) the measures in 2 plus conditions, 4) the measures in 3 plus interaction terms. All models were weighted for selection probability and evaluated them by Hosmer and Lemeshow test for assess the goodness-of-fit, and by standard methods to assess significance. Data were analyzed using the Statistical Package for Social Sciences (SPSS 18) for Windows.

Results

It was found a prevalence of 30.9% (29.1–32.7 CI 95%) depressive symptomatology. Among women 35.1% showed depressive symptomatology, 24.2% of men. There were significant differences by gender, age, education, marital status, main occupation during working life, comorbidiy, functional (ADL and IADL) and cognitive status ($p<.001$).

Chart 1. Participant's socio-demographic and health characteristics

Variable	Non -Depressive symptomatology n= 1765 (%)	Depressive symptomatology n= 788 (%)	Total n= 2553 (%)	p
Gender				
Women	1014 (64.9)	548 (35.1)	1562 (61.2)	<.001
Men	751 (75.8)	240 (24.2)	991 (38.8)	
Age groups, years (Mean= 71.6,SD= 8.7)				
60 – 64	491 (73.6)	176 (26.4)	667 (26.1)	<.001
65 – 69	394 (73.5)	142 (26.5)	536 (21.0)	
70 – 74	309 (70.2)	131 (29.8)	440 (17.2)	
75 – 79	256 (64.6)	140 (35.4)	396 (15.5)	
≥ 80	315 (61.3)	199 (38.7)	514 (20.1)	
Education, years (Mean= 3.6, SD= 3.8)				
0	414 (59.7)	280 (40.3)	694 (27.2)	<.001
1 – 4	679 (66.6)	341 (33.4)	1020 (40.0)	
5 – 6	391 (78.7)	106 (21.3)	497 (19.5)	
≥ 7	281 (82.2)	61 (17.8)	342 (13.3)	
Marital Status				
Single	148 (67.3)	72 (32.7)	220 (8.6)	<.001
Widowed	499 (6.0.6)	325 (39.4)	824 (32.3)	
Divorced	79 (66.4)	40 (33.6)	119 (4.6)	
Married	1036 (74.6)	354 (25.4)	1390 (54.4)	
Main occupation during working life				
Farmer	321 (72.5)	122 (27.5)	443 (17.4)	<.001
Factory worker	217 (77.8)	62 (22.2)	279 (10.9)	
Housewife	661 (62.2)	401 (37.8)	1062 (41.6)	
White-collar worker	85 (82.5)	18 (17.5)	103 (4.0)	
Craftsman / shopkeeper	270 (78.3)	75 (21.7)	345 (13.5)	
Elementary occupations	120 (62.8)	71 (37.2)	191 (7.5)	
Other	91 (70.0)	39 (30.0)	130 (5.1)	
Retired status				
Pension	385 (72.6)	145 (27.4)	530 (20.8)	=.051
No pension	1380 (68.2)	643 (31.8)	2023 (79.2)	
Chronic disease (Mean= 1.5, SD= 1.3)				
0	506 (81.5)	115 (18.5)	621 (24.3)	<.001
1	625 (72.9)	232 (27.1)	857 (33.6)	
2	389 (65.9)	201 (34.1)	590 (23.1)	
3	167 (55.7)	133 (44.3)	300 (11.8)	
≥4	78 (42.2)	107 (57.8)	185 (7.2)	
ADL				
Disability	110 (45.5)	132 (54.5)	242 (9.6)	<.001
Independent	1655 (71.6)	656 (28.4)	2304 (90.4)	
IADL				
Disability	432 (53.7)	373 (46.3)	805 (31.5)	<.001
Independent	1333 (76.3)	415 (23.7)	1748 (68.5)	
Cognitive status				
Impaired	175 (48.1)	189 (51.9)	364 (14.3)	<.001
Normal	1590 (72.6)	599 (27.4)	2189 (85.7)	

SD= Standard Deviation. Chronic disease includes: hypertension, diabetes, cardiovascular disease, cerebrovascular stroke, epilepsy, Parkinson's disease, cancer, cholesterol. ADL= Basic activities of daily living. IADL= Instrumental activities of daily living.

Figure 1 shows participant´s socio-demographics and health characteristics. Mean age of participants was 71.6 ± 8.7 years, ranging from 60 to 104 years of age, mostly women (61.2%). Education level was low; mean was 3.6 ± 3.8 years of education. A significant percentage of the sample was illiterate (27.2%), and 40% only studied 1 to 4 years. In terms of marital status, a sizeable percentage has no couple (45.5%), participants were widowed (32.3%), single (8.6%) or divorced (4.6%). They were mainly housewives (41.6%), which was expected given the women-men ratio. Approximately 8 out of 10 were not pensioners (79.2%).

Chart 2. Socio-demographic and health characteristics associated to depressive symptomatology

VARIABLE	Depressive symptomatology	Non-Depressive symptomatology	OR(1)	CI (95%)(2)
GENDER				
Women	69.5	57.5	1.69	1.41 – 2.02
Men	30.5	42.5		
AGE (years)				
≥ 75	43.0	32.4	1.57	1.21 – 1.53
60 – 74	57.0	67.6		
MARITAL STATUS (3)				
Single	55.5	41.1	1.78	1.50 – 2.11
Married	44.5	58.9		
EDUCATION (years)				
Low (0 – 4)	78.8	61.9	2.28	1.87 – 2.78
High (≥ 5)	21.2	38.1		
HAVING AT LEAST ONE DISEASE (4)				
Yes	85.4	71.3	2.35	1.88 – 2.94
No	14.6	28.7		
COGNITIVE IMPAIRMENT				
Yes	23.7	15.3	1.72	1.39 – 2.12
No	76.3	84.7		
ADL DISABILITY				
Yes	16.8	6.2	3.02	2.31 – 3.96
No	83.2	93.8		
IADL DISABILITY				
Yes	56.6	37.5	2.17	1.83 – 2.57
No	43.4	62.5		
OCCUPATION DURING WORKING LIFE (5)				
Housewife				
Physical	50.9	37.5	1.73	1.46 – 2.05
Combined	32.4	36.8	0.82	0.68 – 0.98
Mental	14.3	18.8	0.72	0.57 – 0.91
	2.4	7.0	0.33	0.20 – 0.35

OR= Odds Ratio, (2) CI= Confidence interval, (3) Single includes people living alone (single, widowed, divorced). (4) Includes at least hypertension, diabetes, cardiovascular disease, cerebrovascular stroke, epilepsy, Parkinson's disease, cancer, cholesterol. ADL= Basic activities of daily living. IADL= Instrumental activities of daily living. (5) Occupations classified according to the type of effort mainly required to perform the activity.

Functional disability prevalence was 31.5% (29.7–33.4, CI 95%) for IADL, 9.6% disability in ADL (8.4–10.7, CI 95%), and 14.3% (12.9-15.7 CI 95%) for cognitive impairment. A mean of 1.5 for chronic diseases was reported by the participants as diagnosed by a doctor; only 1 out of 4 (24.3%) participants remained healthy (without diagnosed chronic disease). Depressive symptoms were associated with socio-demographic and health characteristics. Significant results are shown in Figure 2.

Among socio-demographics factors, gender was found as a risk factor, where women had 1.69 (CI 1.41 - 2.02) more risk than men. Age was a risk factor, the oldest-old were 1.57 (CI 1.3-1.8) times more likely to have depressive symptoms compared with people younger than 75 years. Marital status was also a risk factor, single people had more risk than married (OR = 1.78, CI 1.50 – 2.11). People with less education had 2.28 (CI 1.87 - 2.7) times the risk of depressive symptoms compared to those with a higher educational level. Regarding occupation during working life, housewives had the higher risk, 1.73 (1.46 – 2.05) times the risk of depressive symptoms.

Among health characteristics, elderly with cognitive impairment had 1.72 (CI 1.39 – 2.12) times the risk of depressive symptomatology than those cognitively intact, being dependent on basic activities of daily living (OR= 3.02, CI 2.31 – 3.96) and being dependent on instrumental activities of daily living (OR= 2.17, CI 21.83 – 2.57) were also risk factors, as well as co morbidity OR= 2.35 (CI 1.88 – 2.94).

Depressive symptoms were associated in bivariate analysis with socio-demographic and health characteristics. Variables were entered in blocks, the first of socio-demographic variables (gender and age), the second block included variables related with diseases and impairments, and finally in the third block were added variables related with personal conditions (education and being married). Results are shown in Figure 3.

Chart 3. Adjusted Odds Ratio of depressive symptomatology on socio-demographic and health conditions

Characteristic	Depression			
	Model 1	Model 2	Model 3	Model 4
Gender (women)	1.70 ***	1.28*	0.97	--
Age	1.59 ***	1.10	--	--
Cognitive impairment		1.98 **	1.70 ***	1.71 ***
ADL disability		1.66 ***	1.72 ***	1.73***
IADL disability		1.77 ***	1.63 ***	1.62***
Number of diseases		2.04 ***	2.04 ***	2.04***
Education			1.79 ***	1.79***
Marital status (single)			1.34 **	1.34***
Occupation (housewife)			1.41***	1.39**

*p<.05, **p<.01, p<.001.
ADL= Basic activities of daily living. IADL= Instrumental activities of daily living.

Odds Ratio was adjusted at each step of the analysis to control for potentially confounding factors. Consistently variables such as cognitive impairment, ADL and IADL disability and number of diseases, as well as education, being single and main occupation during working life (housewife) were risk factors for depressive symptoms. It can be observed that age lost strength and significant value in model 2 and gender in model 3.

Conclusion

In this study, the prevalence of depressive symptomatology was 30.9%. Risk factors associated were cognitive impairment, ADL and IADL disability, number of diseases, among those related with diseases and impairments; education, marital status (single), and occupation (housewife) among personal conditions. Age and gender were not risk factors in the adjusted analysis, although they were in the crude analysis.

The coexistence of cognitive impairment and depression in cross sectional studies is identified in various studies (Glasser, Stearns, de Jemp, van Hout, Hott, 1994; Boone, Lesser, Miller, Wohl, Berman, et al., 1994; Arias-Merino, Orozco-Mares, Garabito-Esparza, et al., 2003). In a cohort study it was observed that the risk of cognitive impairment was not associated with concomitant levels of depression after three years, independent of any depressive symptoms at the onset (Dufoil, Fuhrer, Dartigues, and Alperovith, 1996). These results indicate that the association between high depressive symptomatology and poor cognitive function was found in cross sectional studies, showing the importance of adjusting the depressive symptomatology in epidemiological studies in order to measure cognitive function. The findings presented show the coexistence of cognitive impairment, incapacity to perform activities of daily life, and depression.

We also found an association between depressive symptomatology and disability. This contribution of disability (in ADLs and IADLs) to depression –and conversely– suggest a mutually reinforcing relationship. Bruce (2001) offers potential explanations of this issue, the first, argues that disability is a prodromal indicator of underlying physical, cognitive or emotional dysfunction leading to the onset of depression, in its extreme form the argument is that disability is the first observable evidence of a depression; the second, propose that disability is a stressful condition that increases the risk of depression. However the relationship between depression and disability is subtle and complex, alternatively has been suggested that specific depressive symptoms (such as fatigue, sleep disturbance and appetite disruption) have direct debilitating effects resulting over time in functional decline and disability, besides, depression may increase vulnerability to other risk factors for disability, such as medical illness and various life events (Bruce, 2001). Depressive symptoms and disability maintain a reciprocal and potentially spiraling relationship in older adults. The depressed state itself is disabling, and/or depression causes increased disability from other medical conditions, either by increasing the risk of these conditions or by a poorer health behaviors in depressed individuals with these medical conditions (Lenze, et al., 2001).

In our study, marital status was a risk factor, where single people had a higher risk of depressive symptomatology compared with married people, these results are consistent with those reported by Schulman, Gairola, Kuder and McCulloch (2002), where the marital status was significantly different, 18% of married people were depressed in contrast to 37% of the unmarried.

Many of these risk factors can be prevented, Rowe and Kahn (1987) asserts that the effects of aging process itself have been exaggerated, and modifiable factors such as diet, exercise, personal habits and psychosocial factors are underestimated.

Regarding age, in other studies the current prevalence of major depression did not change appreciably with age (Steffens, et al., 2000). Depressive symptoms are more frequent among the oldest elderly, but the higher frequency is explained by factors associated with aging, such as a higher proportion of women, more physical disability, more cognitive impairment, and lower socioeconomic status, when these factors are controlled, there is no relationship between depressive symptoms and age (Blazer, Burchett, Service, and George, 1991).

Among the limitations of this study, it must be considered that this is a cross-sectional study, which limits making assumptions about the progression of depressive symptomatology, besides our findings may be limited by self-report measures that were used. We agree with Blazer and Williams (1980) that it is necessary to take into account that the difficulty of diagnosing depression in older people poses a major threat to epidemiological research, since many of depressive symptoms experienced by the person are attributed to the aging process, illness and even alleged disturbances on the central nervous system.

Finally it is important to emphasize that this results orient to the necessity of prevention and control of the depression in the primary care and to recognize it as a problem of public health.

REFERENCES

Abuli Picart, P., Comas Casanovas, P., Suñer Soler, R., Grau Martín, A. (2003). Niveles de ansiedad y depresión en enfermos hospitalizados y su relación con la gravedad de la enfermedad. *Medicina Clínica*. 120 (10), 370 – 375.

Alexopoulos, G.S. (2005). Depression in the Elderly. *Lancet.* 365, 1961–1970.

American Psychiatric Association. (2002). Manual Diagnóstico y Estadístico de los Trantornos Mentales DSM-IV-TR. Barcelona: Masson.

Andraca, F. (1998). Suicidio en adultos mayores: generalidades. *Geriatrika*. 14,17-23.

Arias Merino, E.D, Ortiz, O.O., Flores-Saiffe, M.E., Morales-Sanchez, A., Maynard, W., Velasquez-Brisuela, I.E., Macias-Islas, M.A., Arias-Merino, M.J., Sanchez-Gonzalez, V.J., Vazquez-Camacho, G. (2006). Prevalence of Cognitive Impairment in Mexican Elderly. In Iqbal, K., Windblad, B. And Avila J. *Alzheimer´s Disease: New Advances.* (pp. 667 – 671). Bologna: Medimond.

Arias Merino, E.D., Orozco Mares, I., Garabito Esparza, L.C. (2003). Correlates of cognitive impairment in elderly residents of long term care institutions in the Metropolitan Area of Guadalajara, México. *The Journal of Nutrition, Health and Aging.* 7(2), 117 – 121.

Beck, A.T., Ward, C.H., Mendelson, M., Mock, J., and Erbaugh, J. (1961). An inventory for measuring depression. *Archives of General Psychiatry.* 4, 561–571

Bermejo, F.P. (2000). Enfermedad de Alzheimer y otras demencias degenerativas. In: *Tratado de Medicina Interna* (14ª ed) Barcelona: Harcourt.

Blazer, D.G. (2001). Depresión. En: Beers, M.H., Berkow, R., (Eds). *Manual Merck de Geriatría.* Madrid: Harcourt (Edición electrónica) (citado 4 Ene 2005): In: http://www2.univadis.net/opencms/opencms/publicaciones/manuales/5/4/Cap_033.

Blazer, D.G. (2003). Depression in late lafe: review and commentary. *The Journal of Gerontology Medical Sciences.* 58(3), 249 – 265.

Blazer, D.G. and Williams, C. (1980). Epidemiology of disphoria and depression in elderly population. *American Journal of Psychiatry.* 137, 439 – 444.

Blazer, Burchett, Service, and George, (1991). The association of age and depression among the elderly: an epidemiologic exploration. *The Journals of Gerontology Medical Sciences.* 46(6), 210 – 215.

Blazer, D., Hughes, D.C., and George, L.K. (1987). The epidemiology of depression in an elderly community population. *The Gerontologist.* 27(3), 281 – 287.

Boone, K.B., Lesser, I., Miller, B., Wohl, M., Berman, N., Lee, A., and Palmer, B. (1994). Cognitive functioning in a mildly to moderately depressed geriatric sample: relationship to chronological age. *The Journal of Neuropsychiatry and Clinical Neurosciences.* 6, 267 – 272.

Bruce, M.L. (2001) Depression and disability in late life: directions for future research. *American Journal of Geriatric Psychiatry.* 9, 102-112.

Butters, M.A., Becker, J.T., Nebes, R.D., Zmuda, M.D., Mulsant, B.H., et al. (2000). Changes in cognitive functioning following treatment of late life depression. *American Journal of Psychiatry.* 157, 1949–1954.

Charney, D.S., Reynolds, C.F., Lewis, L., Lebowitz, B.D., Sunderland, T., Alexopoulos, G.S., et al. (2003). Depression and bipolar support alliance consensus statement on the unmet needs in diagnosis and treatment of mood disorders in late life. *Archives of General Psychiatry.* 60, 664-72.

Christensen, H., Jorm, A.F., Mackinnon, A.J., Korten, A.E., Jacomb, P.A., et al. (1999). Age differences in depression and anxiety symptoms: A structural equation modelling analysis of data from a general population sample. *Psychological Medicine.* 29, 325–339.

Chow, S.M., Hamagami, F., Nesselroade, J.R. (2007). Age differences in dynamical emotion-cognition linkages. *Psychology and Aging.* 22, 765–780.

Cole, M.G., Bellavance, F. and Mansour, A. (1999). Prognosis in elderly community and primary care populations: a systematic review and meta-analysis. *Amercian Journal of Psychiatry.* 156, 1182-1189.

Costa, E., Barreto, S.M., Uchoa, E., Firmo, J.O.A., Lima-Costa, M.F., Prince, M. (2007). Prevalence of diseases, 10th revision common mental disorders in the elderly in a brazilian community: The Bambui Health Ageing Study. *American Journal of Geriatric Psychiatry.* 15, 17 – 27.

Cyr, N. (2007). Depression and older adults. *AORN Journal*, 85(2), 397-401.

Derogatis, L.R., Lipman, R.S., Rickels, K., Uhlenhuth, E.H., and Covi, L. (1974). The Hopkins Symptom Checklist (HSCL): a self-report symptom inventory. *Behavioral Science.* 19(1), 1-15.

Dufoil, C., Fuhrer, R., Dartigues, J.F., and Alperovith, A. (1996). Longitudinal Analysis of the association between depressive symptomatology and cognitive deterioration. *American Journal of Epidemiology.* 144, 634 – 641.

Escobar, J.I., Burnam, A., Karno, M., Forsythe, A., Landsverk, J., Golding, J.M. (1986). Use of the Mini-Mental State Examination (MMSE) in a community population of mixed ethnicity. Cultural and linguistic artifacts. *The Journal of Nervous and Mental Disease.* 174(10), 607 – 614.

First, M., Frances, A. and Pincus H.A. (2001). *DSM-IV-TR: Manual diagnóstico y estadístico de los trastornos mentales.* Barcelona: Masson.

Flores Saiffe-Ruvalcaba, M.E., Mendoza Ruvalcaba, N.M. (2009). La situación emocional de la mujer mayor: al borde de la depression? En: Mendoza Ruvalcaba, N.M. (Ed). *Mujeres Grandes: Las mujeres mayores del municipio de Guadalajara a comienzos del diglo XXI.* Guadalajara: Instituto Municipal de las Mujeres en Guadalajara. Cap. II. 141 – 160.

Folstein, M.F., Folstein, S.E., McHugh, P.R. (1975). Mini-Mental State, a practical method for grading the cognitive state of patients for the clinician. *Journal of Psychiatric Research.* 12, 189-198.

Gallo, J.J., Anthony, J.C., Muthén, B.O. (1994). Age differences in the symptoms of depression: A latent trait analysis. *Journal of Gerontology.* 49, P251–264.

Gallo, J.J., Rabins, P.V., Lyketsos, C.G., Tien, A.Y., Anthony, J.C. (1997). Depression without sadness: Functional outcomes of non-dysphoric depression in later life. *Journal of the American Geriatrics Society.* 45, 570–578.

Gallo, J.J., Cooper-Patrick, L., Lesikar, S. (1998). Depressive symptoms of whites and African Americans aged 60 years and older. *Journal of Gerontology Psychological Sciences.* 53, P277–286.

García Solano, F. (2001). Midiendo la prevalencia de la depresión. *Revista Española de Geriatria y Gerontología.* 36, 127-130.

Glasser, M., Stearns, J.A., de Jemp, E., van Hout, J., Hott, D. (1994). Dementia and depression symptomatology as assessed through screening test of older patients in an outpatient clinic. *Family Practice Research.* 14, 261 – 272.

Hamilton, M. (1960). A rating scale for depression. *Journal of Neurology, Neurosurgery and Psychiatry.* 23, 56 – 62.

Hansen, M.S., Fink, P., Frydenberg, M., Oxhøj, M., Søndergaard, L. and Munk-Jørgennsen, P. (2001). Mental disorders among internal medical inpatients: Prevalence, detection, and treatment status. *Journal of Psychosomatic Research.* 50 (4), 199-204.

Herrera Tejedor, J. (2000). La depresión en el anciano. *Atención Primaria.* 26, 339-346.

Hickie, I., Scott, E., Naismith, S., Ward, P., Turner, K., et al. (2001). Late-onset depression: Genetic, vascular and clinical contributions. *Psychological Medicine,* 31, 1403–1412.

Jansson, M., Gatz, M., Berg, S., Johansson, B., Malmberg, B., et al. (2003). Association between depressed mood in the elderly and a 5-HTR2A gene variant. *American Journal of Medical Genetics Neuropsychiatric Genetics.* 120B, 79–84.

Katz, S., Ford, A.B., Moskowitz, R.W., Jackson, B.A., Jaffe, M.W., Cleveland, M.A. (1963). Studies of illness in the Aged, The Index of ADL: A Standardized Measure of Biological and Psychological Function. *Journal of the American Medical Association.* 185 (12).

Kockler, M., Heun, R. (2002). Gender differences of depressive symptoms in depressed and nondepressed elderly persons. *International Journal of Geriatric Psychiatry.* 17, 65–72.

Kraaij, V., Arensman, E., and Spinhoven, P. (2002). Negative life events and depression in elderly persons: A meta-analysis. *Journal of Gerontology, Psycological Sciences.* 57B, P87-P94.

Lawton, M.P., Brody, E.M. (1969). Assessment of older people: Self-maintaining and instrumental activities of daily living. *Gerontologist.* 9, 179 – 186.

Lenze, E.J., Rogers, J.C., Martire, L.M., Mulsant, B.H., Rollman, B.L., Dew, M.A., Schulz, R., Reynolds, C.F. (2001). The association of late-life depression and anxiety with pshysical disability. A review of the literature and prospectus for future research. *American Journal of Geriatric Psychiatry*. 9, 113-135.

López-Pousa, S., Villalta, J., and Llinás, J. (1996). *Manual de demencias*. Barcelona: Prous Science.

Lozano-Ascencio, R., Frenk-Mora, J., González-Block, M.A. (1996). El peso de la enfermedad en los adultos mayores, México 1994. *Salud Pública de México*. 38, 419-429.

Menendez and San Jose. (1995). In Lucas Vaquero, M.V. *Compilación de técnicas para una evaluación multidimensional en la vejez (Compilation of techniques for a multi-dimensional assessment in old age)*. (2003). http://www.ugr.es/~master/ master/ descargas/LucasVaquero.pdf.

Mohd Sidik, S., Mohd Zulkefli, N.A. and Mustaqim, A. (2003). Prevalence of depression with chronic illness among the elderly in a rural community in Malasya. *Asia Pacific Family Medicine*. 2, 196 – 199.

Oliveira, D.A., Gomes, L., Oliveira. R.F. (2006). Prevalence of depression among the elderly population who frequent community centers. Rev Saúde Pública. 40 (4).

Organización Mundial de la Salud. (1994). CIE-10: Trastornos mentales y del comportamiento. Madrid: Meditor.

Pando Moreno, M., Aranda Beltrán, C., Salazar Estrada, J.G. (1998). *Redes familiares de apoyo y trastornos psicológicos en el adulto mayor en Guadalajara, Jalisco*. Psicología y Salud Nº 12. Veracruz: Nueva Epoca.

Radloff, L.S. (1977). The CES-D: A self-report depression scale for research in the general population. *Applied Psychological Measurement*. 1, 385 – 401.

Ramirez, M., Teresi, J.A., Holmes, D., Gurland, B., Lantigua, R. (2006). Differential Item Functioning (DIF) and the Mini-Mental State Examination (MMSE): overview, sample, and issues of translation. *Medical Care*. 4(3S), S95 – S106.

Salvarezza L. (1993). *Psicogeriatria, Teoría y Clínica*. México: Paidos.

Saz, P., and Dewey, M.E. (2001). Depression, depressive symptoms and mortality in persons aged 65 and over living in the community: a systematic review of the literature. *Internal Journal of Geriatric Psychiatry*. 19, 622 - 630.

Schulman, E., Gairola, G., Kuder, L., and McCulloch, J. (2002). Depression and associated characteristics among community-based elderly people. *Journal of Allied Health*. 31 (3), 140 – 146.

Skarupski, K.A., Mendes de Leon, C.F., Bienias, J.L., Barnes, L.L., Everson-Rose, S.A., Wilson, R.S., Evans, D.A. (2005). Black-white differences in depressive symptoms among older adults over time. *The Journals of Gerontology Psychological Sciences*. 60, 136 – 142.

Steffens, D.C., Skoog, I., Norton, M.C., Hart, A.D., Tschanz, J.T., Plassman, B.L., Wyse, B.W., Welsh-Bohmer, K.A., and Breitner, J.C. (2000). Prevalence of Depression and Its Treatment in an Elderly Population. The Cache County Study. *Archives of General Psychiatry*. 57, 601-607.

Teresi, J.A., Golden, R.P., Gurland, P.C.B., Kleinman, M., Wilder, D. (1995). Item bias in cognitive screening measures: comparisons of elderly white, Afro-American, Hispanic and high and low education subgroups. *Journal of Clinical Epidemiology*. 48 (4), 473 – 483.

Tiemeier, H. (2003). Biological risk factors for late life depression. *European Journal of Epidemiology.* 18, 745–50.

Torres, R.M., and Vázquez, O. (2002). Aspectos epidemiológicos de la depresión en el anciano (23–26). En: Sociedad Española de Geriatría y Gerontología (Ed.). *Depresión en el anciano*. Barcelona: Glosa.

Twedell, D. (2007). Depression in the Elderly. *The Journal of Continuing Education in Nursing.* 38(1), 14-15.

Vázquez-Barquero, J.L. (2008). *Los trastornos depresivos.* Barcelona: Masson.

Vinkers, D.J., Gussekloo, J., Stek, M.L., Westendorp, R.G., and Van der Mast, R.C. (2004). Temporal relation between depression and cognitive impairment in old age: prospective population based study. British Medical Journal. (329), 881.

World Health Organization (2011). Mental Helath. Depression. In: http://www.who.int/mental_health/management/depression/definition/en/ (02/15/2011).

Yesavage, J.A., Brink, T.L., Rose, T.L., Lum, O., Huang, M., Adey, M., Leirer, V.O. (1983). Development and validation of a geriatric depression screening scale: a preliminary report. *Journal of Psychiatric Research.* 17 (1), 37 – 49.

Zung, W.W. (1965). A self rating depression scale. *Archives of General Psychiatry.* 12, 63-70.

In: Depression in the Elderly
Editor: Emaad Abdel-Rahman, pp. 49-66

ISBN 978-1-61324-771-6

Chapter 3

DEPRESSION IN OLDER ADULTS WITH CHRONIC KIDNEY DISEASE

Seki A. Balogun, Rasheed A. Balogun and Emaad M. Abdel-Rahman*
Division of Nephrology, University of Virginia,
Charlottesville, Virginia, USA

ABSTRACT

Older adults with chronic kidney disease (CKD) have a high incidence of clinical depression. This is of great importance as it is associated with increased morbidity and mortality, thereby adversely affecting these and other patient outcomes. Depression in older adults also negatively impacts functional status, quality of life and self-perception of health.

In this chapter, we review and synthesize recent evidence from the literature exploring the impact of depression in older adults with chronic kidney disease (CKD), especially the implications on physical and cognitive functioning, which are of great concern in the geriatric population. For the purposes of this review, CKD refers to predialysis patients with CKD stages 2 to 5, unless otherwise specified.

Optimal management of depressed older adults patients with CKD remains a challenge in the United States. Recent evidence on pharmacological management of depression including selection of drug therapies, non-pharmacological interventions such as psychotherapy, electroconvulsive therapy, physical activity and exercise that enhance the well being of these patients is also reviewed.

BACKGROUND

The World population of older adults continues to increase exponentially. According to a 2001 United Nations report, over 500 million adults were 65 years and older and formed about 8% of the total world population in 2000. They are expected to increase to almost 2

*Phone (434) 243-2671, Fax: (434) 924-5848, Email: ea6n@virginia.edu billion in 2050 and will form about 20% of the total world population [1]. About 35 million (one in eight) Americans are 65 years and older, this is expected to increase to about 55 million in 2020 (an increase of about 36%) [2].

This increase in the number of elderly poses many physical and mental challenges. In parallel to the increase in the number of elderly, there is a noted high percentage of mental problems among these people. In 2003, 1 in 5 Medicare beneficiaries reported mental illness or depression; most of these also had one or more chronic medical condition such as chronic kidney disease (CKD), diabetes mellitus or cardiovascular disease [3]. Recognizing that almost 70% of elderly Americans have CKD [4], and that CKD is the 8th leading cause of mortality in adults aged 65 years and older [5], it becomes crucial to investigate and shed some light on the problems in the elderly with CKD. In this chapter we will focus on depression in the elderly with CKD.

Depression is common in older adults with CKD, particularly those with end stage kidney disease (ESRD). In a 2008 study, almost 24 percent of older adults reported depressed mood at the start of dialysis. Progressive decline in cognitive function and sleep disorders were also noted in these adults [6, 7]. Both CKD and depression are associated with hospitalization and loss of independence. All of which adversely impact self-perception of well-being and quality of life.

While the highest yearly number of inpatient stays and skilled nursing care days in Medicare beneficiaries are in those with CKD, older adults with depression have the second highest number of Medicare covered skilled nursing care days per year [3].

The presence of depression in the elderly also increases the risk of falls almost threefold. By the same token, older adults who fall are twice as likely to be depressed compared to their non-depressed counterparts [8, 9]. Falls are very common in elderly patients, more so, in patients with ESRD on HD.In a recent 2011 study, up to 38.2% of elderly patients on HD fell within a 12-month period [10].

This noted high fall rate in the elderly HD patients further corroborates the high prevalence of depression noted in these patients.In addition, the high incidence of osteoporosis in the elderly, particularly those with advanced CKD, as a result of additional effects of chronic kidney disease-Mineral Bone Disease (CKD-MBD) on bone density, also increases the risk for falls and fractures, thereby significantly impacting functional status, quality of life and mortality in these individuals [10, 11].

Falls and clinical depression are invariably linked in elderly adults with CKD. In addition the treatment of depression using antidepressants can also contribute to falls. Desmet et al studied over three hundred elderly HD patients (median age: 70.9 years) and identified increased age and the use of antidepressants as independent risk factors associated with falls in this population of patients [11]. This may be partly due to the anticholinergic effects of some antidepressants.

Hence, the depressed elderly with CKD are highly susceptible to poorer outcomes and are also especially at high risk for hospitalizations, nursing home admissions and even death. The high incidence of depression in elderly individuals with CKD may be partially explained by the increased prevalence of impaired quality of life, poorer health scores or decreased physical activity [12].

EPEMIOLOGY

I. Elderly without CKD

Epidemiological studies of community-dwelling older adults suggest the prevalence of major depressive symptoms is about 1% - 4%. Depressive symptoms have been reported in up to 8% of elderly postmenopausal women. Furthermore, the prevalence of cognitive impairment in community dwelling older adults is about 18%, though this increases with age and about 5% have both depressive symptoms and cognitive impairment [13].

II. Elderly with CKD

The prevalence of depression in elderly increases further with the presence of one or more co-morbid chronic condition [12, 14, 15]. Examples of these conditions include diabetes mellitus, other psychiatric illnesses and substance abuse as well as CKD [12, 13, 16].

Major Depression is the most common psychiatric diagnosis in adults with CKD [14]. The prevalence of major depression is about 21% in the CKD population, [16] though when other depressive syndromes such as dysthmia are considered, the prevalence of depression increases to about 38% of CKD patients [17].

The strongest predictor of depression in patients with CKD is the presence of other psychiatric illnesses, this increases the risk of depression 12 –fold compared to those who do not have psychiatric illnesses [13, 16]. Furthermore, older adults with CKD and other chronic conditions like diabetes mellitus type 2 have twice the prevalence of depression compared to those without diabetes mellitus [18].

Surprisingly, the presence of depression does not vary significantly with the stage of kidney disease [15]. Given the emotional toll associated with impending dialysis, that is often observed in predialysis patients with CKD stage 4 -5, one would expect that the prevalence of depression would increase as kidney disease worsens. This would be further supported by the increased prevalence of depression in patients with ESRD. In a 2005 study of 51 older ESRD patients (70 years and above) on dialysis, sixty percent had depressive symptoms and almost half of these patients also had cognitive impairment [19]. Thus cognitive impairments and dementia are very common in older adults and often coexists with depression in elderly CKD patients.

Certain predisposing factors are associated with an increased risk of depression in patients with CKD. Depressed patients with CKD tend to be younger, caucasian, female and more likely to be unemployed. They also tend to have lower income, poor functional capacity and lower self-rated quality of life [13, 15, 16]. (Box 1.)

OUTCOMES IN CKD PATIENTS WITH DEPRESSION

The presence of depression in CKD is independently associated with poorer outcomes such as hospitalizations, progression to dialysis and death [20, 21].

Box 1. Predictors of Depression in Elderly Patients with Chronic Kidney Disease [12, 14 -19]

Alcohol or drug abuse
Other psychiatric illnesses
Comorbid chronic medical conditions:
Diabetes mellitus
Cardiovascular diseases
Stroke
Chronic lung disease
Poor functional status
Lower income status
Lower self rated quality of life
Other associated factors:
Caucasian race
Female sex

Table 1. Clinical Outcomes in Elderly Depressed Patients with Chronic Kidney Disease [8,9.15, 21,22,25,26]

CLINICAL OUTCOMES
Increased hospitalization (12,21,22)
Increased mortality (21,22)
Poorer health scores (15)
Decreased physical activity (15)
Impaired quality of life (15)
Increased suicide risk (25)
Increased depressive symptoms in spouse or caregiver (26)
Increased falls (8,9)

CKD patients with major depression are twice as likely to die or be hospitalized [21]. The presence of diabetes mellitus increases mortality almost 3-fold in depressed patients with advanced CKD, independent of age [18, 21, 22].

Though the prevalence of depressive symptoms and poor outcomes related to depression such as death and hospitalization are similar across age groups, older patients with CKD tend to report decreased physical activity and poorer health scores [13] which directly impact their quality of life (Table 1). This suggests that factors other than age play a key role in the impairment in quality of life in elderly patients with CKD. It is also important to note that presence of depression in the elderly is associated with other conditions such as cognitive impairment, sleep disorders and restless leg syndrome, [23] which can also affect quality of life.The presence of comorbid conditions like diabetes mellitus, congestive heart failure also plays a large role in outcomes of depressed elderly patients with CKD.

This is further confirmed by the fact that the risk of suicide in end stage renal disease (ESRD) patients and general population is more common in white males aged 75 years and older. Alcohol or drug abuse, co morbid conditions like diabetes mellitus, congestive heart failure, previous stroke and recent inpatient treatment for a psychiatric illness are other identified independent risk factors for suicide [24]. Depression in the elderly also has implications far beyond the quality of life and health status of patients but also negatively impacts the health and depressive symptoms of spouses or caregivers [25]. The severity of quality of life impairment and presence of depressive symptoms are comparable in older adults with CKD and ESRD populations on peritoneal or hemodialysis [26]. Though depression was found to be associated with an increased risk of peritonitis in ESRD patients on peritoneal dialysis [27].

Clinical Presentation

Depression in the elderly is often unrecognized and under diagnosed as the elderly often focus on somatic symptoms and are less likely to report depressed mood. In addition, medical conditions such as CKD, which is prevalent in the elderly, have somatic symptoms that can mimic symptoms of depression. Some of these somatic symptoms include: decreased activity level, decreased interest in activities previously enjoyed (anhedonia), fatigue, sleep disturbances, anorexia. Symptoms of uremic encephalopathy can also mimic psychomotor retardation or agitation seen in the depressed elderly [28]. This makes it even more difficult to recognize and diagnose in elderly patients with CKD. Often times, depressive symptoms in the elderly are associated with loneliness, social isolation or the loss of partners/spouses, close friends or relatives [29]. Concurrent symptoms of anxiety, more so in the elderly, are also very common and are usually associated with a more severe clinical presentation of depression and associated decreased clinical response to treatment [30].

Sexual dysfunction is a prevalent problem in both men and women with CKD, especially those with ESRD on dialysis. The prevalence ranges from about 30 – 80% and has been shown to consistently correlate with increasing age and presence of depression [31]. Given the high prevalence of sexual dysfunction, elderly patients with CKD should be asked about their sexual function and if any dysfunction exists, this should prompt screening for depressive symptoms.

Diagnosis

Major Depression is diagnosed by medical interview, according to the Diagnostic and Statistical Manual of Mental Disorders, 4th Edition, Text Revision (DSM IV-TR) criteria and requires the presence of at least five out of nine symptoms. Depressed mood or anhedonia must be present. The symptoms of depression must also be present daily for at least 2 weeks and be severe enough to affect activities of daily living [32].

There are several screening tools that are useful in detecting depressive symptoms and help identify patients who are at high risk for depression. Once depression is suspected by using a screening tool, it is then recommended that the presence of major depression be confirmed by thorough clinical interviewing using the DSM IV diagnostic criteria, which is regarded as the gold standard in diagnosing major depression [33-41].

Several screening tools have been validated in the elderly. These include: Two question screener [33, 42], the Geriatric Depression Scale [34-36], Patient Health Questionnaire [37-

39], Cornell Scale for Depression in Dementia, which is especially useful in older adults with dementia and the Center for Epidemiologic Studies Depression Scale (CES-D) [40, 41, 43] (Table 2).

Table 2. Screening Assessment Tools for Depression in the Elderly Patients

Screening tools	Cut off score	Sensitivity (%)	Specificity (%)	Validated in Elderly	Validated in Elderly with CKD
Geriatric Depression Scale (GDS) [37,38] 5-item 15-item	≥2 ≥5	94 63	81 82	Yes	Yes (ESRD patients on dialysis)
Beck Depression Inventory (BDI) [44-46]	≥11	89	88	Yes	Yes
Patient Health Questionnaire (PHQ) [39-41] 2-item 9-item	2 ≥10	100 88	77 88	Yes	No
Center for Epidemiologic Studies Depression Scale (CES-D) [42,43,47]	≥16	69	83	Yes	Yes (ESRD patients on dialysis)

In elderly patients with CKD, the Geriatric Depression Scale and Beck Depression Inventory [20, 44, 45] and the Center for Epidemiologic Studies Depression Scale (CES-D) are common tools that have been validated in screening for depression.

Of these screens, the two-question screener is used very commonly in clinical practice. It has the advantage of brevity and has a sensitivity of 96% – 97% and a specificity of 57% – 67%, which is comparable to other depression screening tools used in the elderly [33, 42]. The two questions in the screen are:

> During the past month, have you been bothered by feeling down, depressed or hopeless?"
> During the past month, have you been bothered by little interest or pleasure in doing things?

Geriatric Depression Scale (GDS)

Several versions of the GDS have been validated in both elderly patients and elderly patients with end stage renal disease. The five-item GDS has been validated in cognitively intact geriatric patients in various care settings such as the outpatient, acute inpatient hospital and nursing homes. It has a sensitivity of 94%, specificity of 81%, positive predictive value of 81% and negative predictive value of 94% [35]. The 15-item GDS-15 has been validated in elderly ESRD patients, a cut off score of ≥5 was shown to have a sensitivity of 63% and specificity of 82%. This compared favorably to the Beck Depression Inventory and the gold standard, a structured clinical interview using the DSM IV criteria, in detecting depressive symptoms [36].

Patient Health Questionnaire (PHQ)

The 9-item Patient Health Questionnaire (PHQ-9) screening tool for depression has been validated in the general population and specifically in the elderly, but not in CKD patients. It is a self-administered tool that is based on depressive symptoms identified in the DSM IV criteria. It is useful clinical because of its brevity and is also used extensively in research. The tool has been also found to be a reliable tool for assessing severity of depression and can be used as a measure in monitoring response to treatment in patient care. With a cut off score of ≥10 out of a maximum score of 27, PHQ-9 has a sensitivity of 88% and a specificity of 88% in screening for major depression. Scores of 5, 10, 15, and 20 are found to be representative of mild, moderate, moderately severe, and severe depression, respectively [37, 38].

The 2-item Patient Health Questionnaire (PHQ-2) has also been shown to be useful in the elderly with a sensitivity of 100% and specificity of 77%, compared to the DSM IV TR criteria for major depression [39].

Center for Epidemiologic Studies Depression Scale (CES-D)

The CES-D Scale is a 20-item screening tool for depression and is used mainly in community-based research. It is not usually used in clinical practice because of its length. It has been validated in older adults mainly in primary care settings [40, 41]. CES-D scale has not been specifically validated in elderly predialysis CKD patients but is used in those with ESRD. Few studies with the ESRD population use the CES-D as a screening tool for depression. In a study in ESRD patients on dialysis, the cut-off score of 18, was found to have a sensitivity and specificity of 69% and 83% respectively [43].

Beck Depression Inventory (BDI)

Beck Depression Inventory, a 21-item screening tool for major depression, has been validated in predialysis elderly patients with CKD and ESRD on dialysis. The sensitivity and specificity with a cut off score of ≥11 in predialysis CKD patients, mean age 64.5 ± 12 years, were 89% and 88% respectively compared to a structured DSM IV based interview [46].

However, in studies in patients with end stage renal disease (ESRD), higher cut off scores are used [44, 45]. This is likely to due to the fact that ESRD patients on dialysis tend to have a number of the somatic symptoms such as sleep disorders, anorexia, fatigue and malaise, as a result of their advanced kidney disease, which could confound typical depressive symptoms assessed with the BDI.

Management

Major depression in the elderly and in the CKD population is grossly undertreated [47, 48], despite the high prevalence of depression and its associated poor outcomes. Effective treatment rates of 17% to 29% have been reported in the elderly [49, 50] and in a 2003 study, only 16% of depressed CKD patients were being treated with antidepressants [47].Under treatment of depression in the elderly and in patients with CKD is likely related to the difficulty in diagnosing depression in these patients, given the presence of confounding somatic symptoms that mimick those found in depression. In addition, studies on efficacy and safety of different treatment modalities for depression often exclude the elderly and those with CKD. This often also results in underdosing of medications in both patient populations because of concerns about adverse effects. Therefore, effective treatment of depression in elderly patients with CKD is uniquely challenging given the very limited research that has been performed in this susceptible subset of patients [51-53].

Given the physiological changes and presence of comorbidities in the elderly, which can alter the pharmacokinetics of certain drug therapies and affect adherence to therapeutic interventions, it is also important to tailor these modalities to individual patient preferences, consider individual contraindications, monitor adverse effects and effectiveness of chosen interventions.

Management of depression in the elderly patient with CKD is similar to other patient populations in that both pharmacological and non-pharmacological interventions are utilized. The non-pharmacological interventions include psychotherapy, which is often a useful adjunct to drug therapy and electroconvulsive therapy, useful in severe cases of major depression, unresponsive to other treatment modalities. Exercise has also been found to be very useful in treating depressive symptoms in the elderly and in CKD patients [54-57].

In a meta-analytic comparison of pharmacotherapy and psychotherapy in treatment of late life depression, there was no significant difference in the effectiveness of the two interventions [58]. Combining both modalities often results in higher treatment success rates and also decreases the recurrence of major depressive episodes [59]. This is of special importance in the elderly as relapse rates are much higher compared to their younger counterparts [60].

Pharmacotherapy

There are four major classes of drugs used in the treatment of depression in the elderly and CKD patients: Selective Serotonin reuptake inhibitors (SSRIs), Tricyclic antidepressants (TCAs), Serotonin-norepinephrine reuptake inhibitors (SNRIs) and Atypical antidepressants (Table 3).

Monoamine Oxidase Inhibitors (MAOI) are rarely used in the elderly and CKD patients because of significant anticholinergic adverse effects such as cardiac conduction abnormalities, orthostatic hypotension, and urinary retention [61]. They also have increased risk of drug-drug interactions and they have to be administered with special dietary restrictions which could be very problematic in both the general elderly population and in

CKD. The following discussion will focus mainly on the four major antidepressant groups mentioned above.

Table 3. Potential Adverse Effects of Common Antidepressants used in Elderly Patients with CKD [58-67]

Medication class	Adverse effects	Clinical Recommendations
Selective Serotonin reuptake inhibitors (citalopram, escitalopram, fluoxetine, paroxetine, sertraline)	Hyponatremia, akathisia, sinus bradycardia, anorexia Sexual dysfunction, risk of bleeding, increased serotonergic activity Drug-drug interactions: (fluoxetine, paroxetine) Risk of fractures Risk of suicide in 1st month of therapy (observational studies)	Monitor closely for adverse effects Use lower doses and titrate slowly
Serotonin-norepinephrine reuptake inhibitors (venlafaxine, duloxetine, mirtazepine)	Diastolic hypertension (venlafaxine), increased sedation, weight gain.	Reduce dose: start with 50% of lowest recommended dose. Titrate slowly Monitor closely for adverse effects
Atypical antidepressants (bupropion, trazodone, nefazodone)	Contraindicated use with seizure disorder/alcohol detoxification Increased anxiety (bupropion) Increased sedation, priapism - rare(trazodone) Significant drug-drug interactions (nefazodone)	Buproprion: Avoid use in elderly with anxiety symptoms Trazodone : Start with lower doses and titrate slowly. Nefazodone: Avoid use in the elderly
Tricyclic antidepressants (TCAs)	Anticholinergic effects: increased confusion, orthostatic hypotension, urinary retention, cardiac conduction abnormalities	Use with caution Use lower doses Monitor closely for adverse effects.

i. Elderly with Depression

SSRIs are considered first line in treatment of depression in the elderly. Of all antidepressant drug classes, they are generally better tolerated, easily administered and have the least risk of adverse effects. Also, newer formulations of SSRIs such as citalopram and escitalopram have fewer drug-drug interactions compared to older SSRIs, which is especially important in elderly patients who are often prescribed other medications for coexisting medical conditions. SSRIs have been shown to be effective in treating depressive symptoms in the elderly [62], though their efficacy compared to other classes of antidepressants is less clear as few comparison studies have been conducted. Adverse effects of SSRIs which are of concern in the elderly include: hyponatremia, akathisia, sinus bradycardia and anorexia [63]. Other reported adverse effects in observational studies include: increased risk of fractures [64] and increased risk of suicide within the first month compared to treatment with other classes of antidepressants, though the overall absolute risk of suicide was very low in all antidepressant groups [65].

SNRIs are also commonly prescribed in elderly patients, often in those whose symptoms are unresponsive to SSRIs. Venlafaxine and duloxetine may be useful in depressed patients with pain symptoms [66]. Mirtazepine, another SNRI, is useful in treating symptoms of anorexia, weight loss and insomnia in depressed elderly, particularly at low doses. SNRIs are generally well tolerated but like the SSRIs can lead serotonin syndrome in any subset of the population, especially when combined with other medications such as opiods [67]. Other adverse effects include dose dependent diastolic hypertension (particularly with venlafaxine), increased sedation and weight gain, which may actually be beneficial in the frail depressed elderly with anorexia and weight loss.

TCAs are effective in treating depressive symptoms in the elderly but their use is limited due to increased risk of adverse effects resulting from their anticholinergic activity, such as increased confusion (particularly in elderly patients with cognitive deficits), orthostatic hypotension, urinary retention, closed angle glaucoma and cardiac conduction abnormalities [68].

Atypical antidepressants such as bupropion and trazodone are also commonly used in the elderly, though few studies have examined their efficacy [69]. Bupropion tends have an activating effect and is therefore useful in depressed patients with psychomotor retardation and fatigue. This activating effect could however increase anxiety symptoms in anxious depressed elderly. It is contraindicated in those with a history of seizures or alcohol detoxification as it lowers the seizure threshold. A common adverse effect in the elderly is dose dependent diastolic hypertension. Trazodone has a sedating effect and is often very useful in treating insomnia associated with depression. It is rarely used as the lone agent for treatment of depression. Adherence to trazodone is often an issue in elderly men because of a potential, but rare, side effect of priapism [67]. Nefazodone is very rarely used in the elderly due to significant drug-drug interactions. It is a potent inhibitor of the CYP450-3A4 isoenzyme and as such interacts with commonly prescribed medications such as macrolide antibiotics and cardiac antiarrythmics. Side effects commonly include restlessness and increased sedation [67].

ii. CKD with Depression

In treating depression in patients with CKD, there are concerns similar to those in elderly patients regarding the safety and tolerability of antidepressants. Of particular importance in CKD is the decreased rate of clearance of these medications and their metabolites, therefore making their half-life uncertain and unpredictable. This further complicates the use of these medications, particularly in those in moderate to severe CKD leading to accumulation of toxic metabolites of medications like nefazodone, venlafaxine and buproprion, significant anticholinergic effects with the use of TCAs, sexual dysfunction, increased bleeding and increased serotonergic activity causing nausea, noted with use of SSRIs. It also leads to increased risk of drug –drug interactions with the use of TCAs, SSRIs and MAOIs [70, 71].

All four major classes of antidepressants are used in patients with CKD, though there is very limited scientific data on the efficacy and safety of these medications [51-53]. No major studies have specifically examined this in elderly patients with CKD, though it is safe to assume that special attention needs to be directed to this subset of the population as they are very susceptible to adverse effects from antidepressant medications given the presence of two notable risk factors: old age and CKD.

Psychotherapy

Cognitive-behavioral therapy and interpersonal psychotherapy have been shown to be effective in treating late life depression, particularly when combined with antidepressant medications [72, 73]. However, the use of psychotherapy in the elderly is limited by the availability of trained psychotherapists and the cost of therapy as Medicare typically reimburses only about 50 percent of the total cost.

Similar studies examining the effectiveness of psychotherapy in patients with CKD have demonstrated efficacy similar to that in the general population [74].

Electroconvulsive Therapy (ECT)

ECT is usually reserved for treatment of major depression that is nonresponsive to all other modalities of treatment and is particularly useful in treating psychotic symptoms that may be present in very severe cases of depression. Several studies have examined the utility of ECT in the elderly and the current body of evidence shows that it is effective in the acute treatment of major depression and is generally safe. Tolerability of ECT in the elderly is similar to that of younger patients but remission rates tend to be higher in older adults compared to younger patients [75-77].

The efficacy of ECT in patients with CKD has not been specifically studied, though given the general tolerability and safety in the elderly, one could hypothesize that it would likely be quite effective in elderly patients with CKD as well.

Exercise

Several studies have looked at the usefulness of exercise in the treatment of depression in the elderly and in CKD patients. Physical activity tends to decrease with age. Up to 75% of end stage renal disease (ESRD) patients report a severe limitation in physical activity. This is more likely in those with depressive symptoms and is associated with an increased mortality risk [78, 79].

In the elderly, exercise programs have been shown to improve mood symptoms and self perception of quality of life [54].

Exercise programs, particularly regular moderate intensity aerobic and strength training programs and tai chi can also increase sleep quality in the elderly, which would likely positively impact mood symptoms as well [55, 56].

Exercise program studies in depressed CKD patients have mainly been confined to younger patients and these have suggested a positive correlation between exercise and improvement in depressive symptoms [57]. No studies have specifically examined the effects of exercise in the depressed elderly patient with CKD.

SUMMARY

Depression is very common in elderly adults with CKD [6] and is associated with grave outcomes [18-27]. As such screening and subsequent management of depression in these adults is extremely important and should be part of routine clinical assessments.

Several factors increase the risk of depression in this subset of population such as the presence of other psychiatric illnesses or chronic medical illnesses (i.e. diabetes mellitus), substance abuse, poor functional status and lower income status [12-19, 47].Depressed elderly with CKD have poorer outcomes compared to non-depressed counterparts. These include poor quality of life, increased hospitalization, increased nursing home admissions, progression to dialysis and even death. Falls, cognitive impairment, sleep disturbances and sexual dysfunction are also closely linked with depression in these adults [18-27].

Inspite of these grave outcomes, depression is often unrecognized, underdiagnosed and undertreated in these patients [28-30]. This is partially due to the fact that the elderly are less likely to report depressed mood and will often focus on somatic symptoms. Also, the presence of other chronic medical conditions may mimic symptoms of depression making it more difficult for medical practitioners to recognize and diagnose. This is made even especially difficult in elderly adults with advanced kidney disease, who also often have uremic symptoms such as psychomotor retardation or agitation, fatigue and anorexia [28].

Hence, it is imperative that medical practitioners routinely assess elderly adults with CKD for depression during each clinical encounter. Several screening tools can be used in clinical practice and have been validated in the elderly. Of these, the two-question screener [33, 42] and the 5-item GDS [34-36] are most commonly used because of their brevity with very comparable sensitivity and specificity to other screening tools and the gold standard for diagnosis, a structured clinical interview using the DSM IV criteria [32]. Specifically, in elderly patients with CKD, the screening tools for depression that have been validated are the GDS [34-36], BDI [44-46] and CES-D [40, 41, 43]. Of the three, the GDS and BDI are used in clinical practice though BDI may be more cumbersome to use because of its length, given time limitations in typical clinical settings.

The treatment of depression in the elderly with CKD also presents another challenge as very little research has been conducted in this subset of the population [51-53]. Most studies on efficacy and safety of treatment modalities for depression often exclude both the elderly and those with CKD, yet these adults are most susceptible to adverse effects, especially from pharmacological agents.

Therefore, treatment modalities in these elderly adults with CKD have to be tailored to individual patient preferences and contraindications. In addition, they have to be closely monitored for adverse effects and efficacy.

Of the pharmacological agents used, SSRIs seem to be the best tolerated in elderly adults [62-65]. SNRI are also commonly used with similar efficacy [66, 67]. Though they both have adverse effects that are of particular concern in the elderly with advanced CKD due to decreased clearance and accumulation of metabolites, especially with venlafaxine. Some of the SSRIs also have significant drug-drug interactions i.e. older SSRIs (paroxetine and fluoxetine).

The use of TCAs in treating depression in the elderly with CKD is limited as a result of their anticholinergic activity resulting in adverse effects such as increased confusion, orthostatic hypotension predisposing to falls and cardiac conduction abnormalities [68].

Atypical antidepressants such as buproprion and trazodone can also be useful in certain elderly adults. For instance, trazodone has a sedating effect that could be effective in treating depressed elderly with insomnia. Though they have significant adverse effects too in elderly adults [67, 69] (Table 3).

Non pharmacological modalities such as psychotherapy and exercise programs are effective adjuncts in treating depression in the elderly and in those with CKD, particularly when combined with antidepressants [54-57, 72-74, 78, 79].

ECT is typically used in very severe cases of depression in the elderly, particularly in those with psychotic symptoms or non responsive to other treatment modalities. Its use in elderly patients with CKD has not been specifically studied [75-77].

Overall, depression in elderly adults with CKD presents a unique blend of challenges not only in detecting and diagnosing clinical depression but also in the management of symptoms in these highly vulnerable adults who are very susceptible to poor outcomes. This combined with very limited data on the efficacy and safety of treatment modalities makes it even more likely for them to have adverse effects. Unfortunately, this can also lead to under treatment as medical practitioners, in trying to avoid adverse effects from different treatment modalities of depression, may be over cautious and prescribe sub optimal doses of antidepressants or forgo other interventions such as psychotherapy, exercise programs and ECT.

With depression being so common in elderly adults with CKD, medical practitioners need to be vigilante in actively screening for symptoms of depression in routine clinical encounters and they need to have a low threshold for treatment of these symptoms, coupled with very close monitoring for adverse effects and effectiveness of treatment intervention.

REFERENCES

[1] Department of Economic and Social Affairs, Population Division, United Nations. World Population Ageing: 1950-2050. New York: United Nations; 2001.

[2] Administration on Aging, U.S. Department of Health and Human Services. A profile of older Americans: 2006. U.S. *Department of Health and Human Services*; 2006.

[3] Schneider KM, O'Donnell BE, Dean D. Prevalence of multiple chronic conditions in the United States' Medicare population. *Health Qual Life Outcomes*. 2009;7:82.

[4] Coresh J, Selvin E, Stevens LA, Manzi J, Kusek JW, Eggers P, et al. Prevalence of chronic kidney disease in the United States. *JAMA*. 2007;298(17):2038-47.

[5] Heron MP. Table 1. Deaths, percentage of total deaths, and death rates for the 10 leading causes of death in selected age groups, by race and sex: United States, 2004. *National Health Vital Statistics Reports*. 2007;56(5):19.

[6] Kutner NG, Zhang R, Huang Y, Bliwise DL. Patient-reported sleep difficulty and cognitive function during the first year of dialysis. *Int. Urol. Nephrol*. 2008;40(1):203-10.

[7] Kutner NG. Promoting functioning and well-being in older CKD patients: review of recent evidence. *Int. Urol. Nephrol*. 2008;40(4):1151-8.

[8] Byers AL, Sheeran T, Mlodzianowski AE, Meyers BS, Nassisi P, Bruce ML. Depression and risk for adverse falls in older home health care patients. *Res.Gerentol. nurs.* 2008;1(4):245-51.

[9] Sheeran T, Brown EL, Nassisi P, Bruce ML. Does depression predict falls among home health patients? Using a clinical-research partnership to improve the quality of geriatric care. *Home Healthc Nurse.* 2004;22(6):384-9.

[10] Abdel-Rahman EM, Yan G, Turgut F, Balogun RA. Long-Term Morbidity and Mortality Related to Falls in Hemodialysis Patients: Role of Age and Gender - A Pilot Study. *Nephron Clin. Pract.* 2011;118(3):c278-84.

[11] Desmet C, Beguin C, Swine C, Jadoul M, Université Catholique de Louvain Collaborative Group. Falls in hemodialysis patients: prospective study of incidence, risk factors, and complications. *Am. J. Kidney Dis.* 2005;45(1):148-53.

[12] McClellan WM, Abramson J, Newsome B, Temple E, Wadley VG, Audhya P, et al. Physical and psychological burden of chronic kidney disease among older adults. *Am J Nephrol.* 2010;31(4):309-17.

[13] Fiest KM, Currie SR, Williams JV, Wang J. Chronic conditions and major depression in community-dwelling older adults. *J. Affect Disord.* 2010;.

[14] Sermet C. Évolution de l'état de santé des personnes âgées en France. *INSERM.* 1998;.

[15] Goveas JS, Espeland MA, Woods NF, Wassertheil-Smoller S, Kotchen JM. Depressive symptoms and incidence of mild cognitive impairment and probable dementia in elderly women: the Women's Health Initiative Memory Study. *J. Am. Geriatr. Soc.* 2011;59(1):57-66.

[16] Hedayati SS, Minhajuddin AT, Toto RD, Morris DW, Rush AJ. Prevalence of major depressive episode in CKD. *Am. J. Kidney Dis.* 2009;54(3):424-32.

[17] Andrade CP, Cruz MC, Urrutia M, Pereira O, Draibe SA, Nogueira-Martins LA, et al. Evaluation of depressive symptoms in patients with chronic renal failure. JN, *J. nephrol.* 2010;23(2):168-74.

[18] Shehatah A, Rabie MA, Al-Shahry A. Prevalence and correlates of depressive disorders in elderly with type 2 diabetes in primary health care settings. *J. Affect Disord.* 2010;123(1-3):197-201.

[19] Tyrrell J, Paturel L, Cadec B, Capezzali E, Poussin G. Older patients undergoing dialysis treatment: cognitive functioning, depressive mood and health-related quality of life. *Aging Ment Health.* 2005;9(4):374-9.

[20] Hedayati SS, Minhajuddin AT, Afshar M, Toto RD, Trivedi MH, Rush AJ. Association between major depressive episodes in patients with chronic kidney disease and initiation of dialysis, hospitalization, or death. *JAMA.* 2010;303(19):1946-53.

[21] Hedayati SS, Bosworth HB, Briley LP, Sloane RJ, Pieper CF, Kimmel PL, et al. Death or hospitalization of patients on chronic hemodialysis is associated with a physician-based diagnosis of depression. *Kidney Int.* 2008;74(7):930-6.

[22] Young BA, Von Korff M, Heckbert SR, Ludman EJ, Rutter C, Lin EH, et al. Association of major depression and mortality in Stage 5 diabetic chronic kidney disease. *Gen. Hosp. Psychiatry.* 2010;32(2):119-24.

[23] Szentkiralyi A, Molnar MZ, Czira ME, Deak G, Lindner AV, Szeifert L, et al. Association between restless legs syndrome and depression in patients with chronic kidney disease. *J. Psychosom. Res.* 2009;67(2):173-80.

[24] Kurella M, Kimmel PL, Young BS, Chertow GM. Suicide in the United States end-stage renal disease program. *J. Am. Soc. Nephrol.* 2005;16(3):774-81.

[25] Pruchno R, Wilson-Genderson M, Cartwright F. Self-rated health and depressive symptoms in patients with end-stage renal disease and their spouses: a longitudinal dyadic analysis of late-life marriages. *J. Gerontol. B. Psychol. Sci Soc. Sci.* 2009;64(2):212-21.

[26] Abdel-Kader K, Myaskovsky L, Karpov I, Shah J, Hess R, Dew MA, et al. Individual quality of life in chronic kidney disease: influence of age and dialysis modality. *Clin. J. Am. Soc. Nephrol.* 2009;4(4):711-8.

[27] Troidle L, Watnick S, Wuerth DB, Gorban-Brennan N, Kliger AS, Finkelstein FO. Depression and its association with peritonitis in long-term peritoneal dialysis patients. *Am. J. Kidney Dis.* 2003;42(2):350-4.

[28] Kimmel PL. Depression in patients with chronic renal disease: what we know and what we need to know. *J Psychosom Res.* 2002;53(4):951-6.

[29] Muller-Spahn F, Hock C. Clinical presentation of depression in the elderly. *Gerontology.* 1994;40(Suppl 1):10-4.

[30] Lenze EJ, Mulsant BH, Shear MK, Houck P, Reynolds III CF. Anxiety symptoms in elderly patients with depression: what is the best approach to treatment? *Drugs Aging.* 2002;19(10):753-60.

[31] Navaneethan SD, Vecchio M, Johnson DW, Saglimbene V, Graziano G, Pellegrini F, et al. Prevalence and correlates of self-reported sexual dysfunction in CKD: a meta-analysis of observational studies. *Am. J. Kidney Dis.* 2010;56(4):670-85.

[32] American Psychiatric Association. Diagnostic and statistical manual of mental disorders : DSM-IV. 4th ed. Washington, DC: American Psychiatric Association; 1994.

[33] Arroll B, Khin N, Kerse N. Screening for depression in primary care with two verbally asked questions: cross sectional study. *BMJ.* 2003;327(7424):1144-6.

[34] Montorio I, Izal M. The Geriatric Depression Scale: a review of its development and utility. *Int Psychogeriatr.* 1996;8(1):103-12.

[35] Rinaldi P, Mecocci P, Benedetti C, Ercolani S, Bregnocchi M, Menculini G, et al. Validation of the five-item geriatric depression scale in elderly subjects in three different settings. *J.Am. Geriatr. Soc.* 2003;51(5):694-8.

[36] Balogun RA, Turgut F, Balogun SA, Holroyd S, Abdel-Rahman EM. Screening for Depression in Elderly Hemodialysis Patients. *Nephron Clin. Pract.* 2010;118(2):c72-7.

[37] Kroenke K, Spitzer RL, Williams JB. The PHQ-9: validity of a brief depression severity measure. *J. Gen. Intern. Med.* 2001;16(9):606-13.

[38] Lowe B, Unutzer J, Callahan CM, Perkins AJ, Kroenke K. Monitoring depression treatment outcomes with the patient health questionnaire-9. *Med. Care.* 2004;42 (12):1194-201.

[39] Li C, Friedman B, Conwell Y, Fiscella K. Validity of the Patient Health Questionnaire 2 (PHQ-2) in identifying major depression in older people. *J. Am. Geriatr. Soc.* 2007;55 (4):596-602.

[40] Kohout FJ, Berkman LF, Evans DA, Cornoni-Huntley J. Two shorter forms of the CES-D (Center for Epidemiological Studies Depression) depression symptoms index. *J. Aging Health.* 1993;5(2):179-93.

[41] Radloff LS. The CES-D scale: a self report depression scale for research in the general population. *Appl. Psychol.Meas.* 1977;1(3):385-401.

[42] Whooley MA, Avins AL, Miranda J, Browner WS. Case-finding instruments for depression. Two questions are as good as many. *J. Gen. Intern. Med.* 1997;12(7):439-45.

[43] Hedayati SS, Bosworth HB, Kuchibhatla M, Kimmel PL, Szczech LA. The predictive value of self-report scales compared with physician diagnosis of depression in hemodialysis patients. *Kidney Int.* 2006;69(9):1662-8.

[44] Craven JL, Rodin GM, Littlefield C. The Beck Depression Inventory as a screening device for major depression in renal dialysis patients. *Int J Psychiatry Med.* 1988;18(4):365-74.

[45] Watnick S, Wang PL, Demadura T, Ganzini L. Validation of 2 depression screening tools in dialysis patients. *Am. J. Kidney Dis.* 2005;46(5):919-24.

[46] Hedayati SS, Minhajuddin AT, Toto RD, Morris DW, Rush AJ. Validation of depression screening scales in patients with CKD. *Am. J. Kidney Dis.* 2009;54(3):433-9.

[47] Watnick S, Kirwin P, Mahnensmith R, Concato J. The prevalence and treatment of depression among patients starting dialysis. *Am. J. Kidney Dis.* 2003;41(1):105-10.

[48] Lebowitz BD, Pearson JL, Schneider LS, Reynolds CF,3rd, Alexopoulos GS, Bruce ML, et al. Diagnosis and treatment of depression in late life. Consensus statement update. *JAMA*. 1997;278(14):1186-90.

[49] Fyffe DC, Sirey JA, Heo M, Bruce ML. Late-life depression among black and white elderly homecare patients. *Am. J. Geriatr. Psychiatry*. 2004;12(5):531-5.

[50] Unutzer J, Katon W, Callahan CM, Williams JW,Jr, Hunkeler E, Harpole L, et al. Depression treatment in a sample of 1,801 depressed older adults in primary care. *J. Am. Geriatr. Soc.* 2003;51(4):505-14.

[51] Turk S, Atalay H, Altintepe L, Guney I, Okudan N, Tonbul HZ, et al. Treatment with antidepressive drugs improved quality of life in chronic hemodialysis patients. *Clin. Nephrol.* 2006;65(2):113-8.

[52] Finkelstein FO, Finkelstein SH. Depression in chronic dialysis patients: assessment and treatment. *Nephrol Dial. Transplant.* 2000;15(12):1911-3.

[53] Blumenfield M, Levy NB, Spinowitz B, Charytan C, Beasley CM,Jr, Dubey AK, et al. Fluoxetine in depressed patients on dialysis. *Int. J. Psychiatry Med.* 1997;27(1):71-80.

[54] Kerse N, Hayman KJ, Moyes SA, Peri K, Robinson E, Dowell A, et al. Home-based activity program for older people with depressive symptoms: DeLLITE--a randomized controlled trial. *Ann. Fam. Med.* 2010;8(3):214-23.

[55] Li F, Fisher KJ, Harmer P, Irbe D, Tearse RG, Weimer C. Tai chi and self-rated quality of sleep and daytime sleepiness in older adults: a randomized controlled trial. *J. Am.Geriatr. Soc.* 2004;52(6):892-900.

[56] King AC, Oman RF, Brassington GS, Bliwise DL, Haskell WL. Moderate-intensity exercise and self-rated quality of sleep in older adults. A randomized controlled trial. *JAMA*. 1997;277(1):32-7.

[57] Kouidi E, Karagiannis V, Grekas D, Iakovides A, Kaprinis G, Tourkantonis A, et al. Depression, heart rate variability, and exercise training in dialysis patients. *Eur. J. Cardiovasc Prev. Rehabil.* 2010;17(2):160-7.

[58] Pinquart M, Duberstein PR, Lyness JM. Treatments for later-life depressive conditions: a meta-analytic comparison of pharmacotherapy and psychotherapy. *Am. J. Psychiatry*. 2006;163(9):1493-501.

[59] Reynolds CF,3rd, Frank E, Perel JM, Imber SD, Cornes C, Miller MD, et al. Nortriptyline and interpersonal psychotherapy as maintenance therapies for recurrent major depression: a randomized controlled trial in patients older than 59 years. *JAMA*. 1999;281(1):39-45.

[60] Mitchell AJ, Subramaniam H. Prognosis of depression in old age compared to middle age: a systematic review of comparative studies. *Am. J. Psychiatry*. 2005;162(9):1588-601.

[61] Georgotas A, McCue RE, Hapworth W, Friedman E, Kim OM, Welkowitz J, et al. Comparative efficacy and safety of MAOIs versus TCAs in treating depression in the elderly. *Biol. Psychiatry*. 1986;21(12):1155-66.

[62] Solai LK, Mulsant BH, Pollock BG. Selective serotonin reuptake inhibitors for late-life depression: a comparative review. *Drugs Aging*. 2001;18(5):355-68.

[63] Fabian TJ, Amico JA, Kroboth PD, Mulsant BH, Corey SE, Begley AE, et al. Paroxetine-induced hyponatremia in older adults: a 12-week prospective study. *Arch.Intern. Med.* 2004;164(3):327-32.

[64] Richards JB, Papaioannou A, Adachi JD, Joseph L, Whitson HE, Prior JC, et al. Effect of selective serotonin reuptake inhibitors on the risk of fracture. *Arch. Intern. Med.* 2007;167(2):188-94.

[65] Juurlink DN, Mamdani MM, Kopp A, Redelmeier DA. The risk of suicide with selective serotonin reuptake inhibitors in the elderly. *Am. J. Psychiatry*. 2006;163(5):813-21.

[66] Nelson JC, Wohlreich MM, Mallinckrodt CH, Detke MJ, Watkin JG, Kennedy JS. Duloxetine for the treatment of major depressive disorder in older patients. *Am. J. Geriatr. Psychiatry*. 2005;13(3):227-35.

[67] Spina E, Scordo MG. Clinically significant drug interactions with antidepressants in the elderly. *Drugs Aging*. 2002;19(4):299-320.

[68] Mittmann N, Herrmann N, Shulman KI, Silver IL, Busto UE, Borden EK, et al. The effectiveness of antidepressants in elderly depressed outpatients: a prospective case series study. *J. Clin. Psychiatry*. 1999;60(10):690-7.

[69] Steffens DC, Doraiswamy PM, McQuoid DR. Bupropion SR in the naturalistic treatment of elderly patients with major depression. *Int. J. Geriatr. Psychiatry*. 2001;16(9):862-5.

[70] Hedayati SS, Finkelstein FO. Epidemiology, diagnosis, and management of depression in patients with CKD. *Am. J. Kidney Dis.* 2009;54(4):741-52.

[71] Cohen LM, Tessier EG, Germain MJ, Levy NB. Update on psychotropic medication use in renal disease. *Psychosomatics*. 2004;45(1):34-48.

[72] Arean PA, Cook BL. Psychotherapy and combined psychotherapy/pharmacotherapy for late life depression. *Biol. Psychiatry*. 2002;52(3):293-303.

[73] Wilson KC, Mottram PG, Vassilas CA. Psychotherapeutic treatments for older depressed people. *Cochrane Database Syst. Rev.* 2008;(1)(1):CD004853.

[74] Cukor D. Use of CBT to treat depression among patients on hemodialysis. *Psychiatr. Serv.* 2007;58(5):711-2.

[75] van der Wurff FB, Stek ML, Hoogendijk WJ, Beekman AT. The efficacy and safety of ECT in depressed older adults: a literature review. *Int. J. Geriatr. Psychiatry*. 2003;18(10):894-904.

[76] Tew JD,Jr, Mulsant BH, Haskett RF, Prudic J, Thase ME, Crowe RR, et al. Acute efficacy of ECT in the treatment of major depression in the old-old. *Am. J. Psychiatry*. 1999;156 (12):1865-70.

[77] O'Connor MK, Knapp R, Husain M, Rummans TA, Petrides G, Smith G, et al. The influence of age on the response of major depression to electroconvulsive therapy: a C.O.R.E. Report. *Am. J. Geriatr. Psychiatry*. 2001;9(4):382-90.

[78] Stack AG, Murthy B. Exercise and limitations in physical activity levels among new dialysis patients in the United States: an epidemiologic study. *Ann. Epidemiol*. 2008;18 (12):880-8.

[79] Stack AG, Molony DA, Rives T, Tyson J, Murthy BV. Association of physical activity with mortality in the US dialysis population. *Am. J. Kidney Dis*. 2005;45 (4):690-701.

In: Depression in the Elderly
Editor: Emaad Abdel-Rahman, pp. 67-83
ISBN 978-1-61324-771-6

Chapter 4

DEPRESSION IN ELDERLY PATIENTS WITH END STAGE RENAL DISEASE TREATED WITH DIALYSIS OR KIDNEY TRANSPLANTATION

Emaad M. Abdel-Rahman*, Rasheed A. Balogun and Faruk Turgut
Division of Nephrology, University of Virginia,
Charlottesville, Virginia, USA

INTRODUCTION

As individuals and as nations, we are growing older. The elderly, defined as those 65 years of age and above, are the fastest growing population group in America. According to the 2008 United States census bureau report, the number of elders grew from 29.6 million in 1990 to 36.8 million in 2008, representing a 20% incremental growth [1]. This aging of the population is mirrored by an increase in the number of patients with chronic kidney disease (CKD) [2]. Similar trends are noted in patients reaching end stage renal disease (ESRD); USRDS data indicate that the incident ESRD population is aging. In 1990, there were 21,479 incident ESRD patients aged 65 or older in the United States; this number steadily increased to 53,842 by 2006. In fact, older individuals comprise the most rapidly growing segment of the ESRD population in the wealthier countries [3]. In USA, the median age of incident dialysis patients is 64.4 years, and adjusted-incidence rate of ESRD in individuals older than 75 years has grown considerably when compared to subjects in the 20-44 or 45-64 age groups (11% vs. 2.4% vs. 6.1%, respectively) [4].

The course of CKD patients faces many challenges including medical and psychosocial challenges. While the medical factors arising as complications of CKD were vastly studied, we are now realizing the importance of the psychosocial factors associated with CKD. Hence, the impact of psychosocial factors on the outcome of CKD patients has been receiving more attention [5-8]. Depressive symptoms and depression are generally accepted to be the most

* Phone (434) 243-2671, Fax: (434) 924-5848, Email: ea6n@virginia.edu

common psychological problem encountered in CKD patients [9]. Depression is defined by the Diagnostic and Statistical Manual of Mental Disorders, 4th edition (DSM-IV), as having a loss of pleasure or interest for two weeks, accompanied by five or more psychological, somatic and behavioral symptoms [10]. Depression is one of the most common illnesses in the elderly. Under-recognition of depression in the elderly patients is a major concern, particularly given the evidence of its impact on morbidity and mortality.

EPIDEMIOLOGY

Depression was found to occur at a prevalence rate of 8.2% within a community-dwelling elderly population [11]. Although it was hypothesized that elderly patients cope better with critical illness and accept it as part of the aging process, this population are also more likely to underreport depression because of the fear of the stigma of psychiatric disease [12], suggesting that the prevalence of depression in elderly could be even higher.

Further epidemiological studies reported that 15-20% of elderly population experience significant depressive symptoms [13]. Although some studies reported that age was inversely related to depression [14, 15], studies indicate that the elderly, especially those with vascular risk factors, are more prone to depression; thus, elderly CKD patients have a higher risk of developing depression [13]. Depression is common in patients with chronic physical illness, including CKD of all stages (Table 1) [16]. Once these patients reach ESRD, renal replacement therapy (RRT) in the form of either dialysis or kidney transplantation (KT) is usually imperative to stay alive. Regardless of the modality used to manage RRT, depression remains prevalent [5, 17-19].

The incidence and prevalence of depression are highest in those older dialysis patients. One study showed that as many as 61% of elderly hemodialysis (HD) patients were found to be depressed [19]. However, the true prevalence of depression is not known, because its prevalence varies widely across studies, which may reflect in part the use of different diagnostic criteria and screening tools [18, 20, 21].Furthermore, patients treated with peritoneal dialysis (PD) were not included in most of these studies. Few studies have compared the incidence and prevalence of depression, and its outcomes in PD patients [22, 23]. In one study of PD patients, patients with depressive symptoms were older (62.5 vs 52.5 years) with one third of PD patients having symptoms of depression based on a simple self-administered scale [24]. A recent study detected depression in 70% of automated PD and 62.5% of continuous ambulatory PD patients [25].

Similar trends of increased incidence and prevalence of depression are also noted in patients undergoing KT [5, 17-19]. In a retrospective observational study of the USRDS data looking at 47, 899 kidney transplant recipients who underwent KT between 1995 and 2003, depression was identified in 3,360 patients in the 3 years post transplantation. Cumulative incidences were 5.05%, 7.29%, and 9.10% at 1, 2, and 3 years post transplantation [12]. Depression in the elderly was noted in 6.8%. This percentage of depression in elderly was more common than in those patients aged 0-17, 18-34, and 35-49 with depression noted in 5.7%, 6.6% and 4.1% respectively [12].

Furthermore, to study whether there was any difference in psychological adjustment between recipients of kidneys from cadavers versus recipients of kidneys from live related donors, Schlebusch et al compared 10 patients who received living-related kidney versus 30 patients receiving kidneys from cadavers, and found no statistically significant differences in the prevalence of depression between both groups. They also showed that 20% of the patients overall were depressed [26]. Taken together, these results highlight the importance of studying depression prevalence and symptoms in patients after KT, both from living-related donor or cadaver.

Table 1. Percentage of depression in association with renal replacement therapy

Study	Renal replacement therapy	Patient number	Mean age (years) 0-17	Depression (%)	Tool
Dobbels (12)	KT	1437 8526 14753 16573 6658	18-34 35-49 50-64 >65	5.7 6.6 4.1 7.1 6.8	Medicare Claim
Hedayati (16)	CKD (Stage 2-5)	274	64.5	21	DSM-IV
Balogun (18)	HD	62	73	30.6 (DSM-IV) 32.3 (GDS-15) 37.1 (BDI)	DSM-IV GDS-15 BDI
Tyrrell (19)	HD PD	25 26	76 79	43	MADRS
Guney (25)	APD CAPD	20 48	46 53	70 62.5	BDI
Schlebusch (26)	KT	40	37	20	BDI
BOLDE (28)	HD PD	70 70	73 73	26 10	HADS
Spencer (29)	KT	58	49	22.4	BDI
Alavi (30)	KT	100	40	39%	SCL90
Giordano (34)	HD	31	70	61 (BDI) 58 (GDS-15)	BDI GDS-15
Akman (50)	KT	27	29	23.2	BDI
Tsunoda (66)	KT	116	50	41.4	Zung-DS
Novak (72)	KT	84	49	22	CES-D

BOLDE: the Broadening Options for Long-term Dialysis in the Elderly (BOLDE) study, KT: kidney transplantation, MADRS: Montgomery-Asberg Depression Rating Scale, BDI = Beck Depression Inventory; GDS-15 = 15-item Geriatric Depression Scale, HADS: Hospital Anxiety and Depression Scale, SCL-90: Symptom Checklist-90, CES-D: Center foe Epidemiologic Studies-Depression scale, Zung-DS: Zung Self-Rating Depression Scale.

TREATMENT MODALITY AND DEPRESSION

The morbidity and mortality outcomes in elderly patients treated for ESRD with either PD or HD are similar [27]. However, the influence of treatment modality on depression is not fully determined. In the Broadening Options for Long-term Dialysis in the Elderly (BOLDE) study, depressive symptoms (using the Hospital Anxiety and Depression Scale) were similar in PD and HD patients who had been on dialysis for less than a year; however, there was significantly higher depression prevalence in HD patients who have been on dialysis longer than 12 months [28]. Although it was not primarily designed for the elderly population, in a very recent cross-sectional study, the effects of automated PD and continuous ambulatory PD on depression were investigated using Beck Depression Inventory (BDI) and depression was found to be similar in both treatment modalities [25].

The prevalence of depression following kidney transplantation may be similar in the graft recipient group as compared to patients on HD [17]. In a sample of 58 transplant patients, using BDI scores, it was shown that 22.4% of the patients studied had significant depressive symptoms, a percentage comparable to that for depression in HD patients [29]. In contradiction to these results, Alavi et al showed that the prevalence of depression was less is patients receiving KT as compared to those on HD. In their study, they compared the prevalence of depression in hundred patients who underwent KT with 63 HD patients. Though, depression was less prevalent in patients receiving KT, yet these patients were younger, better educated and with fewer comorbidities [30]. Thus, probably the prevalence of depression in modalities, post KT and hemodialysis, are comparable.

In addition to the comparable prevalence of depression in both patients following KT and those on HD, the symptoms of depression are also similar in both groups. Karaminia et al studied 71 patients with ESRD, 32 were kidney transplant recipients and 39 were patients maintained on HD. They compared the symptoms of depression between the groups studied, and showed no significant difference between the two groups in the score for depression. They concluded that depressive symptoms did not seem to improve after KT [17].

I. Depression in Elderly Dialysis Patients

Chronic diseases can cause physical limitations or disabilities, impacting negatively the elderly capacity of being independent. Dialysis is often a lifelong treatment in the elderly due to the reduced suitability for transplantation, with the vast majority of people who are treated for ESRD being maintained on HD. Furthermore, the percent of elderly patients maintained on PD remains strikingly low compared to patients in the 20 to 55-year-old age group [4]. The dialysis changes the life style of patients and family members due to the dedication of time it requires for the sessions, medical appointments, dietary changes and drinking habits. Although depression in the elderly dialysis patients is a common problem, only a small percentage get the help they need [31].

A. Predictors of Depression in Dialysis Patients

Depression is one of the most common illnesses in the elderly, but depression is not a normal or necessary part of aging. The etiology of depression in dialysis patients is multifactorial relating to social, psychological and biological mechanisms (Table 2). Depression can be secondary to loss of independence, problems with mobility and health, a change in the primary role in the family and diminution of cognitive skills [32]. These patients with ESRD on HD often have dietary and fluid restrictions, time constraints, functional limitations, loss of employment, loss of role in workplace, society, change in sexual function and constant fear of death [33]. Multiple factors associated with ESRD may have profound effects on depression (Figure 1). These persistent stressors can finally lead to psychological problems including depression. Many other factors were found to be associated with depression including longer duration of dialysis, comorbid conditions and hypoalbuminemia [31]. But, none of these factors are specific to elderly dialysis patients.

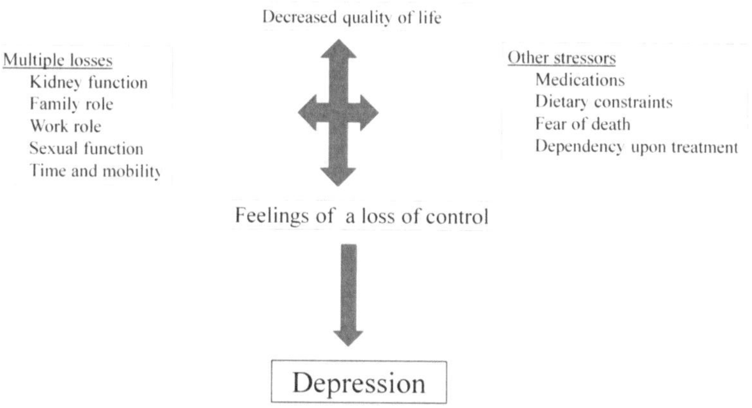

Figure 1.

Table 2. Causes and Predictors of Depression in Association with ESRD

Dialysis-Related	Transplantation-Related
Loss of independence, mobility and health (32) Diminution of cognitive skills Dietary and fluid restrictions, Time constraints Change in sexual function Fear of death Loss of employment Loss of role in workplace, society, and family	Donor's age> 65 years (12) Certain Demographic characteristics (Whites, females, Diabetics, long dialysis vintage) (12) Loss of renal graft and return to dialysis (50) Paradoxical Depression (29, 52) Use of immunosuppressant drugs (53) Being on a waiting list for KT (60) Prior renal graft rejection (66) Socio-economic factors (66) Lack of self-care behavior (68) Decrease level of interest in health-related information(69) Previous psychiatric history (70)

B. Clinical Manifestations and Diagnosis

The overlap between common symptoms related to kidney failure and depressive symptoms are potential confounders of the diagnosis of depression in dialysis patients. Elderly dialysis patients who deny feeling sad or depressed may still have major depression. Therefore, some clues should be looked for in this patient group (Table 3).

Table 3. Depression Diagnostic Clues in the Elderly

Unexplained or aggravated aches and pains	Loss of feeling of pleasure
Hopelessness	Slowed movement
Helplessness	Irritability
Anxiety and worries	Lack of interest in personal care (skipping meals, forgetting medications, neglecting personal hygiene)
Memory problems	

It is important to be clear what exactly is meant by depression. The elderly dialysis patients may manifest an atypical picture or masked depression. Although depression symptoms are commonly encountered in CKD patients, some of these symptoms, including anhedonia and feeling of sadness, helplessness, guilt, hopelessness, etc., are accompanied by changes in sleep, appetite, and libido, which are also the somatic ramifications of uremia in CKD patients. Whether these overlapping symptoms should be removed or included in the diagnostic criteria of depression remains inconclusive [21].

C. Screening for Depression

The gold-standard method for diagnosing depression is a full psychiatric interview by a trained (mental) health professional, usually a psychiatrist [10]. The gold standard for diagnosing depression, the structured psychiatric interview, has been examined in dialysis patients, and proven to be the best for diagnosing depression. Dialysis patients may report depressive symptoms, such as decreased energy, poor appetite and sleep disturbance on self-report depression questionnaires; however, they may not be confirmed as an episode of a major depressive disorder by using a DSM-IV-based structured clinical interview. Unfortunately, this method of structured psychiatric interview is often too time-consuming and impractical to use in everyday practice; thus, various screening tools that identify patients at a high risk of depression have been identified. Although self reported scales are not as accurate as establishing the diagnosis of depressive disorder using the DSM-IV, depression screening tools are usually easy to administer self-reports, requiring the patient to rate symptom frequency or severity [20]. Tools used for the general population may be inapplicable for ESRD patients, and each individual tool has to be validated in this unique group of people with ESRD. The best screening tool for identifying and quantifying depression in CKD patients have not been determined. Some of the tools used to assess depression in these patients are below.

Geriatric Depression Scale

The Geriatric Depression Scale (GDS), specifically developed for older patients in the general population, has been tested in older ESRD patients [18, 34]. Short forms of the GDS with 1, 4, 10 and 15 questions (compared to the 30 questions of the original version) are also available and their use in clinical practice is preferred by busy clinicians because of shorter administration time [18]. We recently investigated and validated the use of the 15-item Geriatric Depression Scale (GDS-15) as an effective screening tool for depression in elderly HD patients [18]. Compared to the gold standard DSM-IV validated psychiatric interview, the results of the GDS-15 questionnaire had a high predictive accuracy of depression in these patients and represents a much simpler, less time-consuming, and valid screening tool developed specifically for older patients.

Beck Depression Inventory

The Beck Depression Inventory, a standard self-administered questionnaire, is considered to be the standard instrument for assessing symptoms of depression and screening clinical depression [35]. The BDI is one such screening tool used in a number of studies in dialysis patients [7, 36]. We further validated it as a tool to screen for depression in elderly patients on HD [18]. The BDI consists of a 21-item questionnaire used to rate the frequency or severity of depressive symptoms, with each item rated on a four-point scale for a total of 0 to 63 [37]. There are at least three different versions BDI I (1961), an amended BDI IA (1979) and then a significantly altered BDI II (1996) version. In short, BDI II was developed to correspond to criteria in the DSM IV whereas the original and amended versions were developed based on descriptive symptoms of depression reported by depressed psychiatric patients. The questionnaires are so different that BDI II scores cannot be directly compared to BDI I /IA scores. Unfortunately, in many of the studies, the version used is not clearly specified and others have noted that researchers unaware of the different versions often cite the original 1961 version by default. This is obviously a major issue.

D. Outcome of Depression in Dialysis Patients

Several outcomes were recognized to be associated with depression in elderly patients on dialysis (table 4). In these patients, depression has been found to be an independent marker of poor prognosis [36]. It is associated with increased medical morbidity and mortality amongst patients with CKD not yet at ESRD [7, 36]. In patients with ESRD, despite the advances in the treatment of these patients, mortality rate remains high. Notably, there is evidence that depression has significant impact on the morbidity and mortality of patients undergoing therapy for ESRD [6, 7, 14, 24]. Physician-diagnosed depression in patients with ESRD was significantly associated with both increased hospitalization rate and length of stay, independent of demographics and comorbidities [6]. The Dialysis Outcomes and Practice Patterns Study (Mean age approximately 60 years) demonstrated that depression was independently related to mortality and hospitalization [14]. Moreover, depression is reported to be associated with markers of poor compliance in dialysis patients [32, 38]. There is also data that depression may impair immune system by decreasing cellular immunity and increasing cytokine levels [39, 40]. An association between depression and the development of peritonitis has been reported in PD patients [22, 23].

Table 4. Outcomes of Depression in Association with Kidney Transplantation

Dialysis-Related	Transplantation-Related
Increased morbidity and mortality (6,7, 14, 24) Increased hospitalization and length of stay (6,14) Poor Compliance (32,38) Impaired immune system (39, 40) Impaired quality of life and suicide (41-44)	Increased renal graft failure (13) Increased mortality (43) Worse quality of life (46)

Overall, patients with depression experience impaired quality of life, anxiety, sleep disturbances, malnutrition, alcohol and drug abuse, and different somatic disorders [41-44]. Furthermore, depression is the most important risk factor for suicide [44].

Conclusion

Depression is not a normal part of aging, and with timely diagnosis and appropriate treatment, the symptoms of depression are often reversible. Depressive disorders can exist not only in patients complaining about depressed mood, but also in patients with medically unexplained symptoms including headache, fatigue, abdominal pain, gastrointestinal symptoms, weight change. Depression in elderly patients with ESRD on dialysis remains under-recognized and undertreated in this vulnerable population group. A program or plan for screening dialysis patients periodically (eg every 6 months) with a valid test should be considered in dialysis units. Patients identified with positive screening tests would benefit from referral to a qualified psychiatric interviewer if this is beyond the scope of practice or competence of the physician in the dialysis unit. If depression is confirmed with further testing, treatment should be implemented. Physicians taking care of CKD patients should have appropriate knowledge about the different therapeutic options (including various antidepressant medications, psychotherapy and other treatment options) to be able to treat their patients properly.

II. Depression in Elderly Renal Transplantation Patients

Kidney transplantation (KT) is the best form of renal replacement therapy (RRT). Transplant as a method of RRT provides a better quality of life (QOL) compared with other replacement methods [45]. Another beneficial effect of KT is that patients who receive a successful kidney transplant gain a survival benefit compared with those remaining on dialysis [46, 47]. Although the survival advantage of transplantation was most pronounced in younger ESRD patients, patients of all ages gained additional years of life with transplant compared with dialysis [46]. Humar et al retrospectively compared patient and graft survival between young KT recipients aged between 18 to 64 years, with a mean age of 42.8 years (n=2746) and older KT recipients 65 years and older , with a mean age of 69.1 years (n=150). They showed that patient and graft survival at 5 years post transplant were 73% and 68% in the older group versus 86% and 79% in the younger group [48]. Though the study showed inferior patient and graft survival in elderly, the 5-year survival in the elderly receiving KT far exceeds the survival of elderly on dialysis.

In spite of the superiority of KT as a form of RRT, elderly patient with ESRD are not getting the maximum benefit of this therapy with limited numbers of elderly receiving KT. Fortunately, the tide is slowly turning. Initially there was a slower increase in kidney transplantation in patients older than age 65, yet the number continues to increase. The number of yearly KT in recipients older than 65 years has nearly doubled from 8878 in 1988 to over 16,000 in 2008 [49].

Transplantation, though a good option for RRT, is not exempt from complications, and the elderly are particularly vulnerable. The most important complication after KT is loss of the function of the transplanted kidney. Multiple factors are known to affect graft survival; in addition to recipient comorbidities other factors can contribute to graft loss. Among these factors are donor quality, immunosuppression, dialysis vintage, and the strength of social support networks. Furthermore, depression has also been cited as a factor that affects graft survival, mortality post KT, and quality of life of KT recipients. In spite of the negative impact that depression can have on elderly receiving KT, very limited literature is available addressing this issue in the elderly. In this segment, we will discuss depression in association with KT affecting recipients, donors, and primary care givers.

A. Depression Related to KT:

i. KT Recipient

Depression in KT recipient can be due to several reasons. One main reason is the rejection of the renal allograft and return to dialysis. Akman et al compared the incidence of depression as evaluated by BDI, between patients who had a successful KT (n=27), patients on a waiting list (n=30), and those who had a failed KT (n=31) and are back on dialysis therapy [50]. They showed that the return to hemodialysis, especially after a short duration of graft function, was associated with depression. They also demonstrated that placing greater numbers of patients on transplant waiting lists decreases depression and might provide a higher quality of life with a better outcome during dialysis therapy [50]. These findings were confirmed by Gill et al who followed a one donor-recipient couple longitudinally. The recipient experienced irreversible graft rejection immediately after a kidney transplant. The graft rejection was devastating, causing feelings of grief, loss, suicide, and depression. Depression improved as physical health and a sense of personal control improved [51].

A peculiar type of depression was identified in KT recipient and was called paradoxical depression. Paradoxical depression occurs despite a completely successful transplantation without complications. Sugawara et al retrospectively studied the occurrence of paradoxical depression among 1139 Japanese who underwent a successful renal transplantation from January 1997 through September 2006. The incidence of psychiatric problems among these patients was 9.04%, 38.8% of those had depression. More than half of the recipients with depressive symptoms had paradoxical depression [52]. Similar results of depression after a successful KT was shown by Spencer et al [29]. They found the prevalence of depression in their patients following a successful KT to be 22.4%. The depressive symptoms correlated with inflammatory markers as shown by high CPR, malnutrition as shown by low albumin and prior history of depression, suggesting that these factors may predict depression [29].

Other causes suggested to contribute in causing depression in patients after KT is the use of immunosuppressive agents. Patients receiving a KT are in need of long term immune-suppression to protect the kidney against rejection. Immunosuppression agents are associated with several adverse effects. To study the stressful adverse effects of immunosuppressive medication Rosenberg et al examined 157 adult kidney transplant recipients from two transplant centers in Slovakia with a functioning graft transplanted less than 7 yr earlier. Patients participated in an interview focusing on stress from adverse effects to these drugs. The researchers found depression to be among these stressful events occurring as an adverse effect to these immunosuppressants [53].

ii. KT Donors

Depression after a kidney transplantation occurs not only to KT recipients, but can affect KT donors, their families as well as patients with ESRD awaiting a KT. Smith et al performed psychiatric assessment of living kidney donors preoperatively and at 4 and 12 months postoperatively. A total of 48 of consecutive donors over a 5-year period were available for follow-up and completed all assessments. At preoperative assessment, 2% were diagnosed with psychiatric disorder. This percentage of psychiatric disorder increased to 31% during the 12 months postoperatively. Depression was noted in 12% of these donors. Thus, the authors recommended assessing risk factors monitoring and managing donors of KT for any psychosocial impairment for at least 12 months [54]. Heck et al further showed that donation of a kidney to a recipient does not have a positive impact on psychological problems, particularly anxiety and depression [55]. Despite these noted psychosocial disorders, especially depression, experienced by KT donors, the majority of KT donors were shown to have excellent quality of life, satisfied, with very limited stresses [56].

iii. Depression in Transplant Candidates

Patients with ESRD, who opt for KT, unless they have a living donor, are placed on a waiting list for a cadaver kidney. Waiting for an organ transplant is a stressful experience frequently associated with symptoms of depression and anxiety [57]. Psychiatric disorders in transplant candidates have been reported to be 11-60% [58, 59]. Corruble et al, assessed depression among 390 patients transplant candidates on the waiting list [60]. Using BDI, they assessed the patients at the time of inclusion on the waiting list, 12 months and 24 months later if still awaiting a kidney transplant, and 3 months after KT. Depression was found to be in 8.7% of patients at inclusion. The percentage of depressed patients increased to 12.4% and

16.7% after 12 months and 24 months on the waiting list respectively [60]. After KT, the percentage decreased to 2.3%. Akman et al [50] showed even a higher percentage of depression among patients on a waiting list for KT, with a percentage reaching 40%. These results highlight the importance of routinely monitoring patients who are on KT waiting lists for symptoms of depression.

Knowing that elderly are have significantly longer median waiting times than younger individuals (1,521 days waiting period in the elderly as compared to 466, 623, 738, and 800 days in patients aged 18-34, 35-49, 50-59 and 60-64 years respectively) [61], leads us to hypothesize that depression is more prevalent in elderly awaiting KT.

iv. Depression in Primary Care Givers

Depression as a result of KT process does not only affect those directly involved in it; donor and recipient, but can extend to involve a wider circle involving primary care giver. A cross-sectional survey was conducted to determine the prevalence of depression among 42 primary caregivers of patients listed for transplantation, either kidney or liver transplantation. The prevalence of depression in primary caregivers was 19%; of these caregivers one third had severe depression [62]. Surprisingly, depression scale scores did not correlate with nature or length of relationship between the primary care giver and the patient. The fact that primary care givers to KT recipient can suffer from depression might be even exaggerated if the KT recipient is elderly. Caring for elderly patients adds extra burden on the primary care giver. Multiple studies have shown that the incidence of depression in caregivers of the elderly is high, ranging from 18 to 47 percent [63-65].

B. Predictors of Depression in KT

Tsunoda et al retrospectively studied a cohort of 116 KT patients aged 50.2 +/- 11.87. They noted that the prevalence of depression in their study was 41.4%. The single best predictor of future depression that they detected was living alone. Other predictors of depression included patients who did not have regular incomes, did not want the KT, as well as those who experienced a rejection episode, thus highlighting the importance of the social environment as a predictor of depression following KT [66]. Other researchers failed to show any association between depression in patients receiving KT and their income. Tavallaii et al categorized 240 KT recipients based on their income. They found that depression symptom scores were not significantly different between the income groups (low-moderate- and high-income) [67].

Another predictor of depression in KT recipients is the lack of self –care behavior. Weng et al studied 177 KT recipients using a cross-sectional survey and showed that patients who have higher self-efficacy and higher self-care behavior had lower depressive symptoms [68].

Similarly, the patient's level of interest for health-related information seems to predict depression in KTR. Christensen et al screened sixty patients for depression while on the waiting list for a cadaveric renal transplant, and 12 months later. Among the 33 patients who received a transplant during the follow-up period, those with a high preference for health-related information exhibited a substantial reduction in depression. In contrast, patients low in preference for information showed a slight increase in depression [69]. In an older study, Sensky showed that previous psychiatric history was the main predictor of future psychiatric symptoms including depression [70]. Dobbels et al identified white race, female sex, diabetes as primary cause of kidney disease, dialysis vintage, certain immunosuppressant agents as well as donor age of 65 years or older as predictors of depression as identified in Medicare claims during the first 3 years post transplantation [12].

C. Outcome of Depression in KT Recipient

Depressive Symptoms (DS) are associated with poor prognosis (Table 4). Among patients with ESRD, depression has been linked to poor quality of life [43, 71], increased rates of hospitalization [14] and mortality [7, 14, 71]. Furthermore, Boulware and colleagues showed that DS are strongly associated with all-cause deaths, cardiovascular disease deaths, and cardiovascular events in patients with ESRD on HD [36].

Similar results were shown for patients receiving KT. Dobbels et al, examining Medicare claims 3 years post transplantation showed that depression was associated with increased graft failure, return to dialysis therapy and death with a functioning graft [12]. More recently, Novak and colleagues prospectively studied 840 transplanted patients followed at a single outpatient transplant center. The prevalence of depression in this cohort was 22%. The researchers showed the mortality to be higher (21% versus 13%; p = .004) in patients with versus without depression. These results lead them to conclude that depressive symptoms are an independent predictor of mortality in kidney transplanted patients [72].

The impact of KT on the quality of life (QOL) among elderly ESRD patients has been poorly studied. Seedat and colleagues examined a group of 128 patients in an ESRD program comparing the impact of different treatment modalities, dialysis versus KT on the quality of life. They showed that KT achieved the best quality of life in patients with ESRD in regard to employability and social, psychological and medical status [42].The finding of better QOL in patients receiving KT as compared to dialytic therapy was confirmed by Gudex and colleagues who studied 997 adult dialysis and transplant patients from twenty-four British renal units. They showed that the KT recipients reported better HRQOL than dialysis patients. KT recipients also reported fewer problems with physical mobility, self-care, social and personal relationships and usual activities [73].

In spite of the superior QOL in patients receiving KT as compared with patients with ESRD on dialysis, the presence of depression in patients who received KT impacts negatively on the patient's QOL. In a Lithuanian study examining 61 KT recipients aiming to evaluate the association between depression and quality of life, depression was found in 20% of patients using BDI. The BDI score correlated inversely with these quality-of-life domains: physical functioning, limitations in physical activities because of physical problems, bodily pain and limitations in usual role activities because of emotional problems. Age was a factor that correlated with depression, with subjects with BDI score higher than 15 being significantly older [41].

Summary and Conclusion

Depression is highly prevalent in relation to KT ranging from 4.1% to 41.4%. It affects a wide variety of individuals; kidney recipients, kidney donors, those with ESRD awaiting kidney transplantation as well as the primary care givers of patients receiving kidney transplantation. The number of elderly patients with ESRD is on the rise and so is the number of elderly patients undergoing KT. In spite of that, there is paucity of literature focusing on the problem of depression in elderly in association with KT. Recognizing that depression in patients in association with KT is associated with poor outcome, should prompt the health care professionals; nephrologists, geriatricians and psychiatrists, to wage several studies focusing on methods to easily diagnose and manage depression in the elderly in association with KT.

References

[1] http://www.census.gov/compendia/statab/2010/tables/10s0034.pdf. 2010.

[2] Garg AX, Papaioannou A, Ferko N, Campbell G, Clarke JA, Ray JG. Estimating the prevalence of renal insufficiency in seniors requiring long-term care. *Kidney Int.* 2004 Feb;65(2):649-53.

[3] USRD 2009. Am J Kidney Dis. 2010;55(Supplement 1):S1-S420.

[4] USRDS 2009 annual data report: Atlas of chronic kidney disease and end-stage renal disease in the United States [database on the Internet]. National Institutes of Health, National Institute of Diabetes and Digestive and Kidney Diseases, Bethesda,. 2009 [cited April 15, 2010]. Available from: http://www.usrds.org/adr.htm.

[5] Weisbord SD, Fried LF, Arnold RM, Fine MJ, Levenson DJ, Peterson RA, et al. Prevalence, severity, and importance of physical and emotional symptoms in chronic hemodialysis patients. *J. Am. Soc. Nephrol.* 2005 Aug;16(8):2487-94.

[6] Hedayati SS, Grambow SC, Szczech LA, Stechuchak KM, Allen AS, Bosworth HB. Physician-diagnosed depression as a correlate of hospitalizations in patients receiving long-term hemodialysis. *Am. J. Kidney Dis.* 2005 Oct;46(4):642-9.

[7] Kimmel PL, Peterson RA, Weihs KL, Simmens SJ, Alleyne S, Cruz I, et al. Multiple measurements of depression predict mortality in a longitudinal study of chronic hemodialysis outpatients. *Kidney Int.* 2000 May;57(5):2093-8.

[8] Hedayati SS, Minhajuddin AT, Afshar M, Toto RD, Trivedi MH, Rush AJ. Association between major depressive episodes in patients with chronic kidney disease and initiation of dialysis, hospitalization, or death. *JAMA.* 2010 May;303(19):1946-53.

[9] Murtagh FE, Addington-Hall J, Higginson IJ. The prevalence of symptoms in end-stage renal disease: a systematic review. *Adv. Chronic. Kidney Dis.* 2007 Jan;14(1):82-99.

[10] American Psychiatric Association. Diagnostic Statistical Manual (DSM) IV-TR. Washington DC1994.

[11] Graham JE, Rockwood K, Beattie BL, Eastwood R, Gauthier S, Tuokko H, et al. Prevalence and severity of cognitive impairment with and without dementia in an elderly population. *Lancet.* 1997 Jun;349(9068):1793-6.

[12] Dobbels F, Skeans MA, Snyder JJ, Tuomari AV, Maclean JR, Kasiske BL. Depressive disorder in renal transplantation: an analysis of Medicare claims. *Am. J. Kidney Dis.* 2008 May;51(5):819-28.

[13] Beekman AT, Copeland JR, Prince MJ. Review of community prevalence of depression in later life. *Br. J. Psychiatry.* 1999 Apr;174:307-11.

[14] Lopes AA, Bragg J, Young E, Goodkin D, Mapes D, Combe C, et al. Depression as a predictor of mortality and hospitalization among hemodialysis patients in the United States and Europe. *Kidney Int.* 2002 Jul;62(1):199-207.

[15] Henderson AS, Jorm AF, Korten AE, Jacomb P, Christensen H, Rodgers B. Symptoms of depression and anxiety during adult life: evidence for a decline in prevalence with age. *Psychol. Med.* 1998 Nov;28(6):1321-8.

[16] Hedayati SS, Minhajuddin AT, Toto RD, Morris DW, Rush AJ. Prevalence of major depressive episode in CKD. *Am. J. Kidney Dis.* 2009 Sep;54(3):424-32.

[17] Karaminia R, Tavallaii SA, Lorgard-Dezfuli-Nejad M, Moghani Lankarani M, Hadavand Mirzaie H, Einollahi B, et al. Anxiety and depression: a comparison between renal transplant recipients and hemodialysis patients. *Transplant Proc.* 2007 May;39(4):1082-4.

[18] Balogun RA, Turgut F, Balogun SA, Holroyd S, Abdel-Rahman EM. Screening for Depression in Elderly Hemodialysis Patients. *Nephron Clin. Pract.* 2010 Dec;118(2):c72-c7.

[19] Tyrrell J, Paturel L, Cadec B, Capezzali E, Poussin G. Older patients undergoing dialysis treatment: cognitive functioning, depressive mood and health-related quality of life. *Aging Ment. Health.* 2005 Jul;9(4):374-9.

[20] Hedayati SS, Bosworth HB, Kuchibhatla M, Kimmel PL, Szczech LA. The predictive value of self-report scales compared with physician diagnosis of depression in hemodialysis patients. *Kidney Int.* 2006 May;69(9):1662-8.

[21] Abdel-Rahman E BS, Kepple A, Ma J, Turgut F, Kovesdy C, Balogun R. Beck Depression Invententory and Survival in Elderly Hemodialysis Patients. *Nephrol Dial Transplant.* (In press).

[22] Wuerth D, Finkelstein SH, Ciarcia J, Peterson R, Kliger AS, Finkelstein FO. Identification and treatment of depression in a cohort of patients maintained on chronic peritoneal dialysis. *Am. J. Kidney Dis.* 2001 May;37(5):1011-7.

[23] Troidle L, Watnick S, Wuerth DB, Gorban-Brennan N, Kliger AS, Finkelstein FO. Depression and its association with peritonitis in long-term peritoneal dialysis patients. *Am. J. Kidney Dis.* 2003 Aug;42(2):350-4.

[24] Einwohner R, Bernardini J, Fried L, Piraino B. The effect of depressive symptoms on survival in peritoneal dialysis patients. *Perit Dial Int.* 2004 2004 May-Jun;24(3):256-63.

[25] Guney I, Solak Y, Atalay H, Yazici R, Altintepe L, Kara F, et al. Comparison of effects of automated peritoneal dialysis and continuous ambulatory peritoneal dialysis on health-related quality of life, sleep quality, and depression. *Hemodial Int.* 2010 Oct;14(4):515-22.

[26] Schlebusch L, Pillay BJ, Louw J. Depression and self-report disclosure after live related donor and cadaver renal transplants. *S. Afr. Med. J.* 1989 May;75(10):490-3.

[27] Harris SA, Lamping DL, Brown EA, Constantinovici N, Group NTDSN. Clinical outcomes and quality of life in elderly patients on peritoneal dialysis versus hemodialysis. *Perit. Dial Int.* 2002 2002 Jul-Aug;22(4):463-70.
[28] Brown EA, Johansson L, Farrington K, Gallagher H, Sensky T, Gordon F, et al. Broadening Options for Long-term Dialysis in the Elderly (BOLDE): differences in quality of life on peritoneal dialysis compared to haemodialysis for older patients. *Nephrol Dial Transplant.* 2010 Nov;25(11):3755-63.
[29] Spencer BW, Chilcot J, Farrington K. Still sad after successful renal transplantation: are we failing to recognise depression? An audit of depression screening in renal graft recipients. *Nephron Clin. Pract.* 2011;117(2):c106-12.
[30] Alavi NM, Aliakbarzadeh Z, Sharifi K. Depression, anxiety, activities of daily living, and quality of life scores in patients undergoing renal replacement therapies. *Transplant Proc.* 2009 Nov;41(9):3693-6.
[31] Hedayati SS, Finkelstein FO. Epidemiology, diagnosis, and management of depression in patients with CKD. *Am J Kidney Dis.* 2009 Oct;54(4):741-52.
[32] Kimmel PL. Depression in patients with chronic renal disease: what we know and what we need to know. *J. Psychosom. Res.* 2002 Oct;53(4):951-6.
[33] Kim JA, Lee YK, Huh WS, Kim YG, Kim DJ, Oh HY, et al. Analysis of depression in continuous ambulatory peritoneal dialysis patients. *J. Korean Med. Sci.* 2002 Dec;17(6):790-4.
[34] Giordano M, Tirelli P, Ciarambino T, Gambardella A, Ferrara N, Signoriello G, et al. Screening of depressive symptoms in young-old hemodialysis patients: relationship between Beck Depression Inventory and 15-item Geriatric Depression Scale. *Nephron Clin. Pract.* 2007;106(4):c187-92.
[35] Steer RA, Cavalieri TA, Leonard DM, Beck AT. Use of the Beck Depression Inventory for Primary Care to screen for major depression disorders. *Gen. Hosp. Psychiatry.* 1999 1999 Mar-Apr;21(2):106-11.
[36] Boulware LE, Liu Y, Fink NE, Coresh J, Ford DE, Klag MJ, et al. Temporal relation among depression symptoms, cardiovascular disease events, and mortality in end-stage renal disease: contribution of reverse causality. *Clin. J. Am. Soc. Nephrol.* 2006 May;1(3):496-504.
[37] BECK AT, WARD CH, MENDELSON M, MOCK J, ERBAUGH J. An inventory for measuring depression. *Arch. Gen. Psychiatry.* 1961 Jun;4:561-71.
[38] Kaveh K, Kimmel PL. Compliance in hemodialysis patients: multidimensional measures in search of a gold standard. *Am. J. Kidney Dis.* 2001 Feb;37(2):244-66.
[39] Miller GE, Cohen S, Herbert TB. Pathways linking major depression and immunity in ambulatory female patients. *Psychosom Med.* 1999 1999 Nov-Dec;61(6):850-60.
[40] Licinio J, Wong ML. The role of inflammatory mediators in the biology of major depression: central nervous system cytokines modulate the biological substrate of depressive symptoms, regulate stress-responsive systems, and contribute to neurotoxicity and neuroprotection. *Mol. Psychiatry.* 1999 Jul;4(4):317-27.
[41] Kusleikaite N, Bumblyte IA, Pakalnyte R. [Quality of life and depression in renal transplant patients]. *Medicina* (Kaunas). 2007;43 Suppl 1:103-8.
[42] Seedat YK, MacIntosh CG, Subban JV. Quality of life for patients in an end-stage renal disease programme. *S. Afr. Med. J.* 1987 Apr;71(8):500-4.

[43] Koo JR, Yoon JW, Kim SG, Lee YK, Oh KH, Kim GH, et al. Association of depression with malnutrition in chronic hemodialysis patients. *Am. J. Kidney Dis.* 2003 May;41(5):1037-42.

[44] Chen CK, Tsai YC, Hsu HJ, Wu IW, Sun CY, Chou CC, et al. Depression and suicide risk in hemodialysis patients with chronic renal failure. *Psychosomatics.* 2010 Nov;51(6):528-.e6.

[45] Shah VS, Ananth A, Sohal GK, Bertges-Yost W, Eshelman A, Parasuraman RK, et al. Quality of life and psychosocial factors in renal transplant recipients. *Transplant Proc.* 2006 Jun;38(5):1283-5.

[46] Wolfe RA, Ashby VB, Milford EL, Ojo AO, Ettenger RE, Agodoa LY, et al. Comparison of mortality in all patients on dialysis, patients on dialysis awaiting transplantation, and recipients of a first cadaveric transplant. *N. Engl. J. Med.* 1999 Dec;341(23):1725-30.

[47] Rao PS, Merion RM, Ashby VB, Port FK, Wolfe RA, Kayler LK. Renal transplantation in elderly patients older than 70 years of age: results from the Scientific Registry of Transplant Recipients. *Transplantation.* 2007 Apr;83(8):1069-74.

[48] Humar A, Denny R, Matas AJ, Najarian JS. Graft and quality of life outcomes in older recipients of a kidney transplant. *Exp. Clin. Transplant.* 2003 Dec;1(2):69-72.

[49] Annual report of the US Organ Procurement and Transplantation Network and the Scientific Registry of Transplant Recipients: Transplant Data 1998-2007. Rockville, Richmond, VA: Department of Health and Human Services Administration, Health care Systems Bureau, Division of Transplantation. United Network for Organ Sharing; Ann Arbor, MI, University Renal Research and Education Association; 2008.

[50] Akman B, Ozdemir FN, Sezer S, Miçozkadioglu H, Haberal M. Depression levels before and after renal transplantation. *Transplant Proc.* 2004 2004 Jan-Feb;36(1):111-3.

[51] Gill P, Lowes L. The kidney transplant failure experience: a longitudinal case study. *Prog. Transplant.* 2009 Jun;19(2):114-21.

[52] Sugawara H, Nishimura K, Kobayashi S, Ishida H, Tanabe K, Ishigooka J. Paradoxical depression in renal transplant recipients. *Transplant Proc.* 2008 Dec;40(10):3448-50.

[53] Rosenberger J, Geckova AM, Dijk JP, Roland R, Heuvel WJ, Groothof F JW. Factors modifying stress from adverse effects of immunosuppressive medication in kidney transplant recipients. *Clin. Transplant.* 2005 Feb;19(1):70-6.

[54] Smith GC, Trauer T, Kerr PG, Chadban SJ. Prospective psychosocial monitoring of living kidney donors using the Short Form-36 health survey: results at 12 months. *Transplantation.* 2004 Nov;78(9):1384-9.

[55] Heck G, Schweitzer J, Seidel-Wiesel M. Psychological effects of living related kidney transplantation - risks and chances. *Clin. Transplant.* 2004 Dec;18(6):716-21.

[56] Johnson EM, Anderson JK, Jacobs C, Suh G, Humar A, Suhr BD, et al. Long-term follow-up of living kidney donors: quality of life after donation. *Transplantation.* 1999 Mar;67(5):717-21.

[57] Moran PJ, Christensen AJ, Ehlers SL, Bertolatus JA. Family environment, intrusive ideation, and adjustment among renal transplant candidates. *Ann. Behav. Med.* 1999;21(4):311-6.

[58] Fukunishi I, Hasegawa A, Ohara T, Aikawa A, Hatanaka A, Suzuki J, et al. Kidney transplantation and liaison psychiatry, part I: anxiety before, and the prevalence rate of

psychiatric disorders before and after, transplantation. *Psychiatry Clin. Neurosci.* 1997 Oct;51(5):301-4.

[59] Chacko RC, Harper RG, Kunik M, Young J. Relationship of psychiatric morbidity and psychosocial factors in organ transplant candidates. *Psychosomatics.* 1996 1996 Mar-Apr;37(2):100-7.

[60] Corruble E, Durrbach A, Charpentier B, Lang P, Amidi S, Dezamis A, et al. Progressive increase of anxiety and depression in patients waiting for a kidney transplantation. *Behav. Med.* 2010 2010 Jan-Mar;36(1):32-6.

[61] Oniscu GC, Schalkwijk AA, Johnson RJ, Brown H, Forsythe JL. Equity of access to renal transplant waiting list and renal transplantation in Scotland: cohort study. *BMJ.* 2003 Nov;327(7426):1261.

[62] Bolkhir A, Loiselle MM, Evon DM, Hayashi PH. Depression in primary caregivers of patients listed for liver or kidney transplantation. *Prog. Transplant.* 2007 Sep;17(3):193-8.

[63] Rosenthal CJ, Sulman J, Marshall VW. Depressive symptoms in family caregivers of long-stay patients. *Gerontologist.* 1993 Apr;33(2):249-57.

[64] Gallagher D, Rose J, Rivera P, Lovett S, Thompson LW. Prevalence of depression in family caregivers. *Gerontologist.* 1989 Aug;29(4):449-56.

[65] Livingston G, Manela M, Katona C. Depression and other psychiatric morbidity in carers of elderly people living at home. *BMJ.* 1996 Jan;312(7024):153-6.

[66] Tsunoda T, Yamashita R, Kojima Y, Takahara S. Risk factors for depression after kidney transplantation. *Transplant Proc.* 2010 Jun;42(5):1679-81.

[67] Tavallaii SA, Einollahi B, Azizabadi Farahani M, Namdari M. Socioeconomic links to health-related quality of life, anxiety, and depression in kidney transplant recipients. *Iran J. Kidney Dis.* 2009 Jan;3(1):40-4.

[68] Weng LC, Dai YT, Wang YW, Huang HL, Chiang YJ. Effects of self-efficacy, self-care behaviours on depressive symptom of Taiwanese kidney transplant recipients. *J. Clin. Nurs.* 2008 Jul;17(13):1786-94.

[69] Christensen AJ, Ehlers SL, Raichle KA, Bertolatus JA, Lawton WJ. Predicting change in depression following renal transplantation: effect of patient coping preferences. *Health Psychol.* 2000 Jul;19(4):348-53.

[70] Sensky T. Psychiatric morbidity in renal transplantation. *Psychother Psychosom.* 1989;52(1-3):41-6.

[71] Knight EL, Ofsthun N, Teng M, Lazarus JM, Curhan GC. The association between mental health, physical function, and hemodialysis mortality. *Kidney Int.* 2003 May;63(5):1843-51.

[72] Novak M, Molnar MZ, Szeifert L, Kovacs AZ, Vamos EP, Zoller R, et al. Depressive symptoms and mortality in patients after kidney transplantation: a prospective prevalent cohort study. *Psychosom. Med.* 2010 Jul;72(6):527-34.

[73] Gudex CM. Health-related quality of life in endstage renal failure. *Qual Life Res.* 1995 Aug;4(4):359-66.

In: Depression in the Elderly
Editor: Emaad Abdel-Rahman, pp. 85-101

ISBN 978-1-61324-771-6

Chapter 5

THE INFLUENCE OF AGE-RELATED NEUROLOGICAL DISEASES ON THE DEVELOPMENT OF DEPRESSION IN THE ELDERLY

Yaroslav Winter[1] and Tobias Back[2]
[1]Dept. of Neurology, Philipps-University, Marburg, Germany
[2]Dept. of Neurology, Saxon Hospital Arnsdorf, Germany

ABSTRACT

Introduction: The world population is ageing and the prevalence of age-related neurological diseases, such as stroke and neurodegenerative diseases, continuously increases. These diseases lead not only to impairment of motor function but also to development of non-motor disorders, such as depression. Diagnosis of depression in the disorders that produce psychomotor impairment can be challenging and requires particular skills and experience to recognize and treat depression effectively. We investigated the prevalence of depression in patients with most common age-related neurological diseases and estimated the influence of depression on the health-related quality of life in these diseases.

Methods and patients: The prevalence of depression and its influence on the health-related quality of life was estimated in consecutively recruited patients with stroke or transient ischemic attacks (TIA) (n=151), Parkinson's disease (PD) (n=100) and Alzheimer dementia (AD) or vascular dementia (VD) (n= 98), which are the most prevalent neurological diseases of the elderly. Depression was diagnosed according to DSM-IV criteria and scored using the Beck Depression Inventory, the Geriatric Depression Scale and the Hospital Anxiety Depression Scale. The health-related quality of life (HrQoL) was evaluated using the EuroQol (EQ-5D and visual analogue scale). The neurological status was assessed by means of the validated severity scales: Barthel Index and modified Rankin Scale in patients with stroke/TIA, Unified Parkinson's disease Rating Scale (UPDRS) in patients with Parkinson's disease and Mini-Mental State Examination in patients with Alzheimer dementia or vascular dementia.

Results: The age was 72±11 (mean+/-SD) years in patients with stroke/TIA, 69±7 years in patients with Parkinson's disease and 77±8 years in patients with Alzheimer or vascular dementia. The prevalence of depression was 51% in stroke/TIA, 75% in Parkinson's disease and 86% in patients with Alzheimer or vascular dementia. In comparison to general population, HrQoL measured on the visual analogue scale was reduced by 23%, 35% and 54% in stroke/TIA, Parkinson's disease and patients with AD/VD, respectively. In the dimension "anxiety/depression" of the EQ-5D, 50% of patients with stroke/TIA, 86% of PD-patients and 81% of patients with AD/VD had moderate or severe problems. Depression showed significant association with reduced HrQoL in stroke/TIA, Parkinson's disease, Alzheimer and vascular dementia ($p<0.01$). Only 40% of patients with manifest depression received adequate antidepressant treatment.

Conclusions: The presence of age-related neurological diseases, such as cerebrovascular and neurodegenerative diseases, is associated with increased risk of depression in the elderly. Unfortunately, depression is often under-diagnosed in these patients being masked by motor impairment. Depression is a predictor of reduced HrQoL in elder individuals with neurological diseases. Therefore, they should be screened for presence of depressive symptoms and receive adequate antidepressant treatment.

INTRODUCTION

Population ageing is a major demographic trend worldwide. In one sense, it represents a human success story of increasing longevity. But at the same time, the steady growth of older populations poses many challenges to healthcare due to increasing prevalence of age-related diseases. Age-related neurological diseases, such as cerebrovascular and neurodegenerative diseases, are among major causes of disability and death in the elderly. Alzheimer's disease is the most common neurodegenerative disorder and the most prevalent cause of dementia in the elderly followed by vascular dementia. According to the World Alzheimer Report released by Alzheimer Disease International, the estimated number of people with dementia exceeded 35 million in 2010 and will double every 20 years to 65.7 million in 2030 and 115.4 million in 2050. Parkinson's disease is the second most common neurodegenerative disorder and the most prevalent age-associated movement disorder. There are approximately five million people with Parkinson's disease worldwide and this number is going to double by 2030 [1,2]. Stroke is the second leading cause of death in the world and is responsible for 4.4 million deaths each year. [3] About 15 million people suffer a stroke per year. Stroke is the most common cause of severe disability and dependency in adults. Its economic burden is considerable and has been estimated at € 21.9 billion (US$ 32.4 billion) in Europe and at €46.6 billion (US$ 68.9 billion) in the USA [4-7].

Age-related neurological diseases lead not only to impairment of motor function but also to development of non-motor disorders, such as depression. Depression is a severely debilitating psychiatric disorder that involves depressed mood, loss of interest or pleasure in activities of daily living, and leads in its worst case to suicidal ideations or attempts. Diagnosis of depression in the disorders that produce psychomotor impairment can be challenging and requires particular skills and experience to recognise and treat depression effectively. Investigating depression is also important in the context of the health-related quality of life. Recent studies identified depression as an independent factor influencing health-related quality of life in a number of neurological diseases [8-11]. Health-related quality of life encompasses those aspects of self-perceived well-being that are related to health status and can be affected by disease and its treatment. Being a critical measure in healthcare, HRQol is increasingly incorporated as an outcome variable into clinical trials in PD.

We investigated the prevalence of depression in patients with most common age-related neurological diseases and estimated the influence of depression on the health-related quality of life in these diseases.

METHODS

Study Design

We recruited consecutive patients with stroke or transient ischemic attacks (TIA) (n=151), Parkinson's disease (PD) (n=100) and Alzheimer dementia (AD) or vascular dementia (VD) (n= 98), which are the most prevalent neurological diseases of the elderly.

Diagnostic criteria used in the study were as follows:

1) Stroke was diagnosed based on the occurrence of a new and abrupt focal neurological deficit and confirmed by positive CT- or MRI-findings. According to the International Classification of Diseases (ICD-10) patients with cerebrovascular disease were classified into ischemic stroke (IS), intracerebral hemorrhage (ICH), and transient ischemic attack. A transient ischemic attack (TIA) is a brief period of neurologic deficit that persists for less than 24 hours caused by a transient disturbance of local cerebral blood flow.
2) Parkinson's disease was diagnosed based on the clinical diagnostic criteria of the UK Parkinson's Disease Society Brain Bank [12].
3) Alzheimer dementia and vascular dementia were diagnosed based on criteria were proposed by the National Institute of Neurological and Communicative Disorders and Stroke and the Alzheimer's Disease and Related Disorders Association (NINCDS-ADRDA Alzheimer's Criteria) [13,14].

Patients with stroke were recruited in the Department of Neurology, Philipps University Marburg, Germany. PD-patients were recruited in the Department of Neurology, Russian Medical State University, Moscow, Russia. Patients with Alzheimer dementia and vascular dementia were recruited in the Department of Psychiatry and Psychosomatics, Sklifosovski Research Institute, Moscow, Russia. Study design received approval by local ethic committees and all patients gave informed written consent for participation.

Clinical Evaluation

Patients with stroke/TIA, Parkinson's disease and Alzheimer or vascular dementia received a complete medical and neurological examination performed by a specialist (study investigator) with at least 5 years experience in cerebrovascular disease, movement disorder or dementia, respectively.

Study investigator documented demographics (age, gender), social status (marital and employment status, number of persons living in the household, net annual income) as well as clinical data (age at symptom onset, duration of disease, disease severity scales, co-morbidity and complications) in specially developed case report forms (CRF). CRF included the following parts: 1. Demographics and social data. 2. Clinical data (disease onset, duration of disease, time from first manifestation to diagnosis, severity scales and co-morbid disorders) 3. Current and previous medication. 4. Depression scales (Beck Depression Inventory, the Geriatric Depression Scale and the Hospital Anxiety Depression Scale). 5. Measures of the health-related quality of life.

Following disease severity scales and disability measures were used:

1) In stroke/TIA, disability and functional impairment were evaluated by using the Barthel Index (BI) and modified Rankin Scale (mRS) [15,16], which are valid and reliable measures of stroke outcome [17-20]. BI and mRS have been used in large-scale studies in cerebrovascular disease, e.g., NINDS, ATLANTIS, and ECASS trials [21-24]. The Barthel Index evaluates the performance of patients in 10 activities of daily living, ranging in 5-point increments from 0 (totally dependent bedridden state) to 100 (fully independence in physical functioning). The following classification of the Barthel Index was used: patients with BI < 30 were classified as "totally dependent"; BI from 30 to 70 was classified as "help needed"; and patients with BI > 70 were classified as being "functionally independent" [25]. The mRS is a measure of functional status in patients with stroke, ranging from 0 (no symptoms) to 5 (severe impairment). The patients with mRS scores from 0 to 2 were classified as independent; patients with mRS from 3 to 5 was classified as experiencing moderate to severe disability.
2) Patients with Parkinson's disease were evaluated in the clinical 'on' state (i.e. during adequate antiparkinsonian treatment). Disease severity was estimated using the Unified Parkison's Disease Rating Scale (UPDRS) [26] and Hoehn and Yahr stages (HandY) [27], both valid and reliable measures of clinical status for PD.
3) In patients with Alzheimer dementia or vascular dementia, severity of cognitive impairment was assessed using the Mini-Mental State Examination [28], which is a valid and most common test for assessment of cognitive function in dementia.

Evaluation of Depressive Symptoms and Health-Related Quality of Life

Depression was diagnosed according to DSM-IV criteria (Table 1) and scored using the Beck Depression Inventory, the Geriatric Depression Scale and the Hospital Anxiety Depression Scale.

Beck Depression Inventory (BDI) is one of the most widely used instruments for measuring the severity of depression [29]. It is a 21-question multiple-choice self-report inventory. Each question has at least four possible answers, ranging in intensity from 0 to 3. The maximal total score is 63. Higher total scores indicate more severe depression. The standard cut-offs are as follows: 0–9 indicates minimal depression, 10–18 indicates mild depression, 19–29 indicates moderate depression and 30–63 indicates severe depression.

Table 1. DSM-IV criteria for major depressive episode

Five (or more) of the following symptoms have been present during the same two week period and represent a change from previous functioning. At least one of the symptoms is either (1) depressed mood or (2) loss of interest or pleasure
Depressed mood most of the day, nearly every day, as indicated by either subjective report or observation made by others
Markedly diminished interest or pleasure in all, or almost all, activities most of the day, nearly every day
Significant weight loss when not dieting or weight gain, or decrease or increase in appetite, nearly every day
Early insomnia or hypersomnia, nearly every day
Psychomotor agitation, nearly every day
Feelings of worthlessness or excessive or inappropriate guilt, nearly every day
Diminished ability to think or concentrate, or indecisiveness, nearly every day
Recurrent thought of death, recurrent suicidal ideation without a specific plan, or a suicide attempt or specific plan for committing suicide

Geriatric Depression Scale (GDS) is a standardized and validated 30-item self-report instrument used to identify depression in the elderly. It is simplified to be used with ill or cognitively impaired individuals and based upon yes-or-no questions regarding mood over the previous week [30]. The test allows 84% sensitivity and 95% specificity for the diagnosis of depression [30]. Increased scores on the Geriatric Depression Scale indicate more severe depressive symptoms. The cut-off scores are as follows: score of 0–9 is considered normal; 10–19 indicates mild depression, and a score ≥20 indicates severe depression.

Hospital Anxiety Depression Scale (HADS) is a well-known standardized questionnaire, which is a valid measure of anxiety and depression [31]. The term 'hospital' suggests that it was initially developed to be used in a hospital setting but many international studies have confirmed that it is valid when used in community settings and primary care medical practice [32]. Hospital Anxiety Depression Scale consists of 14 questions with four possible answers for each question. Scores on the Hospital Anxiety Depression Scale range from 0 to 21 with higher scores indicating more severe depression or anxiety. HADS total scores were categorized as follows: HADS 0 to 7 normal; HADS 8 to 10 marginal; HADS 11 to 21 pathological.

Health-Related Quality of Life Was Assessed Using the EuroQol

The EuroQol is a valid standardized health state measure [33]. It consists of a self-classifier (EQ-5D) and a visual analogue scale (VAS). The self-classifier evaluates five dimensions of health: mobility, self-care, usual activities, pain/discomfort and anxiety/depression [34,35]. Each dimension is divided into three levels of severity (1=no problem, 2=moderate problem, 3=severe problem). Overall, 243 combinations are possible.

The EQ-5D-index score was calculated according to the European recommendations [36]. Visual analogue scale is a thermometer type scale ranging from 0 (worst imaginable health state) to 100 (best imaginable health state) [37].

Statistical Analysis and Data Presentation

Statistical analysis was performed using SPSS Version 15.0 (SPSS Inc., Chicago, IL, USA). All data are presented as mean, standard deviation (SD) and median. The Kolmogorov Smirnov test was used to test the data for normal distribution. For group comparisons of data not following normal distribution, either the Mann-Whitney U test (two independent groups), the Kruskal Wallis test (more than two independent groups) or the Wilcoxon rank test (two dependent groups) were applied. All statistical inference was based on a significance level of 5%.

Results

Demographics and Clinical Data

The age of study participants was 68.9±7.0 (mean+/-SD) years in patients with Parkinson's disease, 71.7±11.3 years in stroke patients, 77.5±8.8 years in patients with Alzheimer or vascular dementia. The proportion of female patients (54-65%) was slightly larger than male patients. Demographics and clinical data are shown in Table 2. More than 90% of patients were age retired. The proportion of widowed patients increased with growing age. Thirty-one percent of patients with Parkinson's disease (mean age 68.9 years) and 44% of patients with Alzheimer or vascular dementia (mean age 77.5 years) were widowed.

The mean disease severity of patients with Parkinson's disease measured on the UPDRS part II-III was 47.7 (95% CI: 16.0-93.0). The mean score on the UPDRS part II was 14.7 (95% CI: 13.2-16.2) and the mean score on the UPDRS part III was 33.0 (95% CI: 29.3-36.7). The proportion of patients in Hoehn and Yahr stage I-II was 57%, in Hoehn and Yahr stage III 20% and in Hoehn and Yahr stage IV-V 23%. The mean disease duration was 6.7 years. Twenty-nine percent of patients had motor complication (on-off fluctuations, dyskinesias or dystonias), 91% of patients had non-motor complications (e.g., orthostatic dysfunction, insomnia, cognitive impairment, psychotic symptoms).

Among patients with cerebrovascular diseases, 54 (70.1%) patients had ischemic stroke, 5 (6.5%) patients had intracerebral hemorrhage and 18 (23.4%) patients had transient ischemic attacks. According to disease severity measured using Barthel Index, 61 (79.2%) patients were "functionally independent", 9 (11.7%) patients were classified as "help needed" and 7 (9.1%) patients were "totally dependent".

Among patients with Alzheimer or vascular dementia, 83 (84.7%) patients had moderate cognitive impairment (MMSE≥14) and 15 (15.3%) had severe cognitive deficits (MMSE<14). Seventy-two (73.5%) patients with AD/VD had extrapyramidal symptoms. Behavioral disorders were present in 43 (43.9%) patients.

Table 2. Demographics and clinical parameters in study cohort

	Parkinson's disease N (%)/ mean±SD	Stroke/ TIA N (%)/ mean±SD	AD/ VD N (%)/ mean±SD
No. of patients	100	77	98
Age	68.9±7.0	71.7±11.3	77.5±8.8
Gender			
male	38 (38.0%)	35 (45.5%)	34 (34.7%)
female	62 (62.0%)	42 (54.5%)	64 (65.3%)
Marital status			
Married	62 (62.0%)	39 (50.6%)	42 (42.8%)
Divorced	5 (5.0%)	2 (2.6%)	2 (2.0%)
Single	2 (2.0%)	6 (7.8%)	10 (10.2%)
Widowed	31 (31.0%)	30 (39.0%)	44 (44.0%)
Employment			
employed	7 (7.0%)	6 (7.8%)	7 (7.1%)
unemployed	93 (93.0%)	71 (92.2%)	91 (92.9%)
Severity scales			
UPDRS II-III Tertile 1*	20 (20.0%)		
UPDRS II-III Tertile 2*	32 (32.0%)		
UPDRS II-III Tertile 3*	48 (48.0%)		
Hoehn and Yahr I-II	57 (57.0%)		
Hoehn and Yahr III	20 (20.0%)		
Hoehn and Yahr IV-V	23 (23.0%)		
Barthel index >70		61 (79.2%)	
Barthel index 30-70		9 (11.7%)	
Barthel index <30		7 (9.1%)	
mRS 0-2		47 (61.0%)	
mRS 3-6		30 (39.0%)	
MMSE ≥14			83 (84.7%)
MMSE <14			15 (15.3%)

*Cutpoints for UPDRS tertiles: 30.63; 61.27.

DEPRESSION AND HEALTH-RELATED QUALITY OF LIFE

Depression was diagnosed in 75 (75.0%) patients with Parkinson's disease. It was the most prevalent mental disorder in these patients. In comparison, cognitive impairment was found in 71 (71.0%) patients, psychosis in 7 (7.0%) patients and sleep disorders in 48 (48.0%) patients. The prevalence of depression had a biphasic course in Parkinson's disease, with a peak prevalence early in the disease and another gradual increase in latter stages (Figure 1). In stroke/TIA patients, depressive symptoms were present in 16 (20.8%) patients. According to

HADS (part depression), 8 (10.4%) patients were classified as having marginal scores and 8 (10.4%) patients had pathological scores. Anxiety was found in 15 (19.5%) patients, with 12 (15.6%) patients having marginal and 3 (3.9%) patients having pathological HADS (part anxiety) scores.

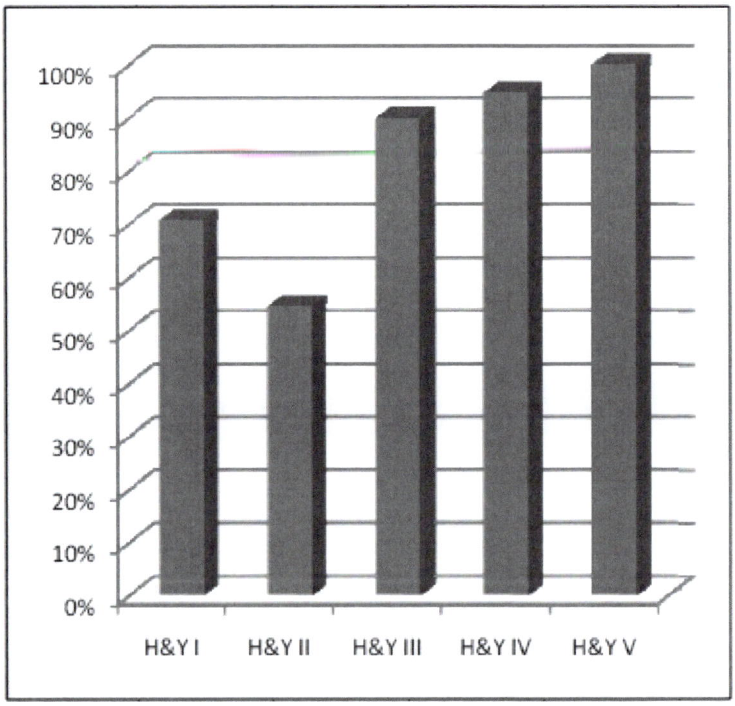

Figure 1. Prevalence of depression in different Hoehn and Yahr stages (HandY) in Parkinson's disease.

A large amount of patients with depressive symptoms was also identified among patients with Alzheimer or vascular dementia (n=85, 86.7%). Fifty-five (56.1%) patients had moderate depression and 35 (35.7%) patients had severe depression as measured on the GDS. The amount of patients with other mental disorders was lower: 30 (30.6%) patients with psychotic symptoms, 43 (43.9%) patients with behavioural disorders, 9 (9.2%) patients with alcohol abuse. Unfortunately, only 40% of patients with manifest depression in our sample received adequate antidepressant treatment.

The health-related quality of life was considerably reduced in all diseased studied (Figure 2). The proportion of patients with Parkinson's disease who reported moderate or severe problems in at least one dimension of the EQ-5D was 24% higher than in general population (98% versus 74%, $p<0.001$). The dimensions "mobility", "pain/discomfort" and "anxiety/depression" showed the most reduction of the HrQoL. In comparison to general population, the proportion of PD-patients with moderate or severe problems was increased by 44%, 30% and 41%, respectively. The mean scores on the EQ VAS in patients Parkinson's disease were significantly lower than in general population (47.7±16.7 versus 77.0±20.8, $p<0.01$) [38]. A comparison of the HrQoL measured on the EQ VAS in study participants and general population is shown in Figure 2.

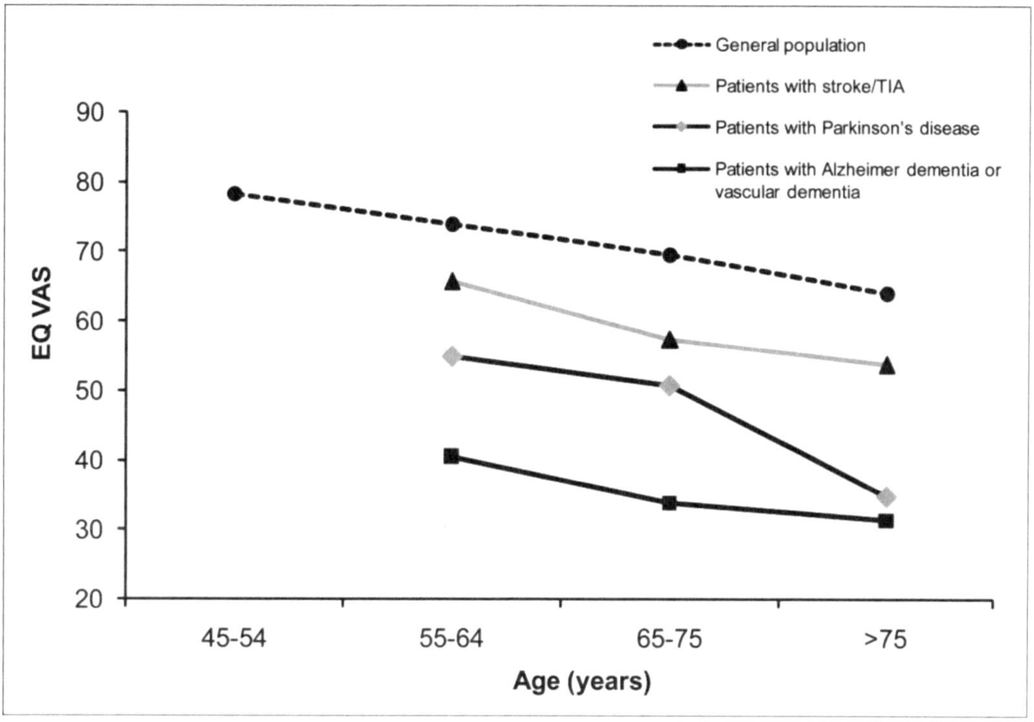

Figure 2. Comparison of health-related quality of life between elderly people with age-related neurological diseases and general population (age-adjusted values).

Considerable reduction of the HrQoL was also found in patients with stroke/TIA. In these patients, mean score on the EQ VAS was decreased by 27% in comparison to general population (56.40±28.7 versus 77.0±20.8, $p<0.01$) [38]. The mean EQ-5D index score was 0.73±0.32. The largest reduction of HrQoL scores was found in patients with intracerebral hemorrhage. The scores on the EQ VAS in different types of cerebrovascular disease were as follows: 54.25±26.18 in intracerebral hemorrhage, 56.74±22.10 in ischemic stroke and 77.67±18.21 in transient ischemic attacks ($p<0.01$).

In patients with Alzheimer or vascular dementia, severe problems in dimensions "mobility", "self-care", "usual activities", "pain/discomfort" and "anxiety/depression" were present in 25.5%, 32.7%, 36.7%, 14.3% and 20.4% of patients, respectively. The mean EQ-5D index score was 36.7±18.5. The mean score on the EQ VAS was significantly lower than in general population (34.0±13.8 versus 77.0±20.8, $p<0.01$) [38].

The association between health-related quality of life and age is shown in Table 3 and 4. The values on the EQ VAS and EQ-5D index decreased with increasing age in all diseases studied. The association between gender and health-related quality of life was found only for EQ-5D index in stroke/TIA. Female patients with stroke/TIA had lower EQ-5D index scores than male patients ($p<0.01$). No other associations between gender and health-related quality of life were found.

In the dimension "anxiety/depression" of the EQ-5D, 50% of patients with stroke/TIA, 86% of PD-patients and 81% of patients with AD/VD had moderate or severe problems. Depression had a strong predictive value for decreased health-related quality of life in all age-associated neurological diseases included in this study (Table 5). The presence of depression reduced health-related quality of life in patients with Parkinson's Disease by 25-30%, in patients with stroke/TIA by 26-34% and in patients with Alzheimer or vascular dementia by 14% ($p<0.01$).

Table 3. Distribution of EQ-VAS scores according to demographic variables

			EQ-VAS			
	Parkinson's disease		Stroke/TIA		Alzheimer/vascular dementia	
	Mean±SD	p-value	Mean±SD	p-value	Mean±SD	p-value
Age groups		<0.01		<0.01		0.025
<65	55.00±14.14		65.71±31.94		40.56±14.23	
65-75	50.80±15.79		57.33±24.56		33.84±11.87	
>75	34.89±14.94		53.74±21.39		31.40±14.57	
Gender		0.516		0.201		0.477
Male	48.16 ±11.70		65.03±22.90		34.76±12.90	
Female	47.45±12.25		57.69±22.85		33.59±14.35	

Table 4. Distribution of EQ-5D index scores according to demographic variables

			EQ-5D Index			
	Parkinson's disease		Stroke/TIA		Alzheimer/vascular dementia	
	Mean±SD	p-value	Mean±SD	p-value	Mean±SD	p-value
Age groups		0.145		<0.01		<0.01
<65	0.50±0.13		0.80±0.16		0.46±0.14	
65-75	0.48±0.16		0.68±0.34		0.40±0.18	
>75	0.39±0.2		0.64±0.33		0.30±0.18	
Gender		0.913		<0.01		0.922
Male	0.46 ±0.18		0.75±0.31		0.36±0.18	
Female	0.46±0.16		0.72±0.32		0.37±0.19	

Table 5. Association between depression and health-related quality of life in age-associated neurological diseases

	EQ VAS	p-value*	EQ-5D index score	p-value*
	Mean±SD		Mean±SD	
Parkinson's disease				
Depression no (n=25)	59.16±11.45	<0.01	0.59±0.9	<0.01
Depression yes (n=75)	43.91±16.45		0.42±0.17	
Stroke/TIA				
Depression no (n=47)	69.26±20.23	<0.01	0.84±0.23	<0.01
Depression yes (n=16)	42.94±14.01		0.50±0.37	
Alzheimer/vascular dementia				
Depression no (n=13)	46.54±17.82	<0.01	0.48±0.18	<0.01
Depression yes (n=85)	32.08±12.00		0.35±0.18	

Discussion

In this study, we investigated the prevalence of depression in most common age-related neurological diseases (Parkinson's disease, stroke/TIA, Alzheimer dementia and vascular dementia) and its influence on the health-related quality of life in these diseases. Depression was found to be the most often psychiatric co-morbidity in these diseases. Depressive symptoms were found in up to 87% of patients depending on disease and its severity. Depression in old age is a challenging condition being associated with increased morbidity and reduced life expectancy [39]. There are difficulties to diagnose depression in the elderly because of factors such as late onset, medical co-morbidity and cognitive impairment [40]. Several studies have been carried out in developed and developing countries to evaluate the prevalence of depression in the geriatric population [41-45]. Depending on the country and study settings (urban versus rural, outpatients versus inpatients) prevalence ranged from 1% to 40% [46]. In the healthy elderly the prevalence of depression usually does not exceed 4% [47].

In elderly, depressive symptoms are often present in people with chronic illnesses or disabled people [39]. Moser et al. found higher prevalence of depression and anxiety in elderly patients with heart failure, myocardial infarction, and a coronary artery bypass graft than in healthy elders [48]. Among these cardiac diseases, the greatest percentage of patients with depressive symptoms was in the heart-failure group (appr. 75%). Depression is also common in elderly people with chronic obstructive pulmonary disease. It was identified in 46% of patients in study by Yohannes et al [49].

Prevalence rates of depression in elderly people with age-related neurological diseases are strikingly high. A recent review, reported prevalence rates of depression in Parkinson's disease and Alzheimer dementia, which are nearly identical with those estimated in our study (75% and 87%, respectively) [50]. In stroke, depression was reported to be even more prevalent (34-79%) than in our sample [50,51]. Diagnosis of depression in neurological disorders that are associated with psychomotor retardation and changes in vegetative function is challenging [51].

Diagnosing depression in Parkinson's disease can be particular difficult due to the overlap between depressive symptoms and symptoms specific for Parkinson's disease, such as slowing of movements, so-called bradykinesia, hypomimia, sleep and appetite disturbances as well as reduced libido. Because of bradykinesia and hypomimia, patients with Parkinson's disease appear to lack an obvious affective response and spontaneity. In fact, they may well have an intact affective response but may not be able to translate this adequately into motor equivalents, such as mimic and gestures. In the literature, following symptoms are suggested to help in the diagnosis of depression in people with Parkinson's disease [51]:

- Persistent low mood with daily variations for at least two weeks
- Waking in the early morning
- Pessimistic thoughts out of context with their level of disability
- Suicidal ideations

Depression may precede the onset of motor symptoms by a number of years. Ishihara et al. performed a systematic review of studies investigating prevalence of depression prior to the onset of Parkinson's disease [52]. The odds ratio for a previous history of depression in patients with Parkinson's disease was around 2 compared to controls from general population. The mean time span between onset of depression and motor symptoms was approximately 6 years. Corresponding with the results of our study, previous studies found a biphasic distribution of prevalence of depression during the course of Parkinson's disease, with a peak shortly before or after diagnosis and another gradual increase with advancing disease [52,53].

The results of the epidemiological studies showing increased prevalence of depression in Parkinson's disease are supported by pathophysiological findings of dopamiergic, noradrenergic and serotoninergic dysfunction in patients with Parkinson's disease and depression [54] and imaging studies suggesting reduced metabolism in the frontal lobe of these patients [55,56]. In comparison to PD-patients without depression, PD patients with depression have reduced cortical 5HT1A receptor binding, which is a sign of postsynaptic 5HT1A receptor dysfunction [57]. All these data indicate that depression is an integral part of brain dysfunction in Parkinson's disease.

In stroke, there are a number of reasons why patients are at increased risk of depression. First, patients experienced a sudden onset of functional deficits, which often affect their employment, social situation or marital status. Six months after stroke onset 48% of stroke patients experience hemiparesis, 22% of patients cannot walk, 2-18% of patients have speech disturbances [58]. Second, stroke and consequences impose long-term economic burden on patients and their families [7]. Finally, stroke may affect areas of the brain directly involved in control of mood and emotions. The diagnosis of post-stroke depression is complicated by speech disturbances, impairment of mimic and gesticulation due to paresis, reduced mobility and cognitive impairments. Therefore post-stroke depression is often under-diagnosed. Only 40% of patients in our study population with manifest depression were received adequate antidepressant treatment. If untreated, post-stroke depression can interfere with recovery and worsen functional and social outcomes [59].

The comparisons between epidemiological studies on post-stroke depression are limited due to heterogeneity of cerebrovascular disease and methodological problems related to ascertainment bias. According to the literature, the point prevalence of post-stroke depression is between 30 and 67% [51,60-62], which is higher than in our study. The differences could be explained by sensitivity of applied depressions scales and severity of post-stroke disability. The peak incidence of post-stroke depression was reported between six months and two years after stroke [51]. The localisation of lesions predicting post-stroke depression was the subject of a lively debate in the last decades. The results of two meta-analyses showed increased risk of post-stroke depression in brain infarcts affecting the left frontal pole and pallidum [63,64].

Patients with Alzheimer dementia or vascular dementia often reveal neuropsychiatric symptoms. A prospective study from the Netherlands, found neuropsychiatric symptoms in all but a few residents (97%) of fourteen dementia special care units in nine nursing homes [65]. Depression is the most prevalent psychiatric co-morbidity in dementia. In our study, 86.7% of patients had depressive symptoms, which was much higher than prevalence of other mental disorders. A recent meta-analysis of 13 cross-sectional and four prospective longitudinal studies identified dementia as a risk for factor for depression in old age [66]. Compared to elderly individuals without dementia, individuals in old age with dementia had both significant higher prevalence and incidence rates of depression (OR: 1.82, 95% CI: 1.15-2.89; OR: 3.92, 95% CI: 1.93-7.99, respectively). Unfortunately, depression is often under-diagnosed in patients with dementia. Not only health professionals but also caregivers providing daily care of demented patients can oversee depressive symptoms or interpret them improperly. For example, loss of interest and apathy can be mistaken for symptoms of cognitive impairment. In the recent study by Watson et al, one third of cases with manifest depression in patients with dementia were not identified by their caregivers [67]. The sensitivity and specificity of caregivers' accuracy in recognizing depression in the patient were 0.65 (95% CI: 0.55, 0.75) and 0.58 (95% CI: 0.50, 0.66), respectively. Caregivers also experienced depression related to caregiving, which was identified in 12% of caregivers.

Depression in elderly people with neurological disease is associated with reduced health-related quality of life. Eighty-six percent of patients with Parkinson's disease in our study reported moderate or severe problems in the dimension "anxiety/depression" of the EQ-5D. The majority of studies identified depression as the main contributor to reduced health-related quality of life in Parkinson's disease [9,68-72]. In our study and study by Chen et al depression was one of the major factors reducing the health-related quality of life in elderly people with cerebrovascular disease [73]. It is also an important factor associated with decreased health-related quality of life in caregivers of stroke patients [73]. Corresponding with results of study by Banerjee et al, depression was a predictor of reduced health-related quality of life in elderly with dementia [74].

In conclusion, age-related neurological diseases, such as cerebrovascular and neuro-degenerative diseases, show association with increased risk of depression in the elderly. Unfortunately, depression is often under-diagnosed in these diseases being masked by motor impairment. Depression is a predictor of reduced HrQoL in elder individuals with neurological diseases, therefore, they should be screened for presence of depressive symptoms and receive adequate antidepressant treatment.

REFERENCES

[1] Winter Y, Bezdolnyy Y, Katunina E, et al. Incidence of Parkinson's disease and atypical Parkinsonism: Russian population-based study. *Mov. Disord.* 2010;25:349-356.

[2] Dorsey ER, Constantinescu R, Thompson JP, et al. Projected number of people with Parkinson disease in the most populous nations, 2005 through 2030. *Neurology* 2007;68(5):384-386.

[3] Wolf P, Kannel W, d'Agostino R. Epidemiology of stroke. In: Ginsberg M, Bogousslavsky J eds, Cerebrovascular disease: pathophysiology, diagnosis and management. Malden, Mass: Blackwell Science; 1998:834-850.

[4] Andlin-Sobocki P, Jonsson B, Wittchen HU, Olesen J. Costs of disorders of the brain in Europe. *Eur. J. Neurol.* 2005;12 (Suppl 1):1-27.

[5] Dodel R, Winter Y, Ringel F, et al. Cost of illness in subarachnoid hemorrhage: a german longitudinal study. *Stroke* 2010;41:2918-2923.

[6] Winter Y, Wolfram C, Schaeg M, et al. Evaluation of costs and outcome in cardioembolic stroke or TIA. *J. Neurol.* 2009;256:954-963.

[7] Winter Y, Wolfram C, Schöffski O, Dodel RC, Back T. Long-term disease-related costs 4 years after stroke or TIA in Germany. *Nervenarzt* 2008;79:918-926.

[8] Winter Y, Schepelmann K, Spottke AE, et al. Health-related quality of life in ALS, myasthenia gravis and facioscapulohumeral muscular dystrophy. *J. Neurol.* 2010;257:1473-1481.

[9] Winter Y, von Campenhausen S, Gasser J, et al. Social and clinical determinants of quality of life in Parkinson's disease in Austria: a cohort study. *J. Neurol.* 2010;257:638-645.

[10] Meyer B, Ringel F, Winter Y, et al. Health-Related Quality of Life in Patients with Subarachnoid Haemorrhage. *Cerebrovasc. Dis.* 2010;30:423-431.

[11] Winter Y, von Campenhausen S, Brozova H, et al. Costs of Parkinson's disease in Eastern Europe: A Czech cohort study. *Parkinsonism Relat. Disord* 2010;16:51-56.

[12] Gibb WRG. Accuracy in the clinical diagnosis of parkinsonian syndromes. *Postgrad Med J* 1988;64:345-512.

[13] McKhann G, Drachman D, Folstein M, et al. Clinical diagnosis of Alzheimer's disease: report of the NINCDS-ADRDA Work Group under the auspices of Department of Health and Human Services Task Force on Alzheimer's Disease. *Neurology* 1984;34:939-944.

[14] Roman GC, Tatemichi TK, Erkinjuntti T, et al. Vascular dementia: diagnostic criteria for research studies. Report of the NINDS-AIREN International Workshop. *Neurology* 1993;43:250-260.

[15] Mahoney FI, Barthel DW. Functional evaluation: the Barthel Index. *Md. State Med. J.* 1965;14:61-65.

[16] Rankin J. Cerebral vascular accidents in patients over the age of 60. *Scott Med. J.* 1957;2:200-215.

[17] Collin C, Wade DT, Davies S, Horne V. The Barthel ADL Index: a relability study. *Int-Disabil-Stud* 1988;10(2):61-63.

[18] Wolfe CDA, Taub NA, Woodrow EJ, Burney PGJ. Assessment of scales of disability and handicap for stroke patients. *Stroke* 1991;22:1242-1244.

[19] Hantson L, De Weerdt W, De Keyser J, et al. The European Stroke Scale. *Stroke* 1994;25:2215-2219.

[20] Loewen SC, Anderson BA. Reliability of the Modified Motor Assessment Scale and the Barthel Index. *Phys Ther* 1988;68(7):1077-1081.

[21] The National Institute of Neurological Disorders and Stroke rt-PA Stroke Study Group. Tissue plasminogen activator for acute ischemic stroke. *The New England journal of medicine* 1995;333:1581–1587.

[22] Albers GW, Clark WM, Madden KP, Hamilton S. The ATLANTIS trial: results for patients treated within 3 hours of stroke onset. *Stroke* 2002;33(2):493-495.

[23] Hacke W, Kaste M, Fieschi C, et al. Intravenous thrombolysis with recombinant tissue plasminogen activator for acute hemispheric stroke: the European Cooperative Acute Stroke Study (ECASS). *JAMA* 1995;274:1017-1025.

[24] Hacke W, Kaste M, Fieschi C, et al. Randomised double-blind placebo-controlled trial of thrombolytic therapy with intravenous alteplase in acute ischaemic stroke (ECASS II): Second European-Australasian Acute Stroke Study Investigators. *Lancet* 1998;352:1245-1251.

[25] Janzen RWC, Kugler C. Eine Schlaganfalldatenbank für die Qualitätssicherung beim Hirninfarkt. *Nervenheilkunde* 1998;17:21-25.

[26] Martinez-Martin P, Gil-Nagel A, Gracia LM, et al. Unified Parkinson's Disease Rating Scale characteristics and structure. The Cooperative Multicentric Group. *Mov. Disord.* 1994;9:76-83.

[27] Hoehn MM, Yahr M. Parkinsonism: onset, progression and mortality. *Neurology* 1967;5:427-442.

[28] Folstein MF, Folstein SE, McHugh PR. "Mini-mental state": a practical method for grading the cognitive state of patients for the clinician. *J. Psychiatr. Res.* 1975;12 (3):189-198.

[29] Beck A, Ward CH, Mendelson M, Mock J, Erbaugh J. An inventory for measuring depression. *Arch. Ger. Psychiatry* 1961;4:561-567.

[30] Yesavage JA, Brink TL, Rose TL, et al. Development and validation of a geriatric depression screening scale: a preliminary report. *J. Psychiatr. Res.* 1982;17:37-49.

[31] Zigmond AS, Snaith RP. The hospital anxiety and depression scale. *Acta Psychiatr Scand* 1983;67:361-370.

[32] Bjelland I, Dahl AA, Haug TT, Neckelmann D. The validity of the Hospital Anxiety and Depression Scale. An updated literature review. *J. Psychosom. Res.* 2002;52:69-77.

[33] Brazier J, Jones N, Kind P. Testing the validity of the EuroQoL and comparing it with the SF-36 health survey questionnaire. *Qual Life Res.* 1993;2:169-180.

[34] Kind P. The EuroQol instrument: an index of health-related quality of life. In: Spilker B ed, Quality of life and pharmacoeconomics in clinical trials. Philadelphia: Lippincott-Raven; 1996.

[35] The EuroQol Group. EuroQol - a new facility for the measurement of health-related quality of life. *Health Policy* 1990;16:199-208.

[36] Greiner W, Weijnen T, Nieuwenhuizen M, et al. A single European currency for EQ-5D health states. Results from a six-country study. *Eur. J. Health Econ* 2003 4:222-231.

[37] Koenig HH, Bernert S, Angermeyer MC. [Health Status of the German population: results of a representative survey using the EuroQol questionnaire]. *Gesundheitswesen* 2005;67:173-182.

[38] Konig HH, Bernert S, Angermeyer MC, et al. Comparison of population health status in six european countries: results of a representative survey using the EQ-5D questionnaire. *Med. Care* 2009;47:255-261.

[39] Alexopoulos GS, Buckwalter K, Olin J, et al. Comorbidity of late life depression: an opportunity for research on mechanisms and treatment. *Biol. Psychiatry* 2002;52:543-558.

[40] Nelson JC. Diagnosing and treating depression in the elderly. *J. Clin. Psychiatry* 2001;62 Suppl 24:18-22.

[41] Ganatra HA, Zafar SN, Qidwai W, Rozi S. Prevalence and predictors of depression among an elderly population of Pakistan. *Aging Ment. Health* 2008;12:349-356.

[42] Helvik AS, Skancke RH, Selbaek G. Screening for depression in elderly medical inpatients from rural area of Norway: prevalence and associated factors. *Int. J. Geriatr. Psychiatry* 2010;25:150-159.

[43] Ma X, Xiang YT, Li SR, et al. Prevalence and sociodemographic correlates of depression in an elderly population living with family members in Beijing, China. *Psychol. Med.* 2008;38:1723-1730.

[44] Wada T, Ishine M, Sakagami T, et al. Depression in Japanese community-dwelling elderly--prevalence and association with ADL and QOL. *Arch. Gerontol. Geriatr.* 2004;39:15-23.

[45] Heath JM, Brown M, Kobylarz FA, Castano S. The prevalence of undiagnosed geriatric health conditions among adult protective service clients. *Gerontologist* 2005;45:820-823.

[46] Djernes JK. Prevalence and predictors of depression in populations of elderly: a review. *Acta. Psychiatr. Scand* .2006; 113:372-387.

[47] Blazer D, Williams CD. Epidemiology of dysphoria and depression in an elderly population. *Am. J. Psychiatry* 1980;137:439-444.

[48] Moser DK, Dracup K, Evangelista LS, et al. Comparison of prevalence of symptoms of depression, anxiety, and hostility in elderly patients with heart failure, myocardial infarction, and a coronary artery bypass graft. *Heart Lung* 2010;39:378-385.

[49] Yohannes AM, Baldwin RC, Connolly MJ. Depression and anxiety in elderly outpatients with chronic obstructive pulmonary disease: prevalence, and validation of the BASDEC screening questionnaire. *Int. J. Geriatr. Psychiatry* 2000;15:1090-1096.

[50] Strober LB, Arnett PA. Assessment of depression in three medically ill, elderly populations: Alzheimer's disease, Parkinson's disease, and stroke. *Clin. Neuropsychol* 2009;23:205-230.

[51] Rickards H. Depression in neurological disorders: Parkinson's disease, multiple sclerosis, and stroke. *J. Neurol. Neurosurg Psychiatry* 2005;76 Suppl 1:i48-52.

[52] Ishihara L, Brayne C. A systematic review of depression and mental illness preceding Parkinson's disease. *Acta neurologica Scandinavica* 2006;113:211-220.

[53] Schrag A. Psychiatric aspects of Parkinson's disease--an update. *J. Neurol.* 2004;251:795-804.

[54] Mayeux R. The "serotonin hypothesis" for depression in Parkinson's disease. *Adv Neurol* 1990;53:163-166.

[55] Mayberg HS, Starkstein SE, Sadzot B, et al. Selective hypometabolism in the inferior frontal lobe in depressed patients with Parkinson's disease. *Annals of neurology* 1990;28:57-64.

[56] Ring HA, Bench CJ, Trimble MR, et al. Depression in Parkinson's disease. A positron emission study. *Br. J. Psychiatry* 1994;165:333-339.

[57] Doder M, Rabiner EA, Turjanski N, Lees AJ, Brooks DJ. Tremor in Parkinson's disease and serotonergic dysfunction: an 11C-WAY 100635 PET study. *Neurology* 2003;60:601-605.

[58] Kaste M, Olsen T, Orgogozo J, Bogousslavsky J, Hacke W. Organization of stroke care: education, stroke unites and rehabilitation. *Cerebrovasc. Dis.* 2000;10:1-11.

[59] Suenkeler IH, Nowak M, Misselwitz B, et al. Timecourse of health-related quality of life as determined 3, 6 and 12 months after stroke. Relationship to neurological deficit, disability and depression. *J. Neurol.* 2002;249(9):1160-1167.

[60] Kaste M, Fogelholm R, Rissanen A. Economic burden of stroke and the evaluation of new therapies. *Public Health* 1998;112(2):103-112.

[61] King RB. Quality of life after stroke. *Stroke* 1996;27:1467-1472.

[62] Carod-Artal J, Egido JA, Gonzalez JL, Varela dS. Quality of life among stroke survivors evaluated 1 year after stroke: experience of a stroke unit. *Stroke* 2000;31:2995-3000.

[63] Narushima K, Kosier JT, Robinson RG. A reappraisal of poststroke depression, intra- and inter-hemispheric lesion location using meta-analysis. *J. Neuropsychiatry Clin. Neurosci.* 2003;15:422-430.

[64] Vataja R, Leppavuori A, Pohjasvaara T, et al. Poststroke depression and lesion location revisited. *J. Neuropsychiatry Clin. Neurosci.* 2004;16:156-162.

[65] Wetzels RB, Zuidema SU, de Jonghe JF, Verhey FR, Koopmans RT. Course of neuropsychiatric symptoms in residents with dementia in nursing homes over 2-year period. *Am. J. Geriatr. Psychiatry* 2010;18:1054-1065.

[66] Huang CQ, Wang ZR, Li YH, Xie YZ, Liu QX. Cognitive function and risk for depression in old age: a meta-analysis of published literature. *Int. Psychogeriatr.* 2010:1-10.

[67] Watson LC, Lewis CL, Moore CG, Jeste DV. Perceptions of depression among dementia caregivers: findings from the CATIE-AD trial. *Int. J. Geriatr. Psychiatry* 2010.

[68] Schrag A, Jahanshahi M, Quinn N. How does Parkinson's disease affect quality of life? A comparison with quality of life in the general population. *Mov. Disord.* 2000; 15:1112-1118.

[69] Schrag A, Jahanshahi M, Quinn N. What contributes to quality of life in patients with Parkinson's disease? *J. Neurol. Neurosurg Psychiatry* 2000;69:308-312.

[70] Visser M, van Rooden SM, Verbaan D, et al. A comprehensive model of health-related quality of life in Parkinson's disease. *J. Neurol.* 2008;255:1580-1587.

[71] The Global Parkinson's Disease Survey (GPDS) Steering Committee. Factors impacting on quality of life in Parkinson's disease: results from an international survey. *Mov. Disord.* 2002;17:60-67.

[72] Zach M, Friedman A, Slawek J, Derejko M. Quality of life in Polish patients with long-lasting Parkinson's disease. *Mov. Disord.* 2004;19:667-672.

[73] Chen Y, Lu J, Wong KS, et al. Health-related quality of life in the family caregivers of stroke survivors. *Int. J. Rehabil. Res.;* 33:232-237.

[74] Banerjee S, Smith SC, Lamping DL, et al. Quality of life in dementia: more than just cognition. An analysis of associations with quality of life in dementia. *J. Neurol. Neurosurg. Psychiatry* 2006;77:146-148.

In: Depression in the Elderly
Editor: Emaad Abdel-Rahman, pp. 103-114
ISBN 978-1-61324-771-6

Chapter 6

PSYCHOTIC DEPRESSION IN THE ELDERLY

Rajesh R. Tampi[1] and Deena Williamson[2]
[1]Yale University School of Medicine and Masonicare, Connecticut, USA
[2]St. Francis Hospital and Medical Center, Connecticut, USA

ABSTRACT

Depression is not uncommon in the elderly. Psychotic depression, a major subtype of depression is more commonly seen in the elderly depressed patients than in younger patients with depression. Evidence indicates that psychotic depression in the elderly is associated with specific clinical, neurobiological and neuropsychological changes and has a worse prognosis than depression without psychosis in the elderly. In this chapter we review the epidemiology, clinical features, neurobiology, neuropsychology, assessment and treatments for this important psychiatric disorder in the elderly.

INTRODUCTION

Depression is not uncommon, occurring in approximately 2% of all community-dwelling elderly [1-3]. In primary care clinics, its prevalence increases to approximately 6-9%, while among the patients admitted to acute care hospitals, the prevalence is approximately 10-12% [3]. Among all nursing home residents, 12-14% meet the criteria for major depressive disorder (MDD) [4]. However, the rates of depressive symptoms in general are much higher, with studies showing prevalence rates between 30% and 45% [2, 5].

The elderly patients with depression remain at very high risk of committing suicide. The elderly are two times more likely to commit suicide than their younger counterparts [6]. Of these, approximately 80% suffered from a depressive syndrome [4]. Presence of psychotic features increases the severity of depression.

Population studies reveal that the presentation profile of depression in later life is distinct from that of the younger population. In general, these patients are less likely to have a family history of depression than their younger counterparts [6]. The symptoms of depression are more likely to develop insidiously, and these patients are less likely than their younger counterparts to attribute their symptoms to depression as opposed to "the normal aging process" [2].

Elderly patients with depression usually present with higher rates of psychotic symptoms as compared to their younger counterparts [7] [8]. Proposed explanations for this disparity include age-related deterioration of cortical areas, neurochemical changes common in aging, comorbid physical illnesses, social isolation, sensory deficits, cognitive changes, and polypharmacy [6]. In this chapter, we review the available data on the psychotic depression in the elderly and its treatments.

EPIDEMIOLOGY

A Finnish community study indicated that the prevalence of psychotic depression in the elderly was 6 per 1,000 for men, 12 per 1,000 for women and 10 per 1,000 for both sexes put together [9]. The Epidemiologic Catchment Area survey reported a range of psychosis from 16% to 23% in an older adult population [10]. In addition, psychotic late-onset depression accounts for nearly 25-50% of admissions to the inpatient geriatric psychiatry units [10]. Studies have also noted that psychotic symptoms generally occur in those elderly depressed patients who are single, widowed, or living alone [9] [11].

CLINICAL FEATURES

A recent study noted that elderly patients suffered from more gastrointestinal symptoms and severe depression compared to younger patients [12]. Additionally, elderly patients expressed significantly more frequently delusions of somatic content and higher scores on the Hamilton Rating Scale for Depression (HRSD) item of hypochondriasis than their young early-onset counterparts [12].

Earlier studies had noted that elderly patients with psychotic depression have higher depressive symptomatology as measured by the HSRD [9] [11]. Elderly patients with psychotic depression also present with increased feelings of guilt, anxiety, hypochondriacal symptoms and reduced insight into their symptoms [9] [11] [13]. Delusional guilt is present in one-third of these patients [14]. Some studies have shown that hypochondrical delusions are more prominent in men and paranoid delusions are more common in women [9] [11]. In the study by Gournellis et al, one-third of the elderly patients with depression had auditory hallucinations but visual and olfactory hallucinations were seen less frequently [11].

Psychomotor activity in patients with psychotic depression is variable, with one study showing agitation, one study showing retardation and one study showing no difference in psychomotor activity [9] [11] [13].

Studies evaluating the age of onset of psychotic depression have found mixed results. Myers and Greenberg in their study found that patients with psychotic depression were older than patients with non-psychotic depression at the onset of symptoms [14]. A later study by Nelson et al did not find any difference between the age of onset of symptoms in elderly patients with psychotic depression compared to those without psychotic symptoms [15]. The study by Gournellis et al found that in the elderly, psychotic depression has a later age at onset of symptoms [11].

Nelson et al found that elderly patients with psychotic depression have more previous hospitalizations but Gournelli et al and Lee et al did not in their studies [15] [11] [13].

Studies evaluating suicidality in elderly depressed patients with psychotic symptoms have provided mixed results. In a retrospective chart review Lyness et al found that among elderly patients who attempted suicide, eighty percent of the attempters had a major depressive disorder and among patients with affective disorders, the presence of an attempt was significantly associated with a later age of onset and those who had made more severe attempts were more likely to be diagnosed as psychotic depression, although this trend was not significant [16]. Lee et al also found that in their sample of elderly patients with psychotic depression the suicide risk was higher [13]. However, a study by Lykouras et al found that psychotic depression does not increase the risk for elderly depressed patients attempting suicide [17]. Gender, age of onset of depression, severity of the episode and melancholic features were also not correlated with higher suicide risk in this study. A recent study noted that although psychotic depression is associated greater intensity of current suicidality, older age was not independently associated higher risk of suicide [18].

Family studies of elderly patients with psychotic depression indicate mixed results. The study by Simpson et al indicated that patients with psychotic depression had more family history of depression than non-psychotic depressed patients and controls [19]. However, studies by O'Brien et al and Gournellis et al did not find any difference in family psychiatric history between psychotic and non-psychotic depressed patients [20] [11].

Prognostic studies in elderly patients with psychotic depression have also yielded mixed results; with some studies indicating no difference, while others indicating a worse prognosis when compared to non-psychotic patients. In the study by Baldwin, two groups of 24 patients with late-onset depression, one with and one without delusions were compared retrospectively. At the index admission, deluded patients were significantly more depressed, were in hospital for longer, responded poorly to antidepressants alone and required more physical treatments, especially ECT and major tranquilizers [21]. Although illness severity was a major factor accounting for these differences, the finding that only the deluded group experienced delusional relapses suggests an underlying intrinsic susceptibility. The discharge status was similar for both groups, as were relapse rates over 48 months and the clinical course of depressive symptoms over 42-104 months. However, in the study by Flint and Rifat, patients with psychotic depression had a substantially higher frequency of relapse and recurrence of depression and a shorter time to these events than non-psychotic depressed patients [22]. At index assessment, patients with psychosis were more severely depressed and had had more prior episodes of depression, but these factors did not account for the difference in outcome between the two groups. Furthermore, before entering the study, none of the psychotic patients had received adequate treatment for the index episode of depression, and so their poor outcome could not be attributed to prior treatment resistance [22]. In the study by Gourellis et al, a previous psychotic episode was the strongest predictors of developing psychotic features during the current episode [11].

NEUROBIOLOGY

Although not specific to the elderly, current evidence indicates that psychotic depression is associated with abnormalities of the hypothalamo-pituitary-adrenal (HPA) axis and dopaminergic system [23]. Patients with psychotic depression have among the highest rates of non-suppression on the dexamethasone suppression test [24]. These patients also have significant elevations in serum cortisol levels [25]. Chronic elevation of cortisol may also lead to dopaminergic dysfunction in patients with psychotic depression although this may not be true in all cases [26] [27].

Neuroimaging studies indicate that depressed patients with psychotic symptoms have enlarged cerebral ventricles and sulcal CSF volumes [28]. These patients have decreased prefrontal cortex volume and reduced amygdala volume compared to non-psychotic depressed patients [29].

An electroencephalographic study has shown that patients with psychotic depression have increased wakefulness, decreased rapid eye movement (REM) sleep percentage and extremely short sleep-onset REM latencies [30].

Several studies completed in elderly patient with psychotic depression indicate that these patients have specific neural correlates that distinguish them from non-psychotic depressed elderly and controls. In a study by Zubenko et al, the investigators specifically tested the hypothesis that the frequency of the APOE epsilon 4 allele is elevated in depressed elders with cognitive impairment or psychotic features [31]. The frequency of epsilon 4 allele was not elevated in the overall group of 45 inpatients and contrary to expectation it was not associated with cognitive impairment in this group. In contrast, the epsilon 4 allele frequency for patients with psychotic features was nearly four times that for the patients without psychotic features and nearly double that for the elderly controls.This data suggested that elderly depressed with psychotic features are at risk for developing Alzheimer's disease (AD) by an epsilon 4-dependent pathway. These findings also suggest that subtypes of idiopathic major depression in late life may serve as landmarks that distinguish separable pathogenetic pathways to AD [31].

In a study by O' Brien et al elderly patients with delusional depression had significantly more vascular risk factors than those without delusions [20]. However, there were no differences on measures of temporal lobe atrophy, periventricular lesions (PVL), deep white matter lesions (DWML) or a standard dexamethasone suppression test (DST) or cognitive test scores, although there was a non-significant trend for DWML to be more prevalent in those with delusions. Delusional depression was however associated with a shorter duration of history and more frequent treatment with ECT [20].

Dopamine beta-hydroxylase (DBH) is the enzyme that converts dopamine to norepinephrine and the peripheral and cerebral spinal fluid DBH activity are significantly correlated in drug-free patients [32]. Although serum DBH is largely under genetic control reports suggest that treatment with psychopharmacologic medications can affect the activity of this enzyme [33]. In a study by Meyers et al, fifteen elderly patients with psychotic depression were compared to 20 non-psychotic depressed patients and 22 control subjects on dopamine beta-hydroxylase (DBH) activity [34]. Baseline and predischarge DBH assays were lower in subjects with delusional depression than in either comparison group. Despite high intraindividual correlation, treatment was associated with significant increases in activity in the clinical groups [34].

In a study by Kim et al, the investigators performed magnetic resonance (MR) morphometry on nineteen deluded depressed patients and 26 non-deluded depressed patients, all older than 55 years of age [35]. Subjects were administered a neuropsychological test battery and measures of depression. The absolute volume of prefrontal cortex (PFC) was smaller in the deluded depressed group than in non-deluded depressed group (131.79 +/- 37.26 ml vs. 152.65 +/- 26.13 ml, $p = 0.03$); a difference that was statistically significant even after adjusting for the effect of whole brain volume, $P= 0.01$. No group differences were observed in the volumes of the basal ganglia, the temporal lobes, the superior temporal gyri, the amygdala-hippocampal complex, the lateral ventricles, or whole brain. The investigators concluded that PFC may be one of the candidate neuroanatomic substrates underlying psychotic depression in the elderly [35].

In a study by Simpson et al of the ninety-nine elderly patients diagnosed with DSM-III-R major depression, eighteen had psychotic symptoms [19]. Sixty-six patients were given a neuropsychological test battery and 44 had a magnetic resonance imaging brain scan. The subgroup of patients with psychotic depression was characterized by worse physical health, more family history of depression, a poorer response to antidepressant drugs, and more severe lowering of mood; however, the strongest predictors of the presence of delusions were diencephalic atrophy, reticular activating system lesions, brain stem atrophy, and left-sided frontotemporal atrophy. The authors concluded that in the elderly, psychotic depression is etiologically, clinically, and neuroradiologically distinct, and has different treatment requirements, from non-psychotic major depression [19].

These studies indicate that elderly patient with psychotic depression have specific neurochemical, neurogenetic, neruroanatomic and neurofunctional changes that distinguish them from non-psychotically depressed patients and controls.

Neuropsychology

Some studies in elderly patients with psychotic depression indicate that these patients perform less well on tests of cognitive functioning. In a study by Miller et al., fourteen patients who developed a psychotic depression after age 45 year were compared with 72 non-psychiatrically ill elderly control subjects using neuroimaging and neuropsychological (NP) tests [36]. Structural brain abnormalities were found in approximately two-thirds of patients and in less than 10% of controls. The most common abnormality, subcortical white matter (WM) lesions, was thought to be vascular in etiology. Also, tumor and primary degenerative dementia were found more frequently in these patients. Compared to an age-, sex-, and education-matched control group, the patients performed more poorly on NP tests of frontal lobe, memory, and visual spatial abilities [36]. In the study by Simpson et al, elderly depressed patients with psychotic symptoms had poorer performance on tests of frontal lobe function and mental processing speed [19]. In the study by Kim et al, the relative volume of PFC correlated inversely and significantly with the index of Wisconsin Card Sorting Test (WCST) performance ($r= -0.76$, $P< 0.01$) in depressed patients with psychosis [35]. However the study by O'Brien et al, did not find any difference between the cognitive test scores of the psychotic versus non-psychotic depressed elderly [20]. The study by Gournellis et al, also found that elderly patients with psychotic depression did not differ in their cognitive functioning compared to their non-psychotic counterparts [11].

ASSESSMENT

The assessment of elderly patients with psychotic depression should begin with a thorough medical and psychiatric history [37]. History should evaluate for previous episodes of depression with or without psychotic features. Medical and psychiatric comorbidities should also be carefully assessed [37]. Adequacy of previous treatments should be thoroughly evaluated. A careful review of medications should be completed and those medications that are causing or worsening depression and/or psychosis should be eliminated [37]. Rating scales like the Geriatric Depression Scale (GDS), Hamilton Rating Scale for Depression (HAM-D), Cornell Scale for Depression in Dementia (CSDD), Brief Psychiatric Rating Scale (BPRS) should be completed to assess the severity of the illness and associated symptoms [38]. An assessment of cognitive functioning should be done as elderly patients with depression often present with cognitive dysfunction and patients with dementia have comorbid depression [38]. Common screening tools like the Mini Mental State Examination (MMSE) or Montreal Cognitive Assessment (MOCA) could be used to screen for cognitive dysfunction. A focused physical examination should be done to rule out cardiovascular and cerebrovascular disorders that can cause depression i.e., coronary artery disease and strokes [38]. Laboratory examination should focus on ruling out infectious and metabolic disorders that could lead to depression i.e., pneumonia, hypothyroidsm and diabetes etc [37] [38]. Neuroimaging, preferably magnetic resonance imaging (MRI) should used in to rule out cerebrovascular causes of depression and psychosis [39]. Neuropsychological testing should be completed in patients where underlying cognitive dysfunction, personality dysfunction or neuropsychiatric disorders like Parkinson's disease is suspected. Once a thorough assessment is completed, all relevant comorbidities have been evaluated and the severity of psychotic depression assessed, the next step is to decide on the appropriate treatment [37].

TREATMENTS

Available data indicates the pharmacotherapy and/or electroconvulsive therapy (ECT) forms the basis for the treatment of psychotic depression in the elderly. The data on psychotherapy for psychotic depression in the elderly is limited. In this section, we will review the available data for psychotherapy, pharmacotherapy and ECT for the treatment of psychotic depression in the elderly.

PSYCHOTHERAPY

Review of literature indicates that there are no randomized controlled trials of psychotherapy for psychotic depression in the elderly. But available data indicates that cognitive behavioral therapy (CBT), interpersonal therapy (ITP), problem solving therapy (PST) are effective and well tolerated in elderly depressed patients [40-43]. Given this data, there is no reason to believe that CBT, IPT and PST will not be effective at least as an adjunct to pharmacotherapy in the treatment of psychotic depression in the elderly.

PHARMACOTHERAPY

The data for the pharmacotherapy of psychotic depression in the elderly is limited by the number of controlled trials. Our review of the literature found a total of six controlled studies for treatment of this condition.

In the first trial, Navarro et al evaluated the use of nortriptyline alone versus nortriptyline and electroconvulsive therapy (ECT) combined in late life depression (age >60 years) in a two year randomized study [44]. The investigators found that patients who had only pharmacologic therapy alone had an eight fold higher chance of relapse or recurrence. This study also showed a high remission rate after ECT of 86.8%. The authors report that the treatments were well tolerated and the adverse effects were only of mild or moderate intensity. There were no significant difference was found in EKG recordings or blood pressure recordings between treatments.

Birkenhager et al compared the efficacy of imipramine in psychotic versus non-psychotically depressed patients [45]. The average age of the patients was between 48.9 and 49.5 years in both the groups. In this study there was a decrease in the Hamilton Scale score of more than 50% in 55% of the psychotic depression group, compared to 39% in the non-psychotic depression group.

A double blind, randomized, placebo controlled study by DeBattista et al included 221 patients aged 19 to 75 years [46]. They met the diagnostic and Statistical Manual (DSM-IV) and Structured Clinical Interview for DSM-IV (SCID) criteria for psychotic major depression (PMD) and were not receiving any antidepressant or antipsychotic medications. [46]. Patients were randomly assigned to either 7 days of mifepristone (n = 105) or placebo (n = 116). Patients treated with mifepristone were significantly more likely to achieve response, defined as a 30% reduction in the Brief Psychiatric Rating Scale (BPRS). In addition, mifepristone treated patients were significantly more likely to achieve a 50% reduction in the BPRS Positive Symptom Scale (PSS). The study concluded that a seven-day course of mifepristone appears to be effective and well tolerated in the treatment of psychosis in PMD. This study suggests that the antiglucocorticoid, mifepristone, might represent an alternative to traditional treatments of psychosis in psychotic depression. The authors report that mifepristone appeared to be well tolerated. The adverse effects were not significantly higher in the mefipristone group than in the placebo group although the mifepristone group did have higher rates of constipation and dyspepsia. The rate of withdrawal due to adverse effects was very low with one patient withdrawing from both the placebo am treatment groups.

In the study by Mulsant et al the investigators conducted a randomized controlled trial comparing the efficacy of an antidepressant alone versus an antidepressant plus an antipsychotic in the treatment of late-life psychotic depression [47]. The efficacy of nortriptyline with placebo versus nortriptyline with perphenazine was compared in 36 patients aged 50 years or older presenting with a major depressive episode with psychotic features

(DSM-III R criteria). Thirty patients were treated with nortriptyline for at least 4 weeks combined with either perphenazine (n=14) or placebo (n=16) for at least 2 weeks (median =9 weeks). No significant difference were noted between the completers in the 2 treatment groups when comparing their scores on the Hamilton Depression Scale (HAM-D), the BPRS-psychoticism subscale, or any side effects measure. Rates of response (defined as resolution of both depression and psychosis) did not differ significantly in the 2 groups (nortriptyline-plus-perphenazine group, 50% vs. nortriptyline-plus-placebo group, 44%). The investigators concluded that when treating older patients with psychotic depression, the addition of a moderate dose of a traditional neuroleptic to a tricyclic antidepressant was well tolerated but did not improve efficacy. Extrapyramidal symptoms (EPS) scores were not significantly different between the two treatment groups although the perphenazine treated group did show a greater trend for EPS.

In a study by Belanoff et al, five patients (44 years, 45 years, 50 years, 57 years, 67 years) with a diagnosis of psychotic major depression, which were confirmed independently by two psychiatrists, were given 600 mg of mifepristone in a 4-day, double blind, placebo-controlled crossover study [48]. In all cases, HAM-D scores declined during mifepristone treatment. In the two cases where the patient received mifepristone first, their HAM-D declined during the placebo treatment also. In the three cases where placebo was given first, HAM-D scores changed very little. The mean decline in HAM-D while receiving mifepristone was 8.0 (25.5%), whereas while receiving placebo it was 1.7 (5.8%), $p<0.07$. In all but one case, BPRS scores declined during mifepristone treatment. This preliminary result suggested that short-term use of glucocorticoid receptor antagonists may be effective in the treatment of psychotic major depression.

In a 12-week, double-blind, randomized, controlled trial two hundred fifty-nine subjects with major depression with psychotic features were randomized by age (<60 or > or =60 years) [49]. The intervention target doses were 15 to 20 mg of olanzapine per day plus masked sertraline or placebo at 150 to 200 mg per day. The main outcome measure was the remission rates of major depression with psychotic features. Treatment with olanzapine and sertraline was associated with higher remission rates during the trial than the olanzapine and placebo groups (odds ratio [OR], 1.28,; 95% confidence interval [CI], 1.12-1.47; $p < .001$); 41.9% of subjects who underwent combination therapy were in remission at their last assessment compared with 23.9% of subjects treated with monotherapy ($P= 0.002$). Combination therapy was comparably superior in both younger (OR, 1.25; 95% CI, 1.05-1.50; $P= 0.02$) and older (OR, 1.34; 95% CI, 1.09-1.66; $P= 0.01$) adults. Tolerability was comparable across the age groups. Both age groups had significant increases in cholesterol and triglyceride concentrations, but statistically significant increases in glucose occurred only in younger adults. Younger adults gained significantly more weight than older subjects (mean [SD], 6.5 [6.6] kg vs 3.3 [4.9] kg, $p = .001$). The investigators concluded that combination pharmacotherapy is efficacious for the treatment of major depression with psychotic features in both younger and older patients. However they cautioned that future research must determine the benefits versus risks of continuing atypical antipsychotic medications beyond the 12 week period.

Although a consensus guideline recommends the use of an antipsychotic medication in combination with an antidepressant as first-line treatment for elderly patients with major depression with psychotic features, this recommendation is supported by only one recent controlled trial [49, 50]. Atypical antipsychotics (except clozapine) are clearly preferred in these patients [50]. The choice of antidepressants includes selective serotonin reuptake inhibitor (SSRIs) and venlafaxine as first-line treatment, with tricyclic antidepressants (TCAs) being the alternative [50]. It is recommended that a 4 to7 week trial on the maximally tolerated dose of one medication be achieved before switching to another medication [50]. Suggested duration of treatment for a first major depressive episode is 6 months, assuming that the patient tolerates the medication with no adverse effects [50]. However, recent data indicate that longer treatment (2 years) may prevent a relapse [51]. The study by Rothschild and Duval indicated that majority of patients with psychotic depression do not require treatment with an antipsychotic medication for more than 4 months [52].

As the pathophysiology of psychotic depression is hypothesized to be different from that of primary psychotic disorders such as schizophrenia or schizoaffective disorder, it is worthwhile to explore alternatives to antipsychotics in the treatment protocol. Mifepristone and ECT are alternatives as monotherapy or in combination with antidepressants, but longer-term data for these treatments is lacking at the present time. Extrapyramidal side effects increase the risk of falls in the elderly and every effort should be made to delay antipsychotic treatment in those with risk factors for falls [53, 54]. ECT is certainly an alternative that should be explored in the treatment of these patients. Mifepristone has the potential to be a good alternative in patients who are at risk for complications from general anesthesia, if long term data and larger clinical trials could support its safety and efficacy.

Conclusion

Currently available evidence indicates that psychotic depression is not uncommon in the elderly. This disorder is associated with specific clinical, neurobiological and neuro-psychological features. Psychotic depression in the elderly carries with it a worse prognosis in terms of morbidity and mortality rates. Data on the treatment for this condition is limited by the number of controlled studies that have been done to date. Our review of the literature indicates that there are no controlled psychotherapeutic studies for this condition. However, available evidence indicates that CBT, IPT and PST are all effective in the treatment of non-psychotic depression in the elderly, so there is no reason why these therapies would not be beneficial at least as an adjunct to medications in the treatment of psychotic depression. Data on pharmacotherapy indicates that there are six controlled studies indicating that that a combination of an antidepressant medication with an antipsychotic drug may have the best evidence in the treatment of an episode of psychotic depression. The data to differentiate between the efficacy rates or tolerability of various classes of antidepressants or between typical and atypical antipsychotics in combination with the antidepressants is currently unavailable. Available data indicates that mifepristone and ECT are alternative treatments as monotherapy or in combination with antidepressants or antipsychotic medications for this condition.

REFERENCES

[1] Unützer J, Katon W, Russo J, et al. Patterns of care for depressed older adults in a large-staff model HMO. *Am. J. Geriatr. Psychiatry*. 1999 Summer;7(3):235-43.

[2] Fountoulakis KN, O'Hara R, Iacovides A, et al. Unipolar late-onset depression: A comprehensive review. Ann. Gen. Hosp. Psychiatry. 2003 Dec 16;2(1):11.

[3] Harman JS, Schulberg HC, Mulsant BH, et al. The effect of patient and visit characteristics on diagnosis of depression in primary care. *J. Fam. Pract*. 2001 Dec; 50(12):1068.

[4] Alexopoulos GS. Depression in the elderly. *Lancet*. 2005 Jun 4-10;365(9475):1961-70.

[5] Alexopoulos GS. New concepts for prevention and treatment of late-life depression. Am. J. Psychiatry. 2001 Jun;158(6):835-8.

[6] Dunner DL. Treatment considerations for depression in the elderly. CNS Spectr. 2003 Dec;8(12 Suppl 3):14-9.

[7] Brodaty H, Peters K, Boyce P, et al. Age and depression. J. Affect Disord. 1991 Nov;23(3):137-49.

[8] Brodaty H, Luscombe G, Parker G, et al. Increased rate of psychosis and psychomotor change in depression with age. Psychol. Med. 1997 Sep;27(5):1205-13.

[9] Kivelä SL, Pahkala K. Delusional depression in the elderly: a community study. Z. Gerontol. 1989 Sep-Oct;22(5):236-41.

[10] Myers JK, Weissman MM, Tischler GL, et al. Six-month prevalence of psychiatric disorders in three communities 1980 to 1982. Arch. Gen. Psychiatry. 1984 Oct;41(10):959-67.

[11] Gournellis R, Lykouras L, Fortos A, et al. Psychotic (delusional) major depression in late life: a clinical study. Int. J. Geriatr. Psychiatry. 2001 Nov;16(11):1085-91.

[12] Gournellis R, Oulis P, Rizos E, et al. Clinical correlates of age of onset in psychotic depression. Arch. Gerontol. Geriatr. 2011 Jan-Feb;52(1):94-8.

[13] Lee TW, Tsai SJ, Yang CH, at al. Clinical and phenomenological comparisons of delusional and non-delusional major depression in the Chinese elderly.. Int. J. Geriatr Psychiatry. 2003 Jun;18(6):486-90.

[14] Meyers BS, Greenberg R Late-life delusional depression. J. Affect Disord. 1986 Sep-Oct;11(2):133-7.

[15] Nelson JC, Conwell Y, Kim K, et al. Age at onset in late-life delusional depression. Am. J. Psychiatry. 1989 Jun;146(6):785-6.

[16] Lyness JM, Conwell Y, Nelson JC. Suicide attempts in elderly psychiatric inpatients. J. Am. Geriatr. Soc. 1992 Apr;40(4):320-4.

[17] Lykouras L, Gournellis R, Fortos A, et al. Psychotic (delusional) major depression in the elderly and suicidal behaviour. J. Affect Disord. 2002 May;69(1-3):225-9.

[18] Schaffer A, Flint AJ, Smith E, et al. Correlates of suicidality among patients with psychotic depression. Meyers BS. Suicide Life Threat Behav. 2008 Aug;38(4):403-14.

[19] Simpson S, Baldwin RC, Jackson A, et al. The differentiation of DSM-III-R psychotic depression in later life from nonpsychotic depression: comparisons of brain changes measured by multispectral analysis of magnetic resonance brain images, neuropsychological findings, and clinical features. Biol. Psychiatry. 1999 Jan 15;45 (2): 193-204.

[20] O'Brien JT, Ames D, Schweitzer I, et al. Clinical, magnetic resonance imaging and endocrinological differences between delusional and non-delusional depression in the elderly. Int J Geriatr Psychiatry. 1997 Feb;12(2):211-8.
[21] Baldwin RC. Delusional and non-delusional depression in late life. Evidence for distinct subtypes. Br. J. Psychiatry. 1988 Jan;152:39-44.
[22] Flint AJ, Rifat SL. Two-year outcome of psychotic depression in late life. Am. J. Psychiatry. 1998 Feb;155(2):178-83.
[23] Rothschild AJ. Challenges in the treatment of depression with psychotic features. Biol. Psychiatry. 2003 Apr 15;53(8):680-90.
[24] Nelson JC, Davis JM. DST studies in psychotic depression: a meta-analysis. Am. J. Psychiatry. 1997 Nov;154(11):1497-503.
[25] Carroll BJ, Cassidy F, Naftolowitz D, et al. Pathophysiology of hypercortisolism in depression. Acta Psychiatr. Scand. Suppl. 2007;(433):90-103.
[26] Duval F, Mokrani MC, Monreal-Ortiz JA, et al.Cortisol hypersecretion in unipolar major depression with melancholic and psychotic features: dopaminergic, noradrenergic and thyroid correlates. Psychoneuroendocrinology. 2006 Aug;31(7):876-88.
[27] Lykouras E, Markianos M, Malliaras D, Stefanis C. Neurochemical variables in delusional depression. Am. J. Psychiatry. 1988 Feb;145(2):214-7.
[28] Salokangas RK, Cannon T, Van Erp T, et al. Structural magnetic resonance imaging in patients with first-episode schizophrenia, psychotic and severe nonpsychotic depression and healthy controls. Results of the schizophrenia and affective psychoses (SAP) project. Br. J. Psychiatry Suppl. 2002 Sep;43:s58-65.
[29] Keller J, Shen L, Gomez RG, et al. Hippocampal and amygdalar volumes in psychotic and nonpsychotic unipolar depression. Am. J. Psychiatry. 2008 Jul;165(7):872-80.
[30] Thase ME, Kupfer DJ, Ulrich RF. Electroencephalographic sleep in psychotic depression. A valid subtype? Arch. Gen. Psychiatry. 1986 Sep;43(9):886-93.
[31] Zubenko GS, Henderson R, Stiffler JS, et al. Association of the APOE epsilon 4 allele with clinical subtypes of late life depression. Biol. Psychiatry. 1996 Nov 15;40 (10): 1008-16.
[32] Lerner P, Goodwin FK, van Kammen DP, et al. Dopamine-beta-hydroxylase in the cerebrospinal fluid of psychiatric patients. Biol. Psychiatry. 1978 Dec;13(6):685-94.
[33] Robertson D, Haile V, Perry SE, et al. Dopamine beta-hydroxylase deficiency. A genetic disorder of cardiovascular regulation. Hypertension. 1991 Jul;18(1):1-8.
[34] Meyers BS, Alexopoulos GS, Kakuma T, et al. Decreased dopamine beta-hydroxylase activity in unipolar geriatric delusional depression. Biol. Psychiatry. 1999 Feb 15;45(4):448-52).
[35] Kim DK, Kim BL, Sohn SE, et al. Candidate neuroanatomic substrates of psychosis in old-aged depression. Prog Neuropsychopharmacol Biol. Psychiatry. 1999 Jul;23(5): 793-807.
[36] Lesser IM, Miller BL, Boone KB, et al. Brain injury and cognitive function in late-onset psychotic depression. J Neuropsychiatry Clin Neurosci. 1991 Winter;3(1):33-40.
[37] Unützer J. Clinical practice. Late-life depression. N. Engl. J. Med. 2007 Nov 29;357(22):2269-76.
[38] Wilkins CH, Mathews J, Sheline YI. Late life depression with cognitive impairment: evaluation and treatment. Clin. Interv. Aging. 2009;4:51-7.

[39] Vaishnavi S, Taylor WD. Neuroimaging in late-life depression. Int. Rev. Psychiatry. 2006 Oct;18 (5):443-510.

[40] Laidlaw K, Davidson K, Toner H, et al. A randomised controlled trial of cognitive behaviour therapy vs treatment as usual in the treatment of mild to moderate late life depression. Int. J. Geriatr. Psychiatry. 2008 Aug;23(8):843-50.

[41] Wilkinson P, Alder N, Juszczak E, et al. A pilot randomised controlled trial of a brief cognitive behavioural group intervention to reduce recurrence rates in late life depression. Int. J. Geriatr. Psychiatry. 2009 Jan;24(1):68-75.

[42] Martire LM, Schulz R, Reynolds CF 3rd, et al. Treatment of late-life depression alleviates caregiver burden. J. Am. Geriatr. Soc. 2010 Jan;58(1):23-9.

[43] Alexopoulos GS, Raue PJ, Kiosses DN, et al. Problem-solving therapy and supportive therapy in older adults with major depression and executive dysfunction: effect on disability. Arch. Gen. Psychiatry. 2011 Jan;68(1):33-41.

[44] Navarro V, Gastó C, Torres X, et al. Continuation/maintenance treatment with nortriptyline versus combined nortriptyline and ECT in late-life psychotic depression: a two-year randomized study. *Am. J. Geriatr. Psychiatry*. 2008 Jun;16(6):498-505.

[45] Birkenhager TK, van den Broek WW, Mulder PG, Moleman P, Bruijn JA. Efficacy of imipramine in psychotic versus nonpsychotic depression. J. Clin. Psychopharmacol. 2008 Apr;28(2):166-70.

[46] DeBattista C, Belanoff J, Glass S, et al. Mifepristone versus placebo in the treatment of psychosis in patients with psychotic major depression. Biol Psychiatry. 2006 Dec 15;60(12):1343-9.

[47] Mulsant BH, Sweet RA, Rosen J, et al. A double-blind randomized comparison of nortriptyline plus perphenazine versus nortriptyline plus placebo in the treatment of psychotic depression in late life. J. Clin. Psychiatry. 2001 Aug;62(8):597-604.

[48] Belanoff JK, Flores BH, Kalezhan M, Sund B, Schatzberg AF. Rapid reversal of psychotic depression using mifepristone. J. Clin. Psychopharmacol. 2001 Oct;21(5): 516-21.

[49] Meyers BS, Flint AJ, Rothschild AJ, et al. A double-blind randomized controlled trial of olanzapine plus sertraline vs olanzapine plus placebo for psychotic depression: the study of pharmacotherapy of psychotic depression (STOP-PD). Arch. Gen. Psychiatry. 2009 Aug;66(8):838-47.

[50] Alexopoulos GS, Katz IR, Reynolds CF 3rd, et al. Pharmacotherapy of depression in older patients: a summary of the expert consensus guidelines. J. Psychiatr. Pract. 2001 Nov;7(6):361-76.

[51] Reynolds CF 3rd, Dew MA, Pollock BG, et al. *Maintenance treatment of major depression in old age*. 2006 Mar 16;354(11):1130-8.

[52] Rothschild AJ, Duval SE. How long should patients with psychotic depression stay on the antipsychotic medication? J. Clin. Psychiatry. 2003 Apr;64(4):390-6.

[53] Thanvi B, Treadwell S. Drug induced parkinsonism: a common cause of parkinsonism in older people. Postgrad. Med. J. 2009 Jun;85(1004):322-6.

[54] Rao SS, Daly JW, Sewell DD. Falls associated with electroconvulsive therapy among the geriatric population: a case report. J. ECT. 2008 Jun;24(2):173-5.

In: Depression in the Elderly
Editor: Emaad Abdel-Rahman, pp. 115-139
ISBN 978-1-61324-771-6

Chapter 7

MANAGEMENT OF DEPRESSION IN OLDER PEOPLE: A ROLE FOR PHYSICAL ACTIVITY

Jane Sims[1], Daniel O'Connor[2] and Colette Browning[3]
[1]Healthy Ageing Research Unit, School of Primary Health Care
and Monash Institute of Health Services Research,
Monash University, Victoria, Australia
[2]Monash University, Victoria. Australia
[3]School of Primary Health Care and Monash Institute
of Health Services Research, Monash University, Victoria, Australia

ABSTRACT

Depressive illness results in considerable functional disability and decreased quality of life. The prevalence of depression in older persons ranges from 5 to 30%. Older people often have depression concurrent with other illnesses, e.g., cardiovascular disease. Depression can also impact adversely on these disorders.

Current management of depression commonly involves drugs and psychotherapies, which whilst effective, have variable adherance rates. Non-pharmacological therapies offer potentially safer alternative management of depression in older people. Of the psychotherapies, cognitive behaviour therapy and reminiscence and life review have the best supporting evidence for older people. Few lifestyle change modalities have been sufficiently tested to recommend their use with older people. An exception is physical activity. Both endurance and resistance type physical activity has anti-depressant effects for older people with depression.

Older depressed people have much to gain from being physically active. Physical activity offers a therapy where negative events are minimal and benefits can accrue for both physical and mental health status. Physical activity may assist both in the prevention and management of depression in older people. As a health promotion intervention, it has the potential to reduce the risk of depression and to ameliorate co-morbid conditions. Using physical activity as an antidepressant can reduce the need for pharmacological intervention, minimizing iatrogenic and polypharmacy risk that is particularly prevalent for older people.

INTRODUCTION

Depression is a major contributor to the chronic burden of disease in a population and a leading cause of loss of disability adjusted-life-years (Snow et al., 2000). As populations age, depression is set to become the main cause of global disability. By 2020, it is expected that depression will be the second most common cause of disability worldwide. Depression poses a significant economic burden at a societal level, being associated with increased rates of hospitalization and emergency service use.

Amongst mental health problems, depression ranks as a high prevalence condition and warrants particular attention using primary, secondary and tertiary prevention measures. There is a growing evidence base about the range of preventive and therapeutic interventions to manage depression. This chapter will discuss measures suitable for older people with depression. Older people often have depression concurrent with other illnesses, such as cardiovascular disease. Depression can impact adversely on these disorders and their prognosis. Having depression can also impact on a person's family life and relationships, influencing the person's overall health status and quality of life.

The reasons for depression in older people will be briefly discussed. The management of depression within the context of co- morbidities will also be considered. Both pharmacological and non-pharmacological therapies will be explored, focusing on the role of lifestyle interventions, namely physical activity and nutrition. We acknowledge the heterogeneity of the older population: interventions suitable for both community-dwelling and institutionalised older people will be highlighted. We will argue that, given the promising effects of physical activity in the prevention and treatment of depression and its far-reaching benefits for overall health, that physical activity be promoted as a key lifestyle behaviour amongst older people.

PREVALENCE

Depressive symptomatology is common amongst older people. Estimates of the actual prevalence of depression among older people living in the community vary widely, from 10% to 35% (Beekman et al., 2002, Baldwin et al., 2002b, Beekman et al., 1999, Sayer et al., 2000, Regier et al., 1988). The prevalence of major depression and dysthmia tends to decline with age in population surveys. Some researchers have posited that the reduced depression prevalence amongst older people reflects greater emotional stability, a honing of coping skills, reduced daily hassles and resilience (Henderson, 1994). An alternative explanation relates to sampling methodology. Most national surveys and many gerontological surveys exclude those living in institutions such as aged care facilities and long stay hospitals and those with cognitive impairment (O'Connor, 2006). As will be discussed below, prevalence rates are higher in these groups. Prevalence amongst older people is therefore likely to be underestimated due to this sampling and case ascertainment bias. A third explanation is that older people are more likely to attribute depressive symptoms to physical illness (Hasin, 1988), making their responses to generic mental health scales less likely to produce a positive diagnostic classification.

SYMPTOMATOLOGY

The presenting symptoms of depression may be different from those in younger adults, making it difficult to detect. The symptoms may be associated with the person's current social circumstances or their physical health status. Indeed, in older people the symptoms may be masked by physical ill health problems. For example, chronic osteoarthritis or respiratory disease can cause fatigue. Cognitive impairment can cause memory and concentration difficulties. Worrying, irritability and agitation may be commoner than low mood in older people (Sable et al., 2002). Some depressive symptoms may be side effects of medication the older person is taking. The interactive effects of psychological and physical health need to be carefully considered. Psychological distress may be due to physical ill health, such as pain. In turn, unresolved depression or anxiety can exacerbate pain. The somatic and psychological symptoms of depression and anxiety can make diagnosis more difficult (Barraclough, 1997).

There remains a societal perspective that feeling down, tired and socially withdrawn is normal amongst older people. This can mean that older people do not present to their doctor with depressive symptoms. The health professional needs to be proactive in assessing older patients for depression so that it is treated appropriately. There have been several public health campaigns to raise awareness and physicians are receiving enhanced training to assist in the detection of depression. Although older age can be a risk factor for depression, the evidence base shows that age itself is *not* a risk factor, once age-associated factors are accounted for.

We need to be aware of the difference between 'normal' distress and psychological disturbance. Older people unhappy with their current situation may speak about wanting to be dead. This expression may capture their perceived burden on others, or a feeling of apathy.

Depression is often associated with suicidal thoughts (Pearson and Brown, 2000). Since suicidal comments may indicate depression, referral for assessment is necessary. Fortunately in recent years, suicide rates among older aged males have continued to decline: for example, in Australia (by 17% since 1997), the United States (by 9%), and in New Zealand (24%). Whilst most countries and regions have reported decreasing trends of suicide mortality amongst those 65 years or older since the early 1990s (Australian Institute for Suicide Research and Prevention, 2003), there remains an increased risk of completed suicides among older people, especially older men. As many as 90% of individuals who complete suicide have at least one diagnosable mental illness, usually depression. Detection and treatment of mental illness is key to suicide prevention. To date there is only limited evidence to support the efficacy of antidepressants in the prevention of suicide among depressed samples. Although the benefit of antidepressants in treating depression is well recognised, several studies have failed to support the efficacy of antidepressants in suicide prevention among depressed adults (Hirsch, 1982, Khan, 2003, Montgomery, 1983). Use of both antidepressants and psychosocial interventions may be a more promising means to prevent suicide. There is a need for greater coordination between general practitioners and allied health professionals in the treatment of high-risk individuals.

Depression's impact amongst older people is compounded by the fact that it sub-optimally diagnosed and treated (McCusker et al., 1998). There are several useful guidelines for the management of depression in older people (Curran et al., 2001, Baldwin et al., 2002a). Assessment tools are useful in screening (Watts et al., 2002), since they enable clinicians to systematically appraise the older person's status. A recent RCT found that screening for depression in long-term care residents increased the frequency of referral and treatment (Soon and Levine, 2002). There are a number of screening tools available (Pomeroy et al., 2001, Holtom and Barraclough, 2000, Lees and Lloyd-Williams, 1999). The Center for Epidemiological Studies Depression Scale (CES-D) and the Geriatric Depression Scale (GDS) (Radloff, 1977, Yesavage, 1983) are the two most widely used scales. The former has been used to identify depressive symptoms in epidemiological samples. The GDS is the commonest clinical screening tool, the 15 item version having the most psychometric testing. The GDS has good cross-cultural validity (Rait et al., 1999). There are a number of short screening tools that are useful in general practice, such as the two-item Patient Health Questionnaire (Li et al., 2007). Assessment tools, whilst valuable in detecting depressive symptoms, should be supported by efforts to obtain a greater understanding of the person's lived experience so as to be able to provide interventions that will best meet their individual needs.

A brief overview follows of the risk and protective factors associated with depression in older people. This knowledge can be used by older people and their formal and informal carers to aid the prevention of depression and assist in aspects of its management.

Risk and Protective Factors

Depressive symptoms are often key markers of broader aspects of emotional health and wellbeing. Working with an individual to address modifiable risk factors and to promote protective factors has the potential not only to improve depressive status, but also overall health and wellbeing.

Factors contributing to depressive symptomatology have been placed into three categories by Jorm and colleagues (Jorm, 2001):

1) Physical health
2) Stressful life events; and
3) Social health.

Compared to younger adults, the absolute risk of physical health problems and their associated effects upon independence via disability and handicap is significant amongst older individuals.

Although older people have a propensity to develop resilience when faced with stressful life events, they are more likely to encounter key events such as the loss of a partner. These losses make them more vulnerable and can in turn influence their emotional health. Life changes are also pertinent to social health, the third category. A person's social connections are important to provide instrumental and emotional support and to maintain a sense of self-worth. An older person's social network may be diminished by bereavement, retirement and relocation.

Residents of Aged Care Facilities

Those living in institutionalised settings are at greater risk of depression. Depression is particularly prevalent amongst residents of aged care facilities, with rates of up to 50% reported (Baldwin et al., 2002a). In a study of depression incidence in those newly admitted to nursing homes in Australia, a quarter (24%) of the sample had major depression at one month post admission and a further 20% had a non-major depressive disorder (McSweeney and O'Connor, 2008). Rates were relatively stable at three and six-month follow-up. A small proportion (13%) showed symptom remission over the follow-up period. Crucially, major depression was only found in those with cognitive impairment (scores of 23 or less on the MMSE). The study is limited by its non-random sampling and 61% response rate, but the findings confirm those elsewhere in the literature highlighting that depression is an issue in aged care facilities (Teresi, 2001).

Depression amongst residents of aged care facilities is likely to be associated with the reduction in autonomy, independence, function and social support commonly experienced by residents. Moving to supported accommodation is a stressful life event. It can alter the person's social networks and lead to a reduction in emotional health. One only needs to consider the reasons for people to be admitted to see that the residents enter the accommodation with greater propensity to either have, or develop depression. Indeed, people living in supported accommodation are at greater risk for depression. In the Amsterdam Groningen Elderly Depression (AGED) study, a range of biological and psychological risk factors for depressive symptomatology were identified (Jongenelis et al., 2004). Prevalence amongst those in residential aged care facilities (RACFs) was three to four times higher that found in community dwelling counterparts. A multivariate logistic regression analysis found pain, history of stroke and visual impairment to be the key risk factors for depression in the 333 residents they assessed. Loneliness was the chief psychological risk factor. Being less than 80 years was also a significant risk factor. Systematic, ongoing assessment and monitoring of residents are therefore crucial. Communication with residents and their families is important. Staff need to explain how any illness is progressing. Residents need to be able to express how they are feeling without fear of censure. For example, a recent study discovered that residents felt reluctant to disclose feelings, for fear of being labelled a bad or weak person (Lloyd-Williams, 2002). This makes it difficult for aged care staff to pick up on depressive symptoms. An open, supportive environment that promotes trust can help overcome this barrier and assist the older person in making life transitions.

Recognition of depression in residents of aged care facilities, particularly those with dementia needs to be improved. The recognition of depression in dementia is challenging given the considerable overlap between depressive symptoms and those of dementia, and the increasingly impaired capacity of the dementia sufferer to reliably report depressive symptoms of depression (Draper, 1999). Comprehensive education regarding depression in dementia and training in the administration of scales such as the Cornell Scale for Depression in Dementia (CSDD) (Alexopoulos, 1998) have the potential to increase recognition and treatment rates greatly within nursing homes.

The management of nursing home residents with co-morbid depression and dementia requires more research. The evidence base to date suggests that for some residents with dementia, antidepressant medications may not prove to be effective in alleviating depression

(McSweeney and O'Connor, 2008). An alternative approach may be the use of psychosocial interventions.

A recent review of the psychosocial treatment of depression in dementia (Teri, 2005) indicated that such interventions have the potential to improve depression greatly, even in the moderately to severely cognitively impaired. The interventions studied were performed in both community and institutional settings. The program components that appeared most effective were the individualization of strategies, using multiple treatment components, enhancing the communication and problem solving capacities of carers, and increasing the exposure of the depressed person to pleasant social interaction. A more recent systematic review of psychosocial treatments for psychological symptoms, including depression, in dementia sufferers confirms the paucity of evidence for such treatments (O'Connor et al., 2009).

Music therapy and recreation therapy produced moderate effect sizes, but the extent of the duration of impact was not measured. More research is needed to enable refinement of techniques and to determine the characteristics of patients most suited to such interventions.

Prevention

Many interventions focus on managing the condition, but a more comprehensive, and potentially more successful approach is to prevent depression from occurring. Interventions to prevent depression have been found to be successful in a variety of studies. Cole and Dendukuri (2004) conducted a systematic review of brief interventions to prevent late life depression.

They found 10 suitable studies with long-term follow up periods. There was general support for the feasibility of a range of interventions, including education and bereavement counselling. The impacts on depression risk were modest.

Management

There are four modes of management of depression: medical, psychological, lifestyle and alternative therapies. Some therapies are specific to depression, whilst others have broader health benefits. It is beyond the scope of this Chapter to review all the therapeutic evidence: a recent systematic review outlines the level of evidence for different antidepressant therapies that can be used with older people (Frazer et al., 2005). Amongst the psychotherapies, cognitive behaviour therapy and reminiscence and life review have the best supporting evidence for older people (Frazer et al., 2005, Jorm, 2002). Few lifestyle change modalities have been sufficiently tested to recommend their use with older people. An exception is physical activity. The following sections will discuss the evidence for antidepressant medications and physical activity, highlighting their advantages and disadvantages for older people. Finally, the importance of complementing any therapy with a balance diet will be noted.

ANTIDEPRESSANTS

Modern antidepressants are more targeted and have fewer side effects than their predecessors. They are an important means of managing major depression. They can be used to temper symptoms from the outset, enabling other therapeutic measures to be more readily adopted by the person.

There is level 1 evidence for the effectiveness of antidepressants in older people (Wilson et al., 2001). These findings apply across tricyclics, selective serotonin reuptake inhibitors (SSRIs) and monoamine oxidase inhibitors (MAOIs) and amongst community dwelling, institutionalised and hospitalised older people. The SSRIs are preferred for older people as they have fewer side effects than other groups. The serotonin and noradrenaline reuptake inhibitors (SNRIs) are effective, but the side effect profile is greater amongst frail older people.

Antidepressants benefit from ease of use. Nevertheless, antidepressant trials have reported high rates of adverse events (around 60%) (Salzman, 1993) and attrition (around 25%) (Mittman et al., 1997). Although most adverse events are mild and transient, for older people with depression side effects such as increased risk of hip fracture (Fiatarone Singh, 2002) need to be borne in mind when deciding treatment options. In older people, where other health problems are more likely to co-exist, there is the also likelihood of the adverse effects of polypharmacy. Depression can be a side effect of certain medications, such as some of those used in the management of arthritis (Leon et al., 2003). Given the risks of antidepressants, it is worth considering that for some people, such as those without major depression, non-pharmacological treatment may suffice. For others, use of adjunct therapies may enable the antidepressant dosage to be minimised.

PHYSICAL ACTIVITY

The following section considers the relationship between physical activity and depression. It explores potential underlying mechanisms for their association and reviews the evidence for the use of physical activity as an adjunct therapy in the management of depression. Depression often coincides with other health conditions. Ill health can lead to depression and depression can exacerbate other health problems. The impact of depression on stroke survivors will be used to illustrate this relationship. Physical activity's role in promoting other aspects of older people's health also will be highlighted. The potential risks of physical activity will be noted.

How Physical Activity Works

Whilst it remains unclear how exercise influences depression, several psychological and physiological mechanisms have been proposed (Lawlor and Hopker, 2001, Craft and Landers, 1998, Mather et al., 2002). Physical activity may provide distraction from negative thoughts. Physical activity is recognised as healthy lifestyle behaviour, so participants may experience positive feedback from others, improving their self esteem and self worth. For older adults adopting an exercise regime, there can be benefits from the mastery of a new skill. From a physiological perspective, in both animal models and depressed people, increased levels of neurotrophic factors in the brain following both exercise and antidepressant medication usage has been reported (Thornen et al., 1990, Duman, 2005). Exercise may also improve depression via social interaction.

The Association between Physical Activity and Depression

Prospective studies demonstrate that people who exercise are less likely to be- or become- depressed (Brosse et al., 2002). Cross-sectional and prospective studies of healthy adult populations have shown an association between physical inactivity and depression (Kritz-Silverstein et al., 2001, Lampinen et al., 2000, Moore et al., 1999, Lindwall et al., 2006) and indicate that a low prevalence of depressive symptomatology is related to exercise behaviour (Baldwin et al., 2002a, Blumenthal, 1999a, Lawlor and Hopker, 2001). Table 1 includes examples of studies that have investigated the relationship between physical activity and depression in older cohorts. Overall, results indicate that exercisers are less likely to have depressive mood, but to date the evidence that exercise protects against future depressed mood amongst the non-clinically depressed remains equivocal.

Data from the Australian Longitudinal Study on Women's Health found that depression scores decreased and mental health scores increased with increasing levels of previous, current and habitual activity (Brown et al., 2005). Women who were active (one hour or more of moderate intensity activity per week) at baseline were 30 to 40% less likely to have poor mental health and depression scores than those less active. Those in the lowest category at baseline who became more active were also at lower risk of poor mental health scores than those who remained inactive. This association was independent of pre-existing physical or psychological health status.

In the Melbourne Longitudinal Studies on Healthy Ageing (MELSHA), both cross sectional and longitudinal analyses of the relationship between physical activity and depression have been conducted (Kendig et al., 1996). Physical activity was measured in terms of both frequency and duration. Both baseline measures of physical activity were significantly negatively correlated with depressive status, measured using the depression subscale of the Psychogeriatric Assessment Scales (PAS-D) (-0.13 and -0.14 respectively). In further analyses, a range of demographic, health and lifestyle factors measured at baseline were used to determine univariate risk ratios for depression incidence two years later (Atlantis, 2009). The analyses excluded those classified as depressed at baseline. Chi square tests showed no significant difference in baseline physical activity frequency in those with depression (symptomatic or antidepressant use) compared to those without. Significant predictors of depression incidence were arthritis and respiratory disease, with prevalent gastrointestinal disease and increasing frequencies of self-reported pain also showing some association, suggesting that chronic disease and poor functional health were predictors of depression incidence at 2-year follow-up. There are various reasons for these conflicting results. The simplest is that during the intervening years, new and chronic health problems have led to the development of depression. There are also methodological bias issues related to self-reported assessment of physical activity and depressive status.

Table 1. The association of physical activity and depression in selected cross-sectional and longitudinal studies

Author	Country	Sample size	Criteria	Odds Ratio/Effect size
Moore et al 1999	USA	146, 50 years + Major depressive disorder	Minnesota Leisure-Time Physical Activity Questionnaire BDI	OR -0.17 (p = .045)
Brown et al 2005	Australia	9207 women 45-55 years	CESD-10 SF-36 Mental health subscale Time spent in vigorous, less vigorous exercise, converted to MET mins	For high levels of physical activity (≥ 1200 or > 300 minutes/week) OR 0.62 for CESD-1- score ε 10 OR 0.55 for MH score δ 52
Lampinen et al 2000	Finland	663, 65 years + 8 year follow up Physical activity behaviour categorised into necessary chores group, regular walking group and strenuous exercise group and change over time assessed in terms of maintained (stable), increased or decreased level (intensity) of physical activity	BDI-13 (Finnish version) Physical activity intensity- necessary chores, regular walking (at least weekly), strenuous physical activity Assessed changes in stability and intensity of physical activity over time	Depressive symptoms at follow-up predicted by necessary chores group: stable intensity 0.96 (NS) regular walking group: reduced intensity 10.56 stable intensity 2.21 (NS) strenuous exercise group: reduced intensity 1.23 (NS)
Kritz-Silverstein et al 2001	USA	2029, 50-89 years 944 at 8 year follow up	BDI Regular strenuous exercise (Y/N), Exercise or labor at least three times/week (Y/N)	Only F tests reported
Lindwall et al, 2006	Sweden	860, 60 years + (mean 75.3, SD 10)	Montgomery Asberg Depression Rating Scale Frequency of light and strenuous intensity activity, change in last 12 months	Light exercise Never vs. every day d = 0.3 Never vs. no change d = 0.3 Strenuous exercise Never vs. every day d = 0.3 Never vs. no change d = 0.2

BDI = Beck Depression Inventory.

Physical Activity in the Prevention and Management of Depression

There is limited trial evidence for physical activity in the primary prevention of mental health problems. A review of interventions to *prevent* depression in older people did not include any physical activity trials (Cole and Dendukuri, 2004). To date, habitual physical activity has not been unequivocally shown to *prevent* the onset of depression.

However, there is growing evidence for the use of physical activity in the *management* of depression. Aerobic and resistance training have both produced benefits (Blumenthal, 1999a, Babyak et al., 2000, Singh et al., 1997, Singh et al., 2001, Singh et al., 2005, Stathopoulou et al., 2006). Both moderate and vigorous levels of exercise shows efficacy in reducing depressive symptoms (Dunn et al., 2001). Secondary analyses in an osteoarthritis trial found improvements in depressive symptoms and disability at 18 months post aerobic, but not resistance, training (Penninx et al., 2002). Even less intensive activity such as walking has been found to be effective (McNeil et al., 1991). Recent meta-analytic and experimental studies show a significant antidepressant effect for physical activity in older adults with clinical depression, supporting the use of physical activity in the management of depression in older people (Taylor et al., 2004, Frazer et al., 2005).

Table 2. Physical activity in the management of depression in older people: randomised trials with nonactive control conditions

Author	Sample	Intervention	Depression measurement tool	Outcome/Effect size
McNeil et al 1991	30, mean age 72.5 years	Walking vs. social contact, waitlist control 6 weeks, no follow-up Attrition 0%	BDI	g 1.02
Singh et al 1997	32, 60-84 years	PRT vs. health education 20 week program, 21 month follow-up Attrition 0%	BDI	g 1.76
Singh et al 2005	60, 60-85 years	High intensity PRT vs. low intensity PRT, usual care 8 weeks, no follow-up Attrition 1%	HRSD	g 1.0
Sims et al 2006	32, ≥ 65 years, mean age 74.3 years	PRT vs. waitlist control 10 weeks, 6 month follow up Attrition 6%	GDS, CES-D, PGMS	d 0.05, 10 weeks d 0. 07, 6 months

BDI = Beck Depression Inventory; CES-D = Center for Epidemiological Studies Depression Scale; GDS= Geriatric Depression Scale; HRSD = Hamilton Rating Scale for Depression; PGMS = Philadelphia Geriatric Morale Scale; PRT = progressive resistance training.

g = Hedges (bias corrected) effect size; d = Cohen's effect size.

The Level 1 evidence suggests that physical activity is preferable to no treatment or social contact alone and that it has a similar effect to standard antidepressant drug or psychological treatments for both adults (North et al., 1990, Craft and Landers, 1998, Lawlor and Hopker, 2001, Brosse et al., 2002) and older adults (Palmer, 2005, Frazer et al., 2005). Reviewers have been critical of the quality of earlier studies (Lawlor and Hopker, 2001). Common methodological weaknesses include a lack of a standard diagnostic process for identifying depression in participants and a short follow up period (Lawlor and Hopker, 2001, Dunn et al., 2001). Table 2 provides examples of studies that have evaluated physical activity in the management of depression in older people with depressive symptoms.

Progressive Resistance Training

The evidence is particularly promising for progressive resistance training (PRT) (Lawlor and Hopker, 2001, Sjosten and Kivela, 2006, Barbour and Blumenthal, 2005). PRT offers an alternative form of physical activity for older people to aerobic physical activity. It has been particularly successful in ameliorating muscle weakness in older people. A decrease in muscle mass and muscle strength is a function of the ageing process, but can be exacerbated by chronic health problems. The weakness contributes to falls and fracture risk and overall disability. There has been substantial research that indicates PRT can improve muscle strength and physiological function. High intensity PRT is a safe, effective means to enhance muscle strength (Seynnes et al., 2004), assisting independence via functional and mobility improvements. In addition, by having a positive effect on bone health, PRT may reduce the potential for falling and osteoporosis.

Use of PRT to promote mental health appears to require high intensity activity to be effective. Singh and colleagues have reported positive effects following PRT in older people with depression. In 32 older people with depression, PRT significantly reduced Beck Depression scores compared to a group receiving health education, demonstrating that physical activity's therapeutic benefit was explained by more than socialisation (Singh et al., 1997). The impact is lasting: Singh and colleagues reported improvements in over 65 year olds' depression scores at 20 weeks (73% no longer depressed following high intensity PRT in a specialist clinic vs. 36% of controls receiving health education classes) (Singh et al., 2001). More recent research highlights the importance of exercise intensity, with a 50% reduction in depressive symptoms in most (61%) of their high intensity group compared to 29% in the low intensity group and 21% in the usual care group (Singh et al., 2005). The reduction was associated with actual strength gain, suggestive of an underlying biological mechanism. There were indications that vitality and sleep quality were particularly improved in the high intensity PRT group. Although social contact in exercise programs for older people with depression may contribute to the outcome, in Singh and colleague's research, the socialization at the exercise program did not seem to explain the impact of PRT: only the high intensity group achieved clinically significant benefits (Singh et al., 2005). Interestingly, belief in the perceived gains from the program seemed to produce a placebo effect for the low intensity group, whereas efficacy belief did not predict outcome in the high intensity group.

In contrast, elsewhere both high intensity and variable intensity PRT were found to improve measures of mood amongst sedentary, healthy older people (McLafferty et al., 2004). There were also gains in strength and lean body mass. Whilst many PRT programs have included healthy older people, benefits have also been seen for those with chronic disease e.g. osteoarthritis and chronic heart failure - and disability (Latham et al., 2005).

Although these trials provide support for PRT's use with older depressed people, translation of such evidence into routine practice has been limited. Access to specialist clinics and laboratories is less feasible for older people with mobility problems, or those living in rural and remote areas. The UPLIFT pilot study assessed the feasibility of older depressed people attending a community-based progressive resistance training (PRT) program (Sims, 2006). The randomised controlled trial also aimed to determine whether PRT improved depressive status in older depressed patients. People aged ≥ 65 years with depressive symptoms were recruited via general practices and randomly allocated to attend a local PRT program three times per week for 10 weeks or a brief advice control group. Depressive status, physical and psychological health, functional and quality of life status were re-assessed post intervention and at six months follow-up. Three hundred and forty six people responded to the study invitation, of whom 22% had depressive symptoms (GDS-30 score ≥ 11). A sample size of 130 was needed to detect a clinically significant (30%) group difference in depression rates, but unfortunately only 32 people entered the trial, so it was underpowered. There were no significant group differences on the GDS at follow-up. At six months there was a trend for the PRT group to have lower GDS scores than the comparison group, but this finding did not reach significance. More of the PRT group (57%) had a reduction in depressive symptoms post program, compared to 44% of the control group. It was not possible to discern which specific components of the program influenced its impact, but in post hoc analyses, improvement in depressive status was significantly associated with the number of exercise sessions completed (r = -0.8). Fifty eight percent met the adherence criterion of 60% or more sessions completed. This compares favourably with effectiveness studies, where participants attend a program at no cost and often with transport provided. There is scope for such a program to be offered by existing community-based facilities who have suitably trained exercise facilitators. More extensive implementation research will be needed to fully examine the effectiveness of such interventions when delivered in the community setting.

Other Forms of Physical Activity

Dance and movement therapy has been suggested as a potential means to reduce depressive symptoms. A therapist facilitates people to express themselves in movement and this is proposed to elevate mood. There are also potential benefits from the associated social interaction and listening to music. To our knowledge this therapy has not been evaluated in older adults. One study found that mood improved on the days the therapy occurred compared to other days, but no long term impact was assessed (Stewart et al., 1994) . Further research is required to assess the benefits.

Yoga exercises are popular and thought to promote well being. They may assist with the symptoms of stress and anxiety. There is modest, but limited evidence for yogic breathing exercises in adults. One study showed breathing exercises to be as effective as ADM for people with major depression, but less effective than electroconvulsive therapy (Janakiramaiah et al., 2000). However, the researchers did not compare the intervention with placebo treatment.

The evidence arising from physical activity intervention trials needs to be interpreted with caution. Very few studies have ascertained clinical depression using DSM-IV criteria: they tend to focus on symptomatology, generally as measured using an assessment tool such as the GDS. Nevertheless, an improvement in symptomatology is valuable in its own right in promoting mental health and quality of life.

Physical Activity for Comorbid Conditions

Over half of older Australians are sedentary (Bauman, 2004). Given their absolute morbidity risk, sedentary older people have the potential to benefit from physical activity more than any other population sub-group. For older people with depression, physical activity may not only assist depression management: it can assist in the prevention and management of other health conditions.

There are many trials where people with a variety of conditions (e.g. coronary heart disease, chronic obstructive pulmonary disease, cancer, arthritis, multiple sclerosis, chronic fatigue syndrome), have demonstrated reduced levels of depressive symptoms following a physical activity program. Interpretation of these findings has to be sensitive not only to methodological constraints, but also to the fact that not all participants were clinically depressed at the time of the physical activity intervention (Paluska and Schwenk, 2000). To posit a clearer association, more studies using clinically depressed people are required.

Physical Activity for Co-Morbid Stroke

Impaired physical fitness can exacerbate disability in people with stroke. The use of physical activity with stroke patients has the potential to improve physical fitness and reduce disability. Coping with the functional impairments of a stroke may influence the onset of depression (Johnson, 1991). Depression is strongly linked with stroke, with comorbidity occurring in around 30% of people with stroke, adding to their disability (Burvill et al., 1995). Depression can therefore have a negative effect on rehabilitation and prognosis.

There is also evidence quality of life (QOL) is affected by stroke (Sturm and Donnan, 2004). People with depression after stroke display poorer social functioning (Clark and Smith, 1998) and poorer functional outcomes than non-depressed patients with stroke (Van de Weg et al., 1999). There has been little exploration of factors that potentially mediate these differences in recovery outcome. Whilst mobility benefits associated with exercise training have been documented (Saunders et al., 2004), there is a paucity of evidence supporting the influence of exercise therapy on post stroke depression or mental health (Morris et al., 2004), Two reviews of post stroke depression treatments failed to examine the use of physical activity (Kneebone and Dunmore, 2000, Whyte and Mulsant, 2002).

A Cochrane review of depression management in stroke patients found no evidence to support routine use of drugs or psychological therapies in this group (Hackett and Anderson, 2004). Whilst it is acknowledged that both therapies are helpful for adult depression, more information is needed on their use in people who have depression after stroke. This is particularly the case for antidepressant use, where there may be the risk of falls and a slight risk of seizures or delirium. As a non-drug treatment, exercise may be useful for stroke patients. Unlike psychotherapy it can impact directly on both mental and physical health. It may also reduce social isolation, a key risk factor for the development of depression after stroke (Ouimet et al., 2001).

The Regenerate study tested the feasibility of implementing a 10-week exercise intervention program for people experiencing clinically significant depressive symptoms post stroke (Sims et al., 2009). The aim of this randomised controlled trial was to examine whether PRT could reduce depressive symptoms and improve mental health, physical and social function, and quality of life amongst chronic stroke survivors. The PRT participants displayed significant improvements in upper and lower body muscle strength over the course of the exercise program, and several chose to continue with the program. However, the exercise group had lower depression scores than the controls at all time points, making an intervention effect difficult to discern. At 10-weeks follow-up, about half of both the exercise group and the control group demonstrated a reduction in their reported symptoms of depression. Twice as many of the exercise group had maintained these reductions at 6-months follow up, but this difference was no longer significant once baseline values were accounted for.

The second aspect of the Regenerate study aimed to examine factors that are associated with better quality of life in chronic stroke survivors 6 to 24 months post stroke (Teoh et al., 2009). Participants completed the study survey forms on three occasions over a six month period. The strongest predictors of post stroke quality of life were stroke severity and depressive status. People with less stroke severity and fewer depressive symptoms were more likely to experience good quality of life. The findings also suggested that being more optimistic, perceiving greater control over one's recovery and exercising regularly are also associated with better quality of life. It was clear that participants with few depressive symptoms following their stroke scored better on all quality of life, mental and physical health aspects of the surveys. Overall, there were significant improvements in participants' depressive status, physical health, emotional health, involvement in social activities and feelings of optimism over the 6-month course of the study. The findings highlight the important role that psychosocial factors play in chronic stroke survivors' quality of life. Targeting post-stroke depression and psychosocial adjustment to stroke within stroke rehabilitation programs has the potential to improve quality of life for chronic stroke survivors, independent of functional impairment. A range of health professionals, including psychiatrists, health psychologists, neurologists and geriatricians have an important role to play in managing the mental health and wellbeing of stroke survivors.

Physical Activity for Co-Morbid Dementia

This chapter has highlighted the greater rates of depressive symptomatology amongst those with dementia. There has been limited investigation of the use of physical activity to improve affect in this group. A recent randomised controlled trial compared a program of strength, balance and flexibility exercises with a supervised walking group and a social conversation control group (Williams, 2007). Ninety nursing home residents with Alzheimer's disease were randomly allocated to one of three groups that met for 15 minutes a day initially, increasing to 30 minutes later. Exercises included knee bends, toe rises and side-stepping plus walking. Walking group participants walked at their usual speed with support and rests as required. Conversation group members engaged in casual discussion of topics of mutual interest. Positive and negative affects were rated by blinded observers using the Alzheimer's Mood Scale (AMS) and the Observed Affect Scale (OAS) before and after the program. Ten weeks later, positive affect as measured by the OAS was significantly higher in the exercise group (15%) than the walking group and than the conversation group (9%). Negative affect scores on the AMS were significantly lower in the exercise group (12%) than the walking group and 21% lower than the conversation group. There were no significant differences for OAS negative affects or AMS positive affects.

Summary

There is growing evidence that physical activity can alleviate depression. In particular, progressive resistance training has been shown to be effective in managing major depression. In summary, many health benefits are associated with increased levels of physical activity in older people: lower rates of hypertension, heart disease, osteoporosis, degenerative arthritis, colonic cancer and diabetes mellitus, improved mood and memory function, and a better and maintained social network (Mazzeo and Tanaka, 2001).

Adherence to Treatment

No intervention is universally effective in the management of depression. Most therapies require to be used for some time before improvement is noted. Adherence is particularly important in the treatment of depression.

Current management of depression commonly involves drugs and psychotherapies, which whilst effective, have variable adherance rates. For some people adherence to physical activity may be easier than adherence to drug treatment. For others, adhering to physical activity regimes will also be challenging. The literature offers promising evidence of adherence amongst people with depression. For example, one study involving people who had not responded to antidepressant treatment (Mather et al., 2002) found that aerobic exercise was of short-term benefit as an adjunct treatment.

Depression has been associated with poor participation in physical activity and health promotion programs (McAuley et al., 1994), making it particularly critical to fully engage participants with depression in enjoyable activity to enable sustained benefits. In the Regenerate study, program adherence amongst stroke survivors with depression was good: on average 75% of the 10 week program was completed (Sims et al., 2009). Attrition was due to circumstances other than lack of motivation to attend. Long term adherence can be improved when the person makes physical activity part of their lifestyle (King, 1991). Some older people may prefer to exercise at home or on their own, for others joining a group based program can assist adherance via social interaction and the mutual commitment amongst participants (King et al., 1998).

Regular physical activity may also reduce the risk of depression relapse, although the evidence is scarce (Babyak et al., 2000). In a trial of older people with major depression, aerobic exercise was found to be of similar benefit to the antidepressant sertraline (Blumenthal, 1999b). At six months follow-up, relapse rates were lower in the exercise group (Babyak et al., 2000).

Risks of Physical Activity Participation for Older People

The risks associated with physical activity in older people are not too dissimilar from those for other adults. There are contraindications to physical activity, such as uncontrolled angina or blood pressure. Clinically these need to be addressed whether or not a person intends to be physical active and should only be temporary. The American College of Sports Medicine's 1998 Position Statement on Physical Activity in Older People (Mazzeo et al., 1998) reviewed the evidence for injury in trials and noted that no serious injury nor cardiovascular event has been reported. There have been isolated reports of minor injury e.g. tripping or sprains, but across the wealth of trials, reporting of adverse events has been rare; whilst this may be partly explained by publication bias, it is likely to reflect reality. For example, in an editorial, McMurdo refers to the exercise program run through the University of Dundee, Scotland. This program sees 1000 older participants per week on a self-referral, no screening, no disclaimer basis. Injuries are scarce. Commonly, modifications have been made to programs to ensure their suitability for people with pre-existing health problems, such as osteoarthritis. Overall, the risks of sedentary behaviour appear to outweigh those associated with physical activity.

Given this evidence, there has perhaps been undue cautiousness surrounding encouraging older people to be physically active. The fears possibly stemmed from the reports of adverse events associated with vigorous activity (as encouraged by previous guidelines). There is evidence from the Framingham Study that strenuous activity may be detrimental to older women's mortality rates (Sherman et al., 1994). Vigorous physical activity can increase the risk of sudden death, but the individual level risk is outweighed by the benefits (Bauman et al., 2002). The current Australian recommendations for older people advise beginning exercising gradually and with moderate intensity to promote safe physical activity (Sims et al., 2006).

Progression in physical activity intensity is vital. For older people starting or recommencing physical activity, beginning at a low intensity and gradually increasing to a moderate intensity will manage risk. Moderate intensity physical activity has greater potential to produce health benefits. The Australian National Heart Foundation guidelines for physical activity discuss indications for specific sub-groups of those with cardiovascular disease requiring medical clearance before commencing physical activity (Briffa et al., 2006). It is encouraging to note that across published chronic heart failure (CHF) trials, very few adverse events have been reported, no deaths or cardiac arrest and minimal orthopaedic injuries or serious arrhythmic events during training itself and few deaths during the studies (Witham et al., 2003). In a systematic review (Smart and Marwick, 2004) of 81 studies, representing 2387 people and more than 60,000 person-hours of physical activity there was no significant difference in the likelihood of deaths or adverse events between exercisers and controls with CHF during the trial period and an odds ratio of 0.71 for deaths in exercisers, indicating improved survival. These findings are particularly encouraging since many schemes have been conducted in the home, without telemetric monitoring.

Frail Older People

Older people are not to be excluded from physical activity solely on the basis of frailty. The American College of Sports Medicine's 1998 Position Statement on Physical Activity in Older People (Mazzeo et al., 1998) provided an overview of the evidence for physical activity adoption amongst frail older people. A growing number of studies have focused upon physical activity for older people in residential aged care facilities. Several of these are critiqued in a recent update of the literature (Cyarto et al., 2004). Unfortunately, many of the studies have had small sample sizes. An exception is a trial that involved 468 people which compared different types of physical activity programs for nursing home residents (Morris et al., 1999). In this cluster randomised trial, one group received mobility and strengthening program, another functional rehabilitation provided by nursing staff and the third received usual care. At 10 months follow up, there was a significant reduction in functional decline in the two intervention groups compared to the usual care group. In particular, declines in locomotion ability were noted. The intervention groups had a slight decline in GDS depression scores, but the difference was not significant. Participants GDS scores were relatively low: they were not clinically depressed, so the impact on depression cannot be determined from this particular study.

Nutrition and Depression Management

Management of the person with depression needs to be holistic and encompass the promotion of a balanced diet. The guidance notes underpinning the current Australian physical activity recommendations emphasise that physical activity adoption should be accompanied by a healthy balanced diet (Sims et al., 2006). This may be particularly important for older people with depression as there are physiological and behavioural links between diet and depression. Two potential pathways will be highlighted here, those involving homocysteine and cortisol respectively. Deficiencies in certain nutrients have been linked to depression, notably B group vitamins and folates. These nutrients are involved in the metabolic pathways that use amino acids methionine and homocysteine. These in turn contribute to the production and activation of neurotransmitters such as serotonin and dopamine. High levels of homocysteine have been implicated in the aetiology of depression. To date, the evidence for dietary supplementation is equivocal. Recent trials using folate, vitamin B6 and B12 supplementation have not markedly reduced risk (Ford et al., 2008). Ford et al (2008) showed no advantage of B vitamin supplementation compared to placebo over two years in reducing depression severity or incidence or promoting remission. There may be some genetic predisposition for raised homocysteine levels: supplementation may prove more helpful in individuals at higher risk. A meta-analysis reported that older people with high homocysteine levels had an increased risk of depression and that those with the methyltetrahydrofolate reductase (MTHFR) C677T genotype (TT) were 22% more likely than CC carriers to have a history of depression or current depression (OR 1.22 95% CI 1.01-1.47) (Almeida et al., 2008). Homocysteine is also implicated in vascular health: lowered levels could contribute to prevention of cardiovascular disease, diabetes and dementia. Whilst there is insufficient evidence for dietary supplementation, ensuring that the individual does not have folate deficiency can protect against a range of health problems.

There is also emerging evidence for an association between certain forms of obesity and depression. Depression can raise cortisol levels, thereby raising blood glucose levels and influencing energy metabolism pathways. Cortisol activates lipoprotein lipase and inhibits lipid mobilisation, leading to fat deposition in the viscera. Low levels of sex steroid hormones (oestrogen and testosterone), also reported in depressed people, inhibits lipid mobilisation. Depression can also lead to people eating more energy rich 'comfort' foods, creating a similar scenario. Certain antidepressants, notably tricyclics, can also raise blood glucose. Dutch researchers recently reported an association between abdominal, visceral fat and depression in a prospective study of women aged 70-79 years (Vogelzangs et al., 2008). There was no association between depression and overall obesity, indicating a specific pathway. The association was significant for those depressed at baseline and for those experiencing recurrent bouts of depression.

Concluding Comments

Depressive illness results in considerable functional disability and decreased quality of life, particularly for older people. A range of approaches has been shown to improve depressive symptomatology. There is strong evidence for the use of antidepressants in the treatment of major depressive disorders. Non-pharmacological therapies such as psychotherapies and physical activity offer alternative or adjunct management of depression in older people.

Physical activity may assist both in the prevention and management of depression in older people. As a health promotion intervention, it has the potential to reduce the risk of depression and to ameliorate co-morbid conditions. Using physical activity as an antidepressant can reduce the need for pharmacological intervention, minimizing iatrogenic and polypharmacy risk that is particularly prevalent for older people.

Older depressed people have much to gain from being physically active. Physical activity offers a therapy where the adverse events are minimal and benefits can accrue for both physical and mental health status. For older people with depression, physical activity accompanied by a balanced diet may not only reduce depressive symptoms, but also improve overall health.

References

Alexopoulos, G. S., Abrams, R. C., Young, R. C., Shamoian, C. A. (1998) Cornell Scale for Depression in Dementia. *Biological Psychiatry,* 23, 271-284.

ATLANTIS, E., GRAYSON, D, BROWNING, C, SIMS, J, and KENDIG, H. (2009) Cardiovascular disease and death associated with depression and antidepressants in the Melbourne Longitudinal Study on Healthy Ageing (MELSHA) *Psychological Medicine*, Submitted.

AUSTRALIAN INSTITUTE FOR SUICIDE RESEARCH AND PREVENTION (2003) International Suicide Rates - Recent Trends and Implications for Australia. Canberra, Australian Government Department of Health and Ageing.

BABYAK, M., BLUMENTHAL, J. A., HERMAN, S., KHATRI, P., DORAISWAMY, M., MOORE, K., CRAIGHEAD, W. E., BALDEWICZ, T. T. and KRISHNAN, K. R. (2000) Exercise treatment for major depression: maintenance of therapeutic benefit at 10 months. *Psychosomatic Medicine,* 62, 633-8.

BALDWIN, R., CHIU, E., KATONA, C. and GRAHAM, N. (2002a) *Guidelines on depression in older people,* London, Martin Dunitz Ltd.

BALDWIN, R., CHIU, E., KATONA, C. and GRAHAM, N. (2002b) *Guidelines on depression in older people: practising the evidence,* London, Martin Dunitz Ltd.

BARBOUR, K. and BLUMENTHAL, J. (2005) Exercise training and depression in older adults. *Neurobiology of aging,* 26S, S119-S123.

BARRACLOUGH, J. (1997) ABC of palliative care: depression, anxiety and confusion. *British Medical Journal,* 315, 1365-1368.

BAUMAN, A. (2004) Health benefits of physical activity for older adults- epidemiological approaches to the evidence. IN MORRIS, M. and SCHOO, A. (Eds.) *Optimizing exercise and physical activity in older people.* Edinburgh, Butterman Heinemann.

BAUMAN, A., BELLEW, B., VITA, P., BROWN, W. and OWEN, N. (2002) Getting Australia active: Towards better practice for the promotion of physical activity. Melbourne, Australia, National Public Health Partnership.

BEEKMAN, A., COPELAND, J. and PRINCE, M. (1999) Review of community prevalence of depression in later life. *British Journal of Psychiatry,* 174, 307-311.

BEEKMAN, A. F., GEERLINGS, S., DEEG, D. and AL., E. (2002) The natural history of late-life depression. *Arch Gen Psychiatr,* 59, 605-611.

BLUMENTHAL, J. (1999a) The association between physical activity and depression in older depressed adults. *Journal of Ageing and Physical Activity,* 7, 55-61.

BLUMENTHAL, J. (1999b) The association between physical activity and depression in older depressed adults. *Journal of Aging and Physical Activity,* 7, 55-61.

BRIFFA, T. G., MAIORANA, A., SHEERIN, N. J., STUBBS, A. G., OLDENBURG, B. F., SAMMEL, N. L. and ALLAN, R. M. (2006) Physical activity for people with cardiovascular disease: recommendations of the National Heart Foundation of Australia. *Medical Journal of Australia,* 184, 71-75.

BROSSE, A. L., SHEETS, E. S., LETT, H. S. and BLUMENTHAL, J. A. (2002) Exercise and the treatment of clinical depression in adults: recent findings and future directions. *Sports Medicine,* 32, 741-60.

BROWN, W., FORD, J., BURTON, N., MARSHALL, A. and DOBSON, A. (2005) Prospective study of physical activity and depression in middle aged women. *American Journal of Preventive Medicine,* 29, 265-272.

BURVILL, P., JOHNSON, G., JAMROZIK, F., ANDERSON, C., STEWART-WYNNE, E. and CHAKERA, T. (1995) The prevalence of depression following stroke : the Perth Community Stroke Study. *Br. J. Psychiatry,* 166, 320-327.

CLARK, M. S. and SMITH, D. S. (1998) The effects of depression and abnormal illness behaviour on outcome following rehabilitation from stroke. *Clinical Rehabilitation,* 12, 73-80.

COLE, M. G. and DENDUKURI, N. (2004) The feasibility and effectiveness of brief interventions to prevent depression in older subjects: a systematic review. *International Journal of Geriatric Psychiatry,* 19, 1019-25.

CRAFT, L. and LANDERS, D. (1998) The effects of exercise on clinical depression and depression resulting from mental illness: A meta-regression analysis. *Journal of Sports and Exercise Psychology,* 20, 339-357.

CURRAN, J., WATTS, J. P. and LYNCH, S. (2001) Practical Management of Depression in Older People. London, Arnold.

CYARTO, E. V., MOORHEAD, G. E. and BROWN, W. J. (2004) Updating the evidence relating to physical activity intervention studies in older people. *Journal of Science and Medicine in Sport,* 7, 30-8.

DRAPER, B. M. (1999) The diagnosis and treatment of depression in dementia. *Psychiatric Services,* 50, 1151-1153.

DUMAN, R. (2005) Neurotrophic factors and regulation of mood: role of exercise, diet and metabolism. *Neurobiology of Ageing,* 26S, S88-S93.

DUNN, A., TRIVEDI, M. and AL., E. (2001) Physical activity dose-response effects on outcomes of depression and anxiety. *Medicine and Science in Sports and Exercise,* 33, S587-S597.

FIATARONE SINGH, M. A. (2002) Exercise in the oldest old: Some new insights and unanswered questions. *Journal of the American Geriatrics Society,* 50, 2089.

FRAZER, C. J., CHRISTENSEN, H. and GRIFFITHS, K. M. (2005) Effectiveness of treatments for depression in older people. *Medical Journal of Australia.,* 182, 637-32.

HACKETT, M. and ANDERSON, C., ET AL. (2004) Interventions for treating depression after stroke. *Cochrane Database of Systematic Reviews.* Chichester, UK., John Wiley and Sons Ltd.

HASIN, D., LINK, B. (1988) Age and recognition of depression:implications for a cohort effect in major depression. *Psychological Medicine,* 18, 683-688.

HENDERSON, A. S. (1994) Does ageing protect against depression? *Social Psychiatry and Psychiatric Epidemiology,* 29, 107-109.

HIRSCH, S. R., WALSH, C., DRAPER, R. (1982) Parasuicide. A review of treatment interventions. *Journal of Affective Disorders,* 4, 299-311.

HOLTOM, N. and BARRACLOUGH, J. (2000) Is the Hospital Anxiety and Depression Scale (HADS) useful in assessing depression in palliative care? *Palliative Medicine.,* 14, 219-20.

JANAKIRAMAIAH, N., GANGADHAR, B., NAGA, V., MURTHY, P., HARISH, M., SUBBAKRISHNA, D. and AL., E. (2000) Antidepressant efficacy of Sudarshan Kriya Yoga (SKY) in melancholia : a randomised comparison with electroconvulsive therapy (ECT) and imipramine. *J. Affective Disorders,* 57, 255-259.

JOHNSON, G. A. (1991) Research into psychiatric disorder after stroke: the need for further studies. *Australian and New Zealand Journal of Psychiatry,* 25, 358-370.

JONGENELIS, K., POT, A., EISSES, A., BEEKMAN, A., KLUITER, H. and RIBBE, M. (2004) Prevalence and risk indicators of depression in elderly nursing home patients: the AGED study. *Journal of Affective Disorders.,* 83, 135-42.

JORM, A., CHRISTENSEN, H, GRIFFITHS, KM, ET AL. (2001) Help for depression: what works (and what doesn't). . Canberra, Centre for Mental Health Research.

JORM, A., CHRISTENSEN, H, GRIFFITHS, KM, RODGERS, B. (2002) Effectiveness of complementary and self-help treatments for depression. *Medical Journal of Australia.*, 176, S84-S96.

KENDIG, H., HELME, R., TESHUVA, K., OSBORNE, D., FLICKER, L. and BROWNING, C. (1996) *Health status of older people project: data report,* Melbourne, Victorian Health Promotion Foundation.

KHAN, A., KHAN, S.R., WALENS, G., KOLTS, R., GILLER, E.L. (2003) Frequency of positive studies among fixed and flexible dose antidepressant clinical trials: an analysis of the food and drug administration summary basis of approval reports. *Neuropsychopharmacology* 28, 552-557.

KING, A. (1991) Community intervention for promotion of physical activity and fitness. *Exercise and Sports Science Review,* 19, 211-260.

KING, A., RIJESKI, W. and BUCHNER, D. (1998) Physical activity interventions targeting older adults: a critical review and recommendations. *American Journal of Preventive Medicine,* 15, 316-333.

KNEEBONE, I. and DUNMORE, E. (2000) Psychological management of post-stroke depression. *British Journal of Clinical Psychology,* 39, 53-65.

KRITZ-SILVERSTEIN, D., BARRETT-CONNOR, E. and CORBEAU, C. (2001) Cross-sectional and prospective study of exercise and depressed mood in the elderly- the Rancho Bernardo Study. *American Journal of Epidemiology,* 153, 596-603.

LAMPINEN, P., HEIKKINEN, R. and RUOPPILA, I. (2000) Changes in Intensity of Physical Exercise as Predictors of Depressive Symptoms among Older Adults: An Eight-Year Follow-Up. *Preventive Medicine,* 30, 371-380.

LATHAM, N., ANDERSON, C., BENNETT, D. and STRETTON, C. (2005) Progressive resistance strength training for physical disability in older people. *Cochrane Database of Systematic Reviews.*

LAWLOR, D. and HOPKER, S. (2001) The effectiveness of exercise as an intervention in the management of depression: systematic review and meta-regression analysis of randomised controlled trials. *British Medical Journal,* 322, 763-767.

LEES, N. and LLOYD-WILLIAMS, M. (1999) Assessing depression in palliative care patients using the visual analogue scale: a pilot study. *European Journal of Cancer Care (Engl).* 8, 220-3.

LEON, F., ASHTON, A., D'MELLO, D., DANTZ, B., JEFFNER, J., MATSON, G. and AL., E. (2003) Depression and comorbid mental illness; therapeutic and diagnostic challenges. *Journal of Family Practice*, S19-S27.

LI, C., FRIEDMAN, B., CONWELL, Y. and FISCELLA, K. (2007) Validity of the Patient Health Questionnaire 2 (PHQ-2) in identifying major depression in older people. *Journal of the American Geriatric Society,* 55, 596-602.

LINDWALL, M., RENNEMARK, M., HALLING, A., BERGLUND, J. and HASSMEN, P. (2006) Depression and exercise in elderly men and women: findings from the Swedish National Study on Aging and Care. *Journal of Ageing and Physical Activity,* 15, 41-55.

LLOYD-WILLIAMS, M. (2002) Is it appropriate to screen palliative care patients for depression? *American Journal of Hospice Palliative Care.,* 19, 112-4.

MATHER, A., RODRIGUEZ, C., GUTHRIE, M., MCHARG, A., REID IC and MCMURDO, M. (2002) Effects of exercise on depressive symptoms in older adults with poorly responsive depressive disorder: Randomised controlled trial. *British Journal of Psychiatry,* 180, 411-415.

MAZZEO, R. S., CAVANAGH, P., EVANS, W. J., FIATARONE, M., HAGBERG, J., MCAULEY, E. and STARTZELL, J. (1998) Exercise and physical activity for older adults. *Medicine and Science in Sports and Exercise,* 30, 992-1008.

MAZZEO, R. S. and TANAKA, H. (2001) Exercise prescription for the elderly. *Sports Medicine,* 31, 809-818.

MCAULEY, E., COURNEYA, K., RUDOLPH, D. and LOX, C. (1994) Enhancing exercise adherence in middle-aged males and females. *Preventive Medicine,* 23, 498-506.

MCCUSKER, J., COLE, M. and KELLER, E. (1998) Effectiveness of Treatments of Depression in Older Ambulatory Patients. *Archives of Internal Medicine,* 158, 705-712.

MCLAFFERTY, C., WETZSTEIN, C. and HUNTER, G. (2004) Resistance training is associated with improved mood in healthy older adults. *Perceptual and Motor Skills,* 98, 947-957.

MCNEIL, J., LEBLANC, E. and AL., E. (1991) The effect of exercise on depressive symptoms in the moderately depressed elderly. *Psychology and Aging,* 6, 487-488.

MCSWEENEY, K. and O'CONNOR, D. (2008) Depression among newly admitted Australian nursing home residents. *International Psychogeraitrics,* 20, 724-737.

MITTMAN, N., HERRNANN, N., EINARSON, T., BUSTO, U., LANCTOT, K., LIU, B., SHULMAN, K., SILVER, I., NARANJO, C. and SHEAR, N. (1997) The efficacy, safety and tolerability of antidepressants in late life depression: a meta-analysis. *Journal of Affective Disorders,* 46, 191-217.

MONTGOMERY, S. A., ROY, D., MONTGOMERY, D.B. (1983) The prevention of recurrent suicidal acts. *British Journal of Clinical Pharmacology,* 15, 183s-188s.

MOORE, K. A., BABYAK, M. A., WOOD, C. E., NAPOLITANO, M. A., KHATRI, P., CRAIGHEAD, W. E., HERMAN, S., KRISHNAN, R. and BLUMENTHAL, J. A. (1999) The association between physical activity and depression in older depressed adults. *Journal of Ageing and Physical Activity,* 7, 55-61.

MORRIS, J., FIATARONE, M., KIELY, D., BELLEVILLE-TAYLOR, P., MURPHY, K., LITTLEHALE, S., OOI, W., O'NEILL, E. and DOYLE, N. (1999) Nursing rehabilitation and exercise strategies in the nursing home. *Journals of Gerontology. Series B, Psychological Sciences and Social Sciences* 54, M494.

MORRIS, S., DODD, K. and MORRIS, M. (2004) Outcomes of progressive resistance strength training following stroke: a systematic review. *Clinical Rehabilitation,* 18, 27-39.

NORTH, T. C., MCCULLAGH, P. and TRAN, Z. V. (1990) The effect of exercise on depression. *Exercise and Sports Science Review,* 18, 379-415.

O'CONNOR, D. (2006) Do older Australians truly have low rates of anxiety and depression? A critique of the 1997 National Survey of Mental Health and Wellbeing. *Australian and New Zealand Journal of Psychiatry,* 40, 623-631.

O'CONNOR, D., AMES, D., GARDNER, B. and KING, M. (2009) Psychosocial treatments of psychological symptoms in dementia: a systematic review of reports meeting quality standards. *International Psychogeraitrics*, 1-11.

OUIMET, M. A., PRIMEAU, F. and COLE, M. G. (2001) Psychosocial risk factors in poststroke depression: A systematic review *Canadian Journal of Psychiatry,* 46, 819-828.

PALMER, C. (2005) Exercise as a treatment for depression in elders. *Journal of the American Academy of Nurse Practitioners,* 17, 60-6.

PALUSKA , S. and SCHWENK, T. (2000) Physical activity and mental health: current concepts. *Sports Medicine,* 29, 167-180.

PEARSON, J. and BROWN, G. (2000) Suicide prevention in later life: directions for science and practice. *Clinical Psychology Reviews,* 20, 685-705.

PENNINX, B., REJESKI, W., PANDYA, J., MILLER, M. and AL., E. (2002) Exercise and depressive symptoms: A comparison of aerobic and resistance exercise effects on emotional and physical function in older persons with high and low depressive symptomatology. *Journals of Gerontology (B),* 57B, 24-132.

POMEROY, I. M., CLARK, C. R. and PHILLIP, I. (2001) The effectiveness of very short scales for depression screening in elderly medical patients. *International Journal of Geriatric Psychiatry,* 16.

RADLOFF, L. S. (1977) The CES-D scale: A self-report depression scale for research in the general population. *Applied Psychophysiological Measurement,* 1, 385-401.

RAIT, G., BURNS, A., BALDWIN, R. and AL., E. (1999) Screening for depression in African-Caribbean elders. *Family Practice,* 16, 591-595.

REGIER, D., BOYD, J., BURKE J and AL., E. (1988) One month prevalence of mental disorders in the United States. *Arch Gen Psychiatr,* 45, 977-986.

SABLE, J., DUNN, L. and ZISOOK, S. (2002) Late-life depression: how to identify its symptoms and provide effective treatment. *Geriatrics,* 57, 18-32.

SALZMAN, C., SCHNEIDER, L, LEBOWITZ, B. (1993) Antidepressant treatment of very old patients. *Am J Geriatr Psychiatry,* 1, 21-29.

SAUNDERS, D., GRIEG, C., YOUNG, A. and MEAD, G. (2004) Physical fitness training for stroke patients. (Cochrane Review). *The Cochrane Library.* Chichester, UK, John Wiley and Sons Ltd.

SAYER, G. P., BRITT, H., HORN, F., BHASALE, A., MCGEECHAN, K., CHARLES, J., MILLER, G. C., HULL, B. and SCAHILL, S. (2000) Measures of health and health care delivery in general practice in Australia. Canberra, Australian Institute of Health and Welfare and the University of Sydney.

SEYNNES, O., FIATRONE SINGH, M., HUE, O., PRAS, P., LEGROS, P. and BERNARD, P. (2004) Physiological and functional responses to low-moderate versus high-intensity progressive resistance training in frail elders. *Journal of Gerontology. Series A, Biological Sciences and Medical Sciences,* 59A, 503-509.

SHERMAN, S., D'AGOSTINO, R., COBB, J. and KANNELL, W. (1994) Does exercise reduce mortality rates in the elderly? Experience from the Framingham Heart Study. *American Heart Journal,* 128, 965-972.

SIMS, J., GALEA, M., TAYLOR, N., DODD, K., JESPERSEN, S., JOUBERT, J. and JOUBERT, L. (2009) Regenerate: assessing the feasibility of using a strength training program to enhance the physical and mental health of chronic post-stroke patients. *Int J. Geriatric Psychiatry,* 24, 76-83.

SIMS, J., HILL K, HUNT S, HARALAMBOUS, B., BROWN A, ENGEL L, HUANG N, KERSE N and M., O. (2006) National physical activity recommendations for older Australians: Discussion document. A Report to the Department of Health and Ageing. April 2006. Melbourne, National Ageing Research Institute.

SIMS, J., HILL, K, DAVIDSON, S, GUNN, J, HUANG, N. (2006) Exploring the feasibility of a community-based strength training program for older people with depressive symptoms and its impact on depressive symptoms. *BMC Geriatrics.*

SINGH, N., CLEMENTS, K. and FIATRONE, M. (1997) A randomized controlled trial of progressive resistance training in depressed elders. *Journal of Gerontology,* 52A, M27-M35.

SINGH, N., CLEMENTS, K. and FIATRONE SINGH, M. (2001) The efficacy of exercise as a long-term antidepressant in elderly subjects: a randomised controlled trial. *Journal of Gerontology. Series A, Biological Sciences and Medical Sciences,* 50, M497-M504.

SINGH, N., STAVRINOS, T., SCARBEK, Y., GALAMBOS, G., LIBER C and FIATRONE SINGH, M. (2005) A randomized controlled trial of high versus low intensity weight training versus general practitioner care for clinical depression in older adults. *Journal of Gerontology. Series A, Biological Sciences and Medical Sciences,* 60A, 768-776.

SJOSTEN, N. and KIVELA, S.-L. (2006) The effects of physical exercise on depressive symptoms among the aged: a systematic review. *Int J Geriatric Psychiatry,* 21, 410-418.

SMART, N. and MARWICK, T. (2004) Exercise training for patients with heart failure: a systematic review of factors that improve mortality and morbidity. *American Journal of Medicine.,* 116, 693-706.

SNOW, V., LASCHER S and MOTTUR-PILSON, C. (2000) Pharmacological treatement of acute major depression and dysthymia. *Annals of Internal Medicine,* 132, 738-742.

SOON, J. and LEVINE, M. (2002) Screening for depression in patients in long-term care facilities: a randomized controlled trial of physician response. *Journal of the American Geriatric Society,* 50, 1092-9.

STATHOPOULOU, G., POWERS, M., BERRY, A., SMITS, J. and OTTO, M. (2006) Exercise interventions for mental health: a quantitative and qualitative review. *Clin Psychol Sci Pract,* 13, 179-193.

STEWART, N., MCMULLEN, L. and RUBIN, L. (1994) Movement therapy with depressed inpatients: a randomised multiple single case design. *Archives of Psychiatric Nursing,* 8, 22-29.

STURM, J. and DONNAN, G., ET AL (2004) Quality of life after stroke: The North East Melbourne Stroke Incidence study (NEMESIS). *Stroke,* 35, 2340-2347.

TAYLOR, A. H., CABLE, N. T., FAULKNER, G., HILLSDON, M., NARICI, M. and VAN DER BIJ, A. (2004) Physical activity and older adults: a review of health benefits and the effectiveness of interventions. *Journal of Sports Sciences,* 22, 703-725.

TEOH, V., SIMS, J. and MILGROM, J. (2009) Psychosocial predictors of quality of life following a stroke. *Topics in Stroke Rehabilitation,* in press.

TERESI, J., ABRAMS, R., HOLMES, D., RAMIREZ, M., EIMICKE, J. (2001) Prevalence of depression and depression recognition in nursing homes. *Social Psychiatry and Psychiatric Epidemiology,* 36, 613-620.

TERI, L., MCKENZIE, G., LAFAZIA, D. (2005) Psychosocial treatment of depression in older adults with dementia. *Clinical Psychology: Science and Practice,* 12, 303-316.

THORNEN, P., FLORAS, J., HOFFMAN, P. and SEALS, D. (1990) Endorphins and exercise: physiological mechanisms and clinical implications. *Med Sci Sports Exerc,* 22, 417-428.

VAN DE WEG, F. B., KUIK, D. J. and LANKHORST, G. J. (1999) Post-stroke depression and functional outcome: a cohort study investigating the influence of depression on functional recovery from stroke. *Clinical Rehabilitation,* 13, 268-272.

VOGELZANGS, N., KRITCHEVSKY, S., BEEKMAN, A., NEWMAN, A., SATTERFIELD, S., SIMONSICK, E., YAFFE, K., HARRIS, T. and PENNINX, B. (2008) Depressive Symptoms and Change in Abdominal Obesity in Older Persons *Arch Gen Psychiatry,* 65, 1386-1393.

WATTS, S., BHUTANI, G., STOUT, I., DUCKER, G., CLEATOR, P., MCGARRY, J. and DAY, M. (2002) Mental health in older adult recipients of primary care services: is depression the key issue? Identification, treatment and the general practitioner. *International Journal of Geriatric Psychiatry.,* 17, 427-37.

WHYTE, E. and MULSANT, B. (2002) Post stroke depression: epidemiology, pathophysiology and biological treatment. *Biological Psychiatry,* 52, 253-264.

WILLIAMS, C. L., TAPPEN, R. M. (2007) Effect of exercise on mood in nursing home residents with Alzheimer's disease. *American Journal of Alzheimer's Disease and Other Dementias,* 22, 389-397.

WILSON, K., MOTTRAM, P., SIVANRANTHAN, A. and A., N. (2001) Antidepressants versus placebo for the depressed elderly. The Cochrane Database of Systematic Reviews.

WITHAM, M. D., STRUTHERS, A. D. and MCMURDO, M. E. (2003) Exercise training as a therapy for chronic heart failure: can older people benefit? *Journal of the American Geriatrics Society,* 51, 699-709.

YESAVAGE, J., ET AL. (1983) Development and validation of a geriatric depression screening scale: a preliminary report *Journal of Psychiatric Research,* 17, 37-49.

In: Depression in the Elderly
Editor: Emaad Abdel-Rahman, pp. 141-158
ISBN 978-1-61324-771-6

Chapter 8

INTERACTIONS BETWEEN DEMENTIA AND DEPRESSION: CAUSES, CONSEQUENCES, AND COMMON MECHANISMS

***Analuiza Camozzato*[1], *Jarbas S. Roriz-Filho*[2], *Idiane Rosset Cruz*[3], *Márcia L. F. Chaves*[4] *and Matheus Roriz-Cruz*[4]**
[1]Division of Geriatric Psychiatry, Department of Psychiatry,
Federal University of Health Sciences of Porto Alegre, Brazil
[2]Division of Geriatric Medicine, Department of Internal Medicine,
University of Sâo Paulo-RP, Brazil
[3]Division of Gerontological Nursing. Faculty of Nursing,
Brazilian Federal University of Rio Grande do Sul State, Brazil
[4]Division of Neurogeriatrics, Department of Neurology, Faculty of Medicine,
Brazilian Federal University of Rio Grande do Sul State, Brazil

ABSTRACT

Severe, major depression is the most common differential diagnosis of dementia. Depression may be diagnosed before, concomitantly, or after the diagnosis of dementia. Generally, ~ 40% of people with dementia have coexistent depression. In most cases depression comes after some degree of cognitive decline and, mainly, functional dependence, in which case depression is said to be 'reactive' to the dementing process. However, depression might also come before dementia, suggesting it may be a prodrome of the dementia syndrome itself. Prevalence of depression seems to be highest during the mid stages of the dementing process. However, many dementia subtypes are intrinsically associated with (organic) depression, i.e., they probably share the same neuropathological processes that leads to both diseases. The coexistence of Vascular Dementia and Vascular Depression is the prototype in this last case, Depression, especially in its aphatic subtype, is more common in vascular dementia than in Alzheimer's Disease (AD). As AD progress through the Braak stages, it starts to involve not only cholinergic neurons, but also the serotoninergic and noradrenergic ones. This seems to be the case also for both Lewy-Body dementia (LBD) and Parkinson's dementia, where the initial cholinergic and dopaminergic deficits, respectively, evolves to compromise other neurotransmitter systems. Depression secondary to dementia may also be the consequence of limited functional independence, which often precedes the diagnosis of dementia. Partial functional dependence may rapidly evolve to full incapacity, further aggravating depression. In very late stages, however, regardless of the dementia subtype, depression is no longer a problem, since it needs some degree of cognitive function to be brought into consciousness. In the coexistence of depression and/or fluctuation of consciousness, visual hallucinations in LBD should not be mistaken for psychotic depression. In summary, depression often precedes and coexists with dementia. The peculiarities of this association are dementia-subtype–specific. In each case, the particularities of the dementia subtype should be taken in consideration in understanding and managing this common association.

1. Introduction

The relationship between depression and dementia in older adults is complex and represents a challenge for all clinicians who deals with them.. Cognitive impairment and frank dementia are often associated with depression, and this association may occur in diverse scenarios, each of them having to be approached differently. Patients with dementia may become depressed in reaction to falling mental capacity or as a biological consequence of the underlying neurologic disorder. In this last scenario, both cognitive and depressive symptoms are thought to be related to the common underlining neuropathologic process. In addition, because both syndromes can have common physiopathology, depression can also be a prodrome or a risk factor for dementia.

Besides, some sub-types of dementia may initially presents with symptoms that mimic depression. Patients with dementia may develop apathy, sleep disturbances and social withdrawal, suggesting depression as the sole diagnosis, but this scenario may be entirely due to cognitive deficits. Furthermore, it can be difficult to discriminate, in the first moment, previously depressed individuals first presenting with dementia from those depressed subjects whose cognitive impairment will show notable improvement with antidepressive treatment. This chapter aims to summarize the scientific evidences for the current ′state of the art′ of this often misconceptualized topic.

2. Cognitive Impairment Secondary to Depression

Some considerations are necessary previous to introduce the issue of cognitive impairment as a consequence of depression itself. Depression is a frequent cause of disability in the elderly.. Some of the consequences of depression in older subjects include reduced life satisfaction, social deprivation, loneliness, increased use of health and home care services, cognitive decline, functional dependence for the Activities of Daily Living (ADL), suicide, and increased nonsuicide mortality (Palsson and Skoog, 1997). The term depression comprehends many disorders, as major depression, subsyndromal or minor depression, nondysphoric depression, late-life depression, vascular depression, among others. The term late-life depression refers to depressive syndromes, as defined by the American Psychiatric Association's Diagnostic and Statistical Manual and/or by the International Classification of Diseases, which have first ocurred in adults older than 65 years of age. The prevalence rate of major depression among healthy independent community-dwelling elderly is about 5% (Blazer et al., 1994; Steffens et al., 2000), being lower than the prevalence in the general adult population. However rates of depression are higher for those older adults with comorbid medical illnesses and for those found in general medical settings (30 to 40%) (Koenig et al., 1997; Burke and Wengel, 2003; Borin et al., 2001).

Table 1. DSM-IV criteria for major depression (APA, 1994)

A. Five (or more) of the following symptoms have been present during the same 2-week period and represent a change from previous functioning; at least one of the symptoms is either (1) depressed mood or (2) loss of interest or pleasure.

(1) depressed mood most of the day, nearly every day, as indicated by either subjective report (e.g., feels sad or empty) or observation made by others (e.g., appears tearful)

(2) markedly diminished interest or pleasure in all, or almost all, activities most of the day, nearly every day (as indicated by either subjective account or observation made by others)

(3) significant weight loss when not dieting or weight gain (e.g., a change of more than 5% of body weight in a month), or decrease or increase in appetite nearly every day

(4) insomnia or hypersomnia nearly every day

(5) psychomotor agitation or retardation nearly every day (observable by others, not merely subjective feelings of restlessness or being slowed down)

(6) fatigue or loss of energy nearly every day

(7) feelings of worthlessness or excessive or inappropriate guilt (which may be delusional) nearly every day (not merely self-reproach or guilt about being sick)

(8) diminished ability to think or concentrate, or indecisiveness, nearly every day (either by subjective account or as observed by others)

(9) recurrent thoughts of death (not just fear of dying), recurrent suicidal ideation without a specific plan, or a suicide attempt or a specific plan for committing suicide

B. The symptoms do not meet criteria for a Mixed Episode

C. The symptoms cause clinically significant distress or impairment in social, occupational, or other important areas of functioning

D. The symptoms are not due to the direct physiological effects of a substance (e.g., a drug of abuse, a medication) or a general medical condition (e.g., hypothyroidism)

E. The symptoms are not better accounted for by Bereavement, i.e., after the loss of a loved one, the symptoms persist for longer than 2 months or are characterized by marked functional impairment, morbid preoccupation with worthlessness, suicidal ideation, psychotic symptoms, or psychomotor retardation

The DSM-IV criteria for major depression (APA, 1994) were not differentiated between young and older adults (Table 1). "Subsyndromal" or minor depression is defined as the presence of clinically significant depressive symptoms which do not meet DSM-IV definition for major depression. It is a particularly important concept to be take into consideration in the elderly population because it carries a similar amount of burden of that of major depression (Lyness et al., 1999, 2006). Psychotic depression, one of the most serious types of this disorder, may occur more commonly in the elderly population,and can course with more memory relapses, incomplete remission, and more significant cognitive impairment (Gournellis et al., 2001).

Depression associated with cerebrovascular disease is frequent among older people, since the prevalence of cerebrovascular disease increases with aging. Depression may develop after an acute cerebrovascular event ("post-stroke depression") (Robinson, 2003) or it may occur in association with chronic ischemic changes in the brain ("(small-vessel) vascular depression") (Alexopoulos et al., 1997; Krishnan et al., 1997). The association with cerebrovascular risk factors is the basis of late-life depression etiopathogeny. Depression of cerebrovascular origin gives higher risk to concomitant or subsequent dementia. Both issues will be discussed below.

Although criteria for major depression for adults and elderly individuals are not differentiated in the DSM IV (APA, 1994), it is reasonable to expect a quite different clinical presentation between the two groups and a higher frequency of cognitive impairment in the late-life depression. To better understand these differences we need to take into account the influence of the aging process upon the Central Nervous System (CNS). . Several lines of evidence suggest that the aging of the CNS, be it associated or not with significative vascular pathology. preferably compromise frontostriatal, amygdalar and hippocampal integrity. Alterations in these brain regions have been associated with mood and behavioral disorders, dysexecutive syndrome, psychomotor lowered speed, functional dependence, and compromised psychosocial functioning. All those, directly or indirectly, may confer vulnerability to late-life depression. These findings can contribute not only to the distinctive course of geriatric depression, but also to the heterogeneity of its clinical presentation (Alexopoulos et al., 2005).

It is important to highlight that cognitive difficulties are frequent complains in young patients with depression, although sometimes objective cognitive deficits are not observed (Reid and Maclullich, 2006). Conversely, cognitive impairment is a common objective finding among elderly patients (Rapp et al., 2005; Elderkin-Thompson et al., 2003; Loockwood et al., 2000; Nebes et al.,2000, 2001, 2002; Alexopoulos et al., 2005; Lesser et al., 1996; Christensen et al., 1997; Forsell et al., 1994; Butters MA et al., 2000; Backman et al., 1996; King et al., 1998). Several studies assessing cognition in patients with late-life depression, have been shown decline in a variety of cognitive domains.

Individuals with late-life depression often presents with memory and attention deficits (Butters et al., 2004; Elderkin-Thompson et al., 2007; Backman et al., 1996; Lesser et al., 1996; Nebes et al., 2000; Lockwood et al., 2000), decreased information processing speed (Nebes et al., 2000, 2002; Lesser et al., 1996; Christensen et al., 1997), and dysfunction in executive function (Rapp et al., 2005; Elderkin-Thompson et al., 2003; Loockwood et al., 2000; Nebes et al.,2000, 2001; Alexopoulos et al., 2005). Poorer performance on measures of executive functioning was the most frequently impairment demonstrated in patients with late life depression. Elderly depressed subjects with executive dysfunction have more pronounced psychomotor retardation and reduced interest in former pleasant activities (Alexopoulos et al. 1997; Krishnan et al. 1997). This clinical presentation is compatible with a medial frontal lobe syndrome, which is characterized by apathy, lack of motivation (avolition), organization, planning, and sequencing (dysexecutive syndrome).

There were several methodological attempts in trying to distinguish neuropsychological patterns of cognitive dysfunction between late-life depression and initial-to-moderate phase dementia (Wright and Persad, 2007). However, considering the broad range of cognitive deficits often found in both depression and dementia, it is often difficult to find a clearly distinctive pattern of cognitive impairment which can differentiate depression from dementia. Differential diagnosis between depression and dementia, therefore, may be very difficult.

In addition, cognitive impairment frequently persists after clinical recovery from depression, after antidepressant drug treatment, particularly in terms of memory and executive functions (Thomas, 2008; Butters et al., 2000). It has been proposed that these persisten, cognitive deficits, could be an indicator of underlying brain structural disease, such as Alzheimer's disease and Vascular dementia (Butters et al., 2000). In fact, cerebrovascular pathology may contribute not only to the poor response to antidepressive drugs, but also to the persistence of neurocognitive deficits after treatment of vascular depression (Thomas, 2008). These findings evidence that the need of longitudinal assessment of older depressed subjects cannot be overemphasized.

2.1. Pathophysiology of Late-Life Depression

Cerebrovascular disease probably is an important contributor for the often coexistence of cognitive impairment in late-life depression. Besides, late-life depression itself is also a common finding among subjects with extensive cerebrovascular disease, even after adjusting for the functional status (Alexopoulos et al., 1997; Rao, 2000. Furthermore, more severe depressive symptoms are observed among individuals with greater cerebrovascular burden. (Sultzer et al,1995; Stefens et al., 1999). Depressed elderly individuals showed more evidence of vascular disease on magnetic resonance imaging (MRI), such as white matter hyper-intensities (WMH) and lacunae (de Groot et al., 2000; Stefens et al., 2002; Thomas et al., 2002). Several imaging studies have evidenced that, besides WMH, Subcortical gray matter lesions, are also associated with geriatric depression (Coffey et al., 1989,1990; Rabins et al., 1991; Greenwald et al., 1996; Nebes et al., 2002; Figiel et al., 1991).

Depressed elderly patients with MRI hyperintensities demonstrated more cognitive difficulties than depressed elderly patients without evidence of such lesions (Hickie et al., 1995; Jenkins et al., 1998; Kramer-Ginsberg et al., 1999; Baldwin et al., 2000). Besides, it is now recognized that vascular changes in the frontostriatal circuits can lead to depression (Alexopoulos, 2006). It has been also suggested that cognitive impairments observed in patients with late-life vascular depression often arises from damage to the frontostriatal and frontolimbic circuits (Alexopoulos , 2006).

Impairments on executive functions are frequently observed in late-life depression (Rapp et al., 2005; Elderkin-Thompson et al., 2003; Loockwood et al., 2000; Nebes et al.,2000, 2001; Alexopoulos et al., 2005). Damage to frontostriatal neural networks and their limbic and hippocampal connections often produces a dysexecutive syndrome. Particularly in subjects with late-life depression, WMH are strongly associated with psychomotor slowing (Hickie et al., 1995) and impairment in executive functions (Salloway et al., 1996). Therefore, vascular-related brain structural modifications probably play an important role in the etiology and pathophysiology of late-life depression.

Besides fronto-striato-limbic dysfunction, other CNS abnormalities can be associated with late-life depression. Pathological modifications in the structure (Frodl et al. 2003; Sheline et al. 1998) and function of the amygdala (Drevets 1999, 2003) have been documented in depressive patients. Relavively common cerebral diseases among the elderly, stroke and subcortical disorders such as Parkinson's disease can damage amygdala conexions (Drevets 1999).

Hippocampal dysfunction has also been related to depression (Bremner et al. 2000; Frodl et al. 2002; MacQueen 2003). Age-related disorders such as AD and cerebrovascular disorder specially renders the hippocampus vulnerable to atrophy, further and beyond the influence of age itself. In fact, the hippocampus is especially vulnerable to ischemia (MacQueen 2003) and to the effect of chronic hypercortisolemia caused by sustained stressing conditions and chronic medical illness (Miller and O'Callaghan 2003). Moreover, Indeed, cortisol hypersecretion was associated with both hippocampal atrophy and cognitive impairment among depressed subjects (Rubinow et al., 1984). Depression was also associated with Hypothalamic-Pituitary-Adrenal axis (HPA) dysfunction (Hatzinger, 2000), hypercortisolism being a common finding among depressed subjects.

2.2. Common Pathophysiology between Depression and Dementia?

In addition of being possible consequences of each other, depression and dementia also appears to have a common pathophysiological process. Cerebrovascular changes are one of the neurobiological variables which may underlie the relationship between depression and dementia (Wright and Persad, 2007). Cerebrovascular disease is associated with a greater risk and severity of cognitive decline, in which extreme vascular dementia will develop (Launer, 2002; DeCarli, 2003; , Vermeer et al., 2003). Cerebrovascular disease is also associated with late-life depression among many elderly patients, especially those oldest-old. Therefore, cerebrovascular disease may be the link that underlies the often co-occurrence between mood and cognitive disorders.

This seems to be a valid argument not only for vascular dementia, but also for Alzheimer Disease (AD). In fact, there is already a large body of epidemiologic evidence linking vascular risk factors to a greater risk of developing AD (Breteler, 2000; Honig et al., 2005). Furthermore, hippocampal atrophy associated with HPA dysfunction in depression may place patients with a history of depression at greater risk for developing AD (Wright and Persad, 2007). Whether alterations in the HPA axis may increase amyloid/tau burden is unknown. However, there are evidences for an indirect mechanism, at least. Hypercortisolism is associated with increased insulin resistance and hyperinsulinism have been shown to be associated with AD, possibly by increasing both amyloid and tau neuropathological burden.

Besides, as AD progress through the Braak stages, it starts to involve not only the cholinergic neurons, but also the serotoninergic and noradrenergic ones (D'Amato, 1987). This seems to be the case also for both Lewy-Body dementia (LBD) and Parkinson's dementia, where the initial cholinergic and dopaminergic deficits, respectively, evolves to compromise other neurotransmitter systems (D'Amato, 1987). In each case, the relative synaptic deficit of serotonin and noradrenalin should certainly have its piece of contribution for the possible co-ocurrence of depression.

3. Depression: Risk Factor or Prodrome to Dementia?

It is still controversial whether depressive symptoms represent a true risk factor for dementia or whether they just share one or more etiopathogenic mechanism, such as in vascular dementia/depression. Many studies have suggested that preexistent depression represents a true risk factor for dementia. A meta-analysis of follow-up studies examining the risk of developing dementia among subjects which first developed depression after the age of 65 years, found that this group has a 1.2 to 3.5 times higher risk of developing dementia

(Jorm et al., 2000). However, many individual population-based longitudinal studies have provided conflicting data.. Some of these studies have encountered that depression was in fact a risk factor for the development of subsequent dementia (Barnes et al., 2006; Geda et al., 2006; Wilson et al., 2002,2004; Yaffe et al., 1999; Berger et al., 1999; Devanand et al., 1996; Green et al., 2003; Geerlings et al., 2000; Modrego and Ferrandez, 2004), whereas other studies did not support this finding (Ganguli et al., 2006, Dufouil et al., 1996, Vinkers et al., 2004, Lindsay et al., 2002; Henderson et al., 1997). One possible explanation for these apparently conflicting findings is that they included, in different proportions, both cases of late-life depression predominantly due to cerebrovascular disease, at one side, and those reactive to external and internal conditions such as social isolation, economic deprivation, institutionalization, organic diseases, functional dependence and incapacity, in another side. Including both subgroups of older depressed subjects in the same group might have weakened or biased the results. Moreover, the nature of the relationship between depression and dementia ought to be different between the several subtypes of dementia. At instance, have no reasons to expect that the nature of these relationships between depression and dementia should be similar between AD and vascular dementia.

Another possibility is depression being in fact an early symptom of neurodegeneration. In this case, depressive symptoms could be a prodrome to dementia. Many studies have suggested that depressive symptoms among older adults can represent an early manifestation of dementia (Chen et al., 1999; Bassuk et al., 1998; Alexopoulos et al., 1993; Heun et al., 2002; Buntinx et al., 1996; Cervilla et al., 2000, Yaffe et al., 1999).

There are several attempts to predict evolution to dementia based on the initial presentation of depression. Depression in those individuals who were eventually diagnosed with dementia first presented with motivation-related symptoms, such as disinterest, low energy, and concentration difficulties (Berger et al.. 1999). Furthermore other study showed that patients with Mild Cognitive Impairment (MCI) with at least one symptom of apathy were at greater risk for developing AD than were those without symptoms of apathy (Robert et al.. 2006). More longitudinal studies are needed to verify the existence of a neuropsychological profile that could be characteristic of this group early in the course of dementia (Wright and Persad, 2007).

Based on these findings, we can conclude that the nature of the relationship between depression and dementia is still not fully understood, and that more longitudinal studies should be specifically designed in order to definitely answer many of the above questions..

4. Depression as a Component of the Dementia Syndrome

Depressive symptoms are common in dementia and can affect approximately 30% of the patients (Lyketsos et al., 2002). Patients with dementia may become depressed reaction to their falling mental habilities, such as memory, or as a direct biological consequence of the same neurodegenerative process.

A "reactive depression" can be the consequence of limited functional independence, which often precedes the diagnosis of dementia. However depressive symptoms are more frequent in middle-stages of dementia (Lövheim et al., 2008).

There are some difficulties in diagnosing depression among patients with dementia. Patients with dementia may develop symptoms like apathy, sleep impairment, and social withdrawal, inducing the clinician to think in depression as the main diagnosis. As mentioned above these symptoms can be mainly related to the cognitive deficits.

The frequency, severity, and functional impact of depressive symptoms upon an underlining clinical picture of dementia can be quite different from that of major depression. Besides, depressive symptoms tend to fluctuate more if underlining dementia is present. Further complicating the issue, patients with depression superposed to a baseline dementing disease cannot be fully aware of the extent of their depressive symptoms and often cannot fully express their own mood state. Depressive symptoms are often modified according to the state of dementia severity. In a cross-sectional study, patients with classic symptoms of depression, such as mood and appetite disturbance, feelings of guilt, and suicidal ideation were less severely demented than patients with symptoms characteristic of motivational disturbance (Forsell et al.. 1993). A changing profile of depressive symptoms was found among depressed elderly people progressing to dementia, with fewer affective symptoms and increased both agitation and motor slowing (Ritchie et al.. 1999).

The lack of reliable tools to measure the relative contributions of depression and dementia to both cognitive dysfunction and behavioral changes in individual patients has been noticed since at least 15 years ago (Jones and Reifler, 1994). One of the practical recommendations of the National Institute of Mental Health conference "Perspectives on Depression, Mild Cognitive Impairment, and Cognitive Decline" was to refine and develop approaches to assessing depression in the context of cognitive impairment (Steffens et al., 2006).

As AD is the most frequent dementia, there is more information about depression in AD than in other dementias. The development of provisional criteria for the diagnosis of depression in the underlining presence of AD (Olin et al.., 2002) (Table 2) were performed taking into account that the depressive symptoms of patients with cognitive impairment are somewhat different from those of cognitively unimpaired depressed older persons. Presentation and treatment responsiveness of depression in AD may significantly differ between early onset and other types of depression (Lyketsos and Olin, 2002).

A study which evaluated the natural course of depression in AD evidenced that the prevalence of depressive symptoms was stable (~40%) over the first 3 years of follow-up(Holtzer et al., 2005). There was a significant drop to 28% and 24% in the fourth and fifth years of follow-up, respectively. AD duration and level of functional activity, but not cognitive status, were significantly related to depressive symptoms over the entire follow-up period (Holtzer et al., 2005). However a systematic review did not find any association between the severity of AD and the prevalence of depressive symptoms or diagnosed depression (Verkaik et al.., 2007). Obviously, in very late stages, regardless of the dementia subtype, depression is no longer a problem, since it seems that at least a minimal degree of cognitive function is necessary in order to suffer from depresion.

Besides the possible co-involvement,of cerebrovascular risk factor, neuropsychiatric symptoms in Alzheimer's disease (AD) can also results from specific alterations on neurotransmitters. An imbalance between the cholinergic and serotonergic systems was related to overactivity and psychosis in post-mortem analysis of the frontal and temporal cortex of 22 AD patients who had been prospectively assessed (Garcia-Alloza et al., 2005). In addition to cholinergic deficits, significant decreases in Gamma-Amino Butyric Acid

(GABA) content associated to no changes in glutamate concentrations were found in the frontal and temporal cortex of depressed AD patients (Garcia-Alloza et al., 2006). Besides, in the same study, both GABA levels and the glutamate/GABA ratio showed significant correlations with the intensity of depressive symptoms in AD (Garcia-Alloza et al., 2006).

Table 2. American Association Geriatric Psychiatry diagnostic criteria for Depression in AD (Olin et al., 2002): Depression in Alzheimer-type dementia

A.	Three or more of the following symptoms, present during the same two-week period, and representing a change from a previous level of functioning. Either item-one or item-two must be included:
1.	Clinically significant depressed mood
2.	Decreased positive affect or pleasure in response to social contacts and usual activities
3.	Social isolation or withdrawal
4.	Disturbed appetite
5.	Disturbed sleep
6.	Psychomotor retardation or agitation
7.	Irritability
8.	Fatigue or loss of energy
9.	Feelings of worthlessness, hopelessness, or inappropriate guilt
10.	Recurrent thoughts of death or suicidal ideation, plan, or any attempt
B.	Meets criteria for Alzheimer-type dementia
C.	Depressive symptoms cause clinically significant distress or disruption in function
D.	Symptoms do not occur exclusively during an episode of delirium
E.	Symptoms are not due to a direct physiological effect from a substance (medication or drug of abuse)
F.	Symptoms are not better accounted for by another condition

In addition to AD, other dementing illnesses can also present with depression or significant depressive symptoms at a give point of their courses. Patients with vascular dementia can present depression during any stage of dementia severity, since both cognitive and affective symptoms often share the same vascular mechanism. Furthermore, prominent depressed mood together with poor executive functioning are important characteristics of vascular dementia (Levy and Chelune, 2007).

The common pathophysiology of vascular dementia and vascular depression was already commented in the above sections. Phenotypic differences on depression presentation seem to exist between the early and late stages of AD and Vascular dementia. Patients with vascular dementia demonstrated increased apathy at mild phase and higher depressive scores (Geriatric Depression Scale-GDS) at moderate-to-severe stages than did patients with AD (Chan et al., 2008). A cross-sectional study had also found higher depressive symptomatology in subjects with vascular dementia, as compared with AD patients, by using another scale (Hamilton Depression Scale - HAM-D) (Kim et al., 2003). A third study has also encountered affective disturbance to be more frequent in vascular dementia in comparison with AD, FrontoTemporal Dementia (FTD), Dementia with Lewy Bodies (DLB), and other dementias in a sample of 155 demented outpatients (Chiu et al., 2006). Together, these studies support the hypothesis of a vascular contribution to late-life depression.

Behavioral features are the core symptoms of FTD, especially in the frontal variant form of FTD. This variant commonly presents with changes in personality and social behavior (Hodges, 2001). In such case emotional blunting, loss of capacity of demonstrate emotions, and a lack of expression of concern or distress when confronted with adversities are often observed (Snowden et al., 2002). These symptoms may be erroneously interpreted as depressive or bipolar symptoms. Furthermore, apathy was two times higher in FTD in comparison with other dementia subtypes (AD, VaD, mixed dementia and DLB) (Engelborghs et al., 2005). On the other hand, apathy can be a depressive symptom or it can occur as a single neuropsychiatry symptom, without other depressive findings.

The presence of dementia with marked fluctuation in cognitive performance, visual hallucinations, and motor symptoms of parkinsonism which are the core features of LBD (Frank, 2003) should not be mistaken with psychotic depression. Depression, anxiety, apathy, and anhedonia are also often seen early in the course of DLB (Rockwell et al., 2000; Ballard et al.., 2001).

The term "Frontal-subcortical dementias" (Bonelli and Cummings, 2008) has grouped distinct neuropathologic disorders which share its primary pathology in the subcortical structure and have a characteristic pattern of neuropsychologic impairment, which include a primary subcortical and a secondarily frontal pattern (due to frontal-subcortical disconnection). These dementias are characterized by important alterations in behavior (apathy, inertia or avolition, anehdonia), an impaired ability to manipulate acquired knowledge, slowed thought processing (bradyphrenia) and marked secondary frontal dysfunction. Included in this group are Vascular dementia, Parkinsonian dementia, Normal Pressure Hydrocephalus among other, less common, causes of dementia, such as Progressive Supranuclear Palsy, Huntington's disease, AIDS dementia complex, thalamic degeneration (Stewart, 1996), Depression is a common characteristic to this group of dementias. , subcortical vascular dementia, multiple sclerosis, and the acquired immunodeficiency syndrome dementia complex are among the "frontal-subcortical dementias" together with some other rare dementias (Bonelli and Cummings, 2008).

The Microvascular "Frontal-Subcortical Syndrome" (FSCS) is a new conceptualized syndrome which tries to link a series of geriatric disorders, such as cognitive impairment, late-onset depression, dysexecutive function, small-stepped frontal gait disorder, repetitive falls, and urge incontinence under a common underlying common pathophysiological process, namely, small-vessel disease compromising the integrity of the group of frontostriatolimbic networks (Pugh and Lipsitz, 2002). Our group was the first to elaborate a clinical criteria for this syndrome, which should also included the presence of at least one frontal release sign (Roriz-Cruz, 2007). In the same study, its prevalence in the community has been found to be around 10%. Of note, dementia including NPH, as well as Parkinson's disease and major, clinical strokes, are the main exclusion criteria for this syndrome. Our group has also evidenced a strong statistical association among all of the above components of the syndrome, which is consistent with the hypothesis that all the FSCS components share a general pattern of frontostriatolimbic compromise.

Moreover, in this study, the FSCS was significantly associated with metabolic syndrome among 422 community-dwelling elderly subjects (Roriz-Cruz et al., 2007). Interestingly, the strong inverse association between the MMSE and GDS scores were restricted exclusively to the metabolic syndrome group, as in the control group there was no association at all between these two variables (flat regression line) (Roriz-Cruz, 2008).

Etiopathogenically and pathophysiologically, the FSCS most probably represents an earlier stage of the cerebral small-vessel pathology found in the Biswanger subtype of vascular dementia.

Conclusion

Depression often coexists with dementia. Approximately 40% of all people with dementia have coexistent depression. The prevalence and peculiarities of this association are dementia-subtype –specific. Depression may be diagnosed before, concomitantly, or after the diagnosis of dementia.

Both diseases can share a common physiopathology linked to subjacent vascular changes, advanced neurodegenerative changes bringing destruction of the serotoninergic or noradrenergic systems, like in AD, or yet alterations on the HPA axis with consequent hypercortisolism.

Besides, does depression represent also an early sign of dementia or a risk factor for the development of cognitive decline"? There is no definite answer for this question as yet. However, there are evidences points to both hypothesis being true, since they are not mutually excluding, as each clinical case have different dynamics. Certainly the answer for this question will open new venues in terms of a more accurate baseline medical diagnosis. This may allow both a more exact prognosis and the correspondent more appropriate treatment for the case. At instance, this may allow the possibility of more appropriated medical interventions aimed to avoid the development of dementia in a given elderly patient with depression.

A more integrated approach among clinical and epidemiological researchers working in the area of depression with those working primarily in the area of memory disorders was recommended by the NIMH conference (above mentioned, Steffens et al., 2006) in order to fulfill the gaps of knowledge in the complex web of possible crossectional and longitudinal relationships between the several subtypes of dementia, at one side, and the various types of depression presentation in the elderly.

References

[1] Alexopoulos, GS; Meyers, BS; Young, RC; Mattis, S; Kakuma, T. The course of geriatric depression with "reversible dementia": a controlled study. *Am. J. Psychiatry*, 1993, 150, 1693-1699.

[2] Alexopoulos, GS; Meyers, BS; Young, RC; Campbell, S; Silbersweig, D; Charlson, M. 'Vascular depression' hypothesis. *Arch. Gen. Psychiatry*, 1997, 54, 915-922.

[3] Alexopoulos, GS; Schultz, SK; Lebowitz, BD. Late-Life Depression: A Model for Medical Classification. *Biol. Psychiatry*, 2005 58, 283-289.

[4] Alexopoulos, GS; Kiosses, DN; Heo, M; Murphy, CF; Shanmugham, B; Gunning-Dixon, F. Executive dysfunction and the course of geriatric depression. *Biol. Psychiatry*, 2005, 58, 204-210.

[5] Alexopoulos, GS. The vascular depression hypothesis: 10 years later. *Biol. Psychiatry*, 2006, 60, 1304-1305.

[6] American Psychiatric Association. *Diagnostic and Statistical Manual of Mental Disorders, Fourth Edition.* Washington, DC: American Psychiatric Association; 1994.

[7] Backman, L; Hill, RD; Forsell, Y. The influence of depressive symptomatology on episodic memory functioning among clinically nondepressed older adults. *J. Abnorm. Psychol.*, 1996, 105, 97-105.

[8] Baldwin, RC; Walker, S; Simpson, SW; Jackson, A; Burns, A. The prognostic significance of abnormalities seen on magnetic resonance imaging in late life depression: clinical outcome, mortality and progression to dementia at three years. *Int. J. Geriatr. Psychiatry*, 2000, 15, 1097-1104.

[9] Ballard, CG; O'Brien, JT; Swann, AG; Thompson, P; Neill, D; McKeith, IG. The natural history of psychosis and depression in dementia with Lewy bodies and Alzheimer's disease: persistence and new cases over 1 year of follow-up. *J. Clin. Psychiatry*, 2001, 62, 46-49.

[10] Barnes, DE; Alexopoulos, GS; Lopez, OL; Williamson, JD; Yaffe, K. Depressive Symptoms, Vascular Disease,and Mild Cognitive Impairment. *Arch. Gen. Psychiatry*, 2006, 63, 273-279.

[11] Bassuk, SS; Berkman, LF; Wypij, D. Depressive symptomatology and incident cognitive decline in an elderly community sample. *Arch. Gen. Psychiatry*, 1998, 55, 1073-1081.

[12] Berger, AK; Fratiglioni, L; Forsell, Y; Winblad, B; Backman, L. The occurrence of depressive symptoms in the preclinical phase of AD: a population-based study. *Neurology*, 1999, 53, 1998-2002.

[13] Blazer, DG; Kessler, RC; McGonagle, KA; Swartz, MS. The prevalence and distribution of major depression in a national community sample: the National Comorbidity Survey. *Am. J. Psychiatry*, 1994, 151, 979-986.

[14] Bonelli, RM; Cummings, JL. Frontal-subcortical dementias. *Neurologist*, 2008, 14, 100-107.

[15] Borin, L; Menon, K; Raskin, A; Ruskin, P. Predictors of depression in geriatric medically ill inpatients. *Int. J. Psychiatry Med.*, 2001, 31, 1-8.

[16] Bremner, J; Narayan, M; Anderson, E; Staib, L; Miller, H; Charney, DS. Hippocampal volume reduction in major depression. *Am J Psychiatry*, 2000, 157, 115-118.

[17] Breteler, MMB. Vascular risk factors for Alzheimer's disease: an epidemiologic perspective. *Neurobiol. Aging*, 2000, 21, 153-160.

[18] Buntinx, F; Kester, A; Bergers, J; Knottnerus, JA. Is depression in elderly people followed by dementia: a retrospective cohort study based in general practice. *Age and Ageing*, 1996, 25, 231-233.

[19] Burke, WJ; Wengel, SP. Late-life mood disorders. *Clin. Geriatr. Med.*, 2003, 19, 777-797.

[20] Butters, MA ; Becker, JT; Nebes, RD; Zmuda, MD; Mulsant, BH; Pollock, BG; Reynolds, CF 3rd. Changes in Cognitive Functioning Following Treatment of Late-Life Depression. *Am. J. Psychiatry*, 2000, 157, 1949-1954.

[21] Butters, MA; Whyte, EM; Nebes, RD; Begley, AE; Dew, MA; Mulsant, BH; Zmuda, MD; Bhalla, R; Meltzer, CC; Pollock, BG; Reynolds, CF; Becker, JT. The nature and

determinants of neuropsychological functioning in late-life ldepression. *Arch. Gen. Psychiatry*, 2004, 61, 587-595.

[22] Cervilla, JA; Prince, M; Joels, S; Mann, A. Does depression predict cognitive outcome 9 to 12 years later? Evidence from a prospective study of elderly hypertensives. *Psychol. Med.*, 2000, 30, 1017-1023.

[23] Chan, M; Lim, WS; Sahadevan, S. Stage-independent and stage-specific phenotypic differences between vascular dementia and Alzheimer's Disease. *Dement Geriatr. Cogn. Disord*, 2008, 26, 513-521.

[24] Chen, P; Ganguli, M; Mulstan, BH; DeKosky, ST. The temporal relationship between depressive symptoms and dementia. *Arch. Gen. Psychiatry*, 1999, 56, 261-266.

[25] Chiu, MJ; Chen, TF; Yip, PK; Hua, MS; Tang, LY. Behavioral and psychologic symptoms in different types of dementia. *J. Formos Med. Assoc.*, 2006, 105, 556-562.

[26] Christensen, H; Griffiths, K; MacKinnon, A; Jacomb, P. A quantitative review of cognitive deficits in depression and Alzheimertype dementia. *J. Int. Neuropsychol. Soc.*, 1997, 3, 631-651.

[27] Coffey, CE; Figiel, GS; Djang, WT; Saunders, WB; Weiner, RD. White matter hyperintensity on magnetic resonance imaging: clinical and neuroanatomic correlates in the depressed elderly. *J. Neuropsychiatry Clin. Neurosci.*, 1989, 1, 135-144.

[28] Coffey, CE; Figiel, GS; Djang, WT; Weiner, RD. Subcortical hyperintensity on magnetic resonance imaging: a comparison of normal and depressed elderly subjects. *Am. J. Psychiatry*, 1990, 147, 187-189.

[29] D'Amato, RJ; Zweig, RM; Whitehouse, PJ; Wenk, GL; Singer, HS; Mayeux, R; Price, DL; Snyder, SH. Aminergic systems in Alzheimer's disease and Parkinson's disease. *Ann. Neurol.*, 1987, Aug, 22(2), 229-36.

[30] DeCarli, C. The role of cerebrovascular disease in dementia. *Neurologist*, 2003, 9, 123-136.

[31] de Groot, JC; de Leeuw, FE; Oudkerk, M; Hofman, A; Jolles, J; Breteler, MM. Cerebral white matter lesions and depressive symptoms in elderly adults. *Arch. Gen. Psychiatry*, 2000, 57, 1071-1076.

[32] Devanand, DP; Sano, M; Tang, MX; Taylor, S; Gurland, BJ; Wilder, D; Stern, Y; Mayeux, R. Depressed mood and the incidence of Alzheimer's disease in the elderly living in the community. *Arch. Gen. Psychiatry*, 1996, 53, 175-182.

[33] Drevets, WC. Prefrontal cortical-amygdalar metabolism in major depression. *Ann. N. Y. Acad. Sci.*, 1999, 877, 614-637.

[34] Drevet,s, WC. Neuroimaging abnormalities in the amygdala in mood disorders. *Ann. N. Y. Acad. Sci.*, 2003, 985, 420-444.

[35] Dufouil, C; Fuhrer, R; Dartigues, JF; Alperovitch, A. Longitudinal analysis of the association between depressive symptomatology and cognitive deterioration. *Am. J. Epidemiol.*, 1996, 144, 634-641.

[36] Elderkin-Thompson, V; Kumar, A; Bilker, WB; Dunkin, JJ; Mintz, J; Moberg, PJ; Mesholam, RI; Gur, RE. Neuropsychological deficits among patients with late-onset minor and major depression. *Arch. Clin. Neuropsychol*, 2003, 18, 529-549.

[37] Elderkin-Thompson, V; Mintz, J; Haroon, E; Lavretsky, H; Kumar, A. xecutive dysfunction and memory in older patients with major and minor depression. *Arch. Clin. Neuropsychol.*, 2007, 22, 261-70.

[38] Engelborghs, S; Maertens, K; Nagels, G; Vloeberghs, E; Mariën, P; Symons, A; Ketels, V; Estercam, S; Somers, N; De Deyn, PP. Neuropsychiatric symptoms of dementia: cross-sectional analysis from a prospective , longitudinal Belgian study. *Int. J. Geriatr. Psychiatry*, 2005, 20, 1028-1037.

[39] Figiel, GS; Krishnan, KR; Koraiswamy, PM; Rao, VP; Nemeroff, CB; Boyko, OB. Subcortical hyperintensities on brain magnetic resonance imaging: a comparison between late age onset and early onset elderly depressed subjects. *Neurbiol. Aging*, 1991, 12, 245-247.

[40] Forsell, Y; Jorm, AF; Fratiglioni, L; Grut, M; Winblad, B. Application of DSM-III-R criteria for major depressive episode to elderly subjects with and without dementia. *Am J. Psychiatry*, 1993, 150, 1199-1202.

[41] Forsell, Y; Jorm, AF; Winblad, B. Association of age, sex, cognitive dysfunction, and disability with major depressive symptoms in an elderly sample. *Am. J. Psychiatry*, 1994, 151, 1600-1604.

[42] Frank, C. Dementia with Lewy bodies. Review of diagnosis and pharmacologic management. *Can. Fam. Physician*, 2003, 49, 1304-1311.

[43] Frodl, T; Meisenzahl, E; Zetzsche, T; Born, C; Groll, C; Jager, M. Hippocampal changes in patients with a first episode of major depression. *Am. J. Psychiatry*, 2002, 159, 1112-1118.

[44] Frodl, T; Meisenzahl, EM; Zetzsche, T; Born, C; Jager, M; Groll, C; Bottlender, R; Leinsinger, G; Möller, HJ. Larger amygdala volumes in first depressive episode as compared to recurrent major depression and healthy control subjects. *Biol. Psychiatry*, 2003, 53, 338-344.

[45] Ganguli, M; Du, Y; Dodge, HH; Ratcliff, GG; Chang, CC. Depressive symptoms and cognitive decline in late life. *Arch. Gen. Psychiatry*, 2006, 63, 153-160.

[46] Garcia-Alloza, M; Gil-Bea, FJ; Diez-Ariza, M; Chen, CP; Francis, PT; Lasheras, B; Ramirez, MJ. Cholinergic-serotonergic imbalance contributes to cognitive and behavioral symptoms in Alzheimer's disease. *Neuropsychologia*, 2005, 43(3), 442-449.

[47] Garcia-Alloza, M; Tsang, SW; Gil-Bea, FJ; Francis, PT; Lai, MK; Marcos, B; Chen, CP; Ramirez, MJ. Involvement of the GABAergic system in depressive symptoms of Alzheimer's disease. *Neurobiol. Aging*, 2006, 27, 1110-1117.

[48] Geda, YE; Knopman, DS; Mrazek, DA; Jicha, GA; Smith, GE; Negash, S; Boeve, BF; Ivnik, RJ; Petersen, RC; Pankratz, VS; Rocca, WA. Depression, Apolipoprotein E Genotype, and the Incidence of Mild Cognitive Impairment. *Arch. Neurol.*, 2006, 63, 435-40.

[49] Geerlings, MI; Schoevers, RA; Beekman, AT; Jonker, C; Deeg, DJ; Schmand, B; Ader, HJ; Bouter, LM; Van Tilburg, W. Depression and risk of cognitive decline and Alzheimer's disease: results of two prospective community-based studies in the Netherlands. *Br. J. Psychiatry*, 2000, 176, 568-575.

[50] Green, RC; Cupples, LA; Kurz, A; Auerbach S; Go, R; Sadovnick, D; Duara, R; Kukull, WA; Chui, H; Edeki, T; Griffith, PA; Friedland, RP; Bachman, D; Farrer, L. Depression as a risk factor for Alzheimer disease: the MIRAGE Study. *Arch. Neurol.*, 2003, 60, 753-759.

[51] Greenwald, BS; Kramer-Ginsberg, E; Krishnan, KRR; et al.. MRI signal hyperintensities in geriatric depression. *Am. J. Psychiatry*, 1996, 153, 1212-1215.

[52] Gournellis, R; Lykouras, L; Fortos, A; Oulis, P; Roumbos, V; Christodoulou, GN. Psychotic (delusional) major depression in late life: a clinical study. *Int. J. Geriatr. Psychiatry*, 2001, *16(11)*, 1085-1091.
[53] Hatzinger, M. Neuropeptides and the hypothalamic-pituitary-adrenocortical (HPA) system: review of recent research strategies in depression. *World J. Biol. Psychiatry*, 2000, 1, 105-111.
[54] Henderson, AS; Korten, AE; Jacomb, PA; et al. The course of depression in the elderly: a longitudinal community-based study in Australia. *Psychol. Med.*, 1997, 27, 119-129.
[55] Heun, R; Kockler; M, Ptok, U. Depression in Alzheimer's disease: is there a temporal relationship between the onset of depression and the onset of dementia? *Eur. Psychiatry*, 2002, 17, 254-258.
[56] Hickie, I; Scott, E; Mitchell, P; et al. Subcortical hyperintensities on magnetic resonance imaging: clinical correlates and prognostic significance in patients with severe depression. *Bio. Psychiatry*, 1995, 37, 151-160.
[57] Hodges, JR. Frontotemporal dementia (Pick's disease): clinical features and assessment. *Neurology*, 2001, *56 (suppl4)*, S6-10.
[58] Holtzer, R; Scarmeas, N; Wegesin, DJ; Albert, M; Brandt, J; Dubois, B; Hadjigeorgiou, GM; Stern, Y. Depressive symptoms in Alzheimer's disease: natural course and temporal relation to function and cognitive status. *J. Am. Geriatr. Soc.*, 2005, 53, 2083-2089.
[59] Honig, LS; Kukull, W; Mayeux, R. Atherosclerosis and AD: analysis of data from the US National Alzheimer's Coordinating Center. *Neurology*, 2005, 64, 494-500.
[60] Jenkins, M; Malloy, P; Salloway, S; et al. Memory processes in depressed geriatric patients with and without subcortical hyperintensities on MRI. *J. Neuroimaging*, 1998, 8, 20-26.
[61] Jones, BN; Reifler, BV. Depression coexisting with dementia. Evaluation and treatment. *Med. Clin. North Am.*, 1994, 78, 823.
[62] Jorm, AF. Is depression a risk factor for dementia or cognitive decline? *Gerontology*, 2000, 2000, 219-227.
[63] Kramer-Ginsberg, E; Greenwald, BS; Krishnan, KRR; et al. Neuropsychological functioning and MRI signal hyperintensities in geriatric depression. *Am. J. Psychiatry*, 1999, 156, 438-444.
[64] Koenig, HG; George, LK; Peterson, BL; Pieper, CF. Depression in medically ill hospitalized older adults: prevalence, characteristics, and course of symptoms according to six diagnostic schemes. *Am. J. Psychiatry*, 1997, 154, 1376-1383.
[65] Levy, JA; Chelune, GJ. Cognitive-behavioral profiles of neurodegenerative dementias: beyond Alzheimer's disease. *J. Geriatr. Psychiatry Neurol.*, 2007, 20, 227-238.
[66] Lindsay, J; Laurin, D; Verreault; R, Hébert; R, Helliwell; B, Hill, GB; McDowell, I. Risk Factors for Alzheimer's Disease: A Prospective Analysis from the Canadian Study of Health and Aging. *Am. J. Epidemiol.*, 2002, 156, 445-53.
[67] Lyness, JM; King, DA; Cox, C; Yoediono, Z; Caine, ED. The importance of subsyndromal depression in older primary care patients: prevalence and associated functional disability. *J. Am. Geriatr. Soc.*, 1999, 47, 647-652.
[68] Lyness, JM; Heo, M; Datto, CJ; Ten Have, TR; Katz, IR; Drayer, R; Reynolds, CF 3rd; Alexopoulos, GS; Bruce, ML. Outcomes of minor and subsyndromal depression among elderly patients in primary care settings. *Ann. Intern. Med.*, 2006, 144, 496-504.

[69] King, DA; Cox, C; Lyness, JM; Conwell, Y; Caine, ED. Quantitative and qualitative differences in the verbal learning performance of elderly epressives and healthy controls. *J. Int. Neuropsychol. Soc.*, 1998, 4, 115-126.

[70] Krishnan, KR; Hays, JC; Blazer, DG. MRI-defined vascular depression. *Am. J. Psychiatry*, 1997, 154, 497-501.

[71] Launer, LJ. Demonstrating the case that AD is a vascular disease: epidemiologic evidence. *Ageing Res. Rev.*, 2002, 1, 61-77.

[72] Lesser, IM; Boone, KB; Mehringer, CM. Cognition and white matter hyperintensities in older depressed patients. *Am. J. Psychiatry*, 1996, 153, 1280-1287.

[73] Lockwood, KA; Alexopoulos, GS; Kakuma, T; Van Gorp, WG. Subtypes of cognitive impairment in depressed older adults. *Am. J. Geriatr. Psychiatry*, 2000, 8, 201-208.

[74] Lövheim, H; Sandman, PO; Karlsson, S; Gustafson, Y. Behavioral and psychological symptoms of dementia in relation to level of cognitive impairment. *Int. Psychogeriatr*, 2008, 20, 777-789.

[75] Lyketsos, CG; Lopez, O; Jones, B; Fitzpatrick, AL; Breitner, J; DeKosky, S. Prevalence of neuropsychiatric symptoms in dementia and mild cognitive impairment: results from the Cardiovascular Health Study. *JAMA*, 2002, 288, 1475- 1483.

[76] Lyketsos, CG; Olin, J. Depression in Alzheimer's disease: overview and treatment. *Biol. Psychiatry*, 2002, 52, 243.

[77] MacQueen, GM; Campell, S; McEwen, BS; Macdonald,, K; Amano, S; Joffe, RT; et al. Course of illness, hippocampal function and hippocampal volume in major depression. *Proc. Natl. Acad. Sci., USA*, 2003, 100, 1387-1392.

[78] Miller, DB; O'Callaghan, JP. Effects of aging and stress on hippocampal structure and function. Metabolism, *2003*, 52, 17-21.

[79] Modrego, PJ; Ferrandez, J. Depression in patients with mild cognitive impairment increases the risk of developing dementia of Alzheimer type: a prospective cohort study. *Arch. Neurol.*, 2004, 61, 1290.

[80] Nebes, RD; Butters, MA; Houck, PR; Zmuda, MD; Aizenstein, HJ; Pollock, BG; Mulsant, BH; Reynolds, CF. Dual-task performance in depressed geriatric patients. *Psychiatry Res.*, 2001, 102, 139-151.

[81] Nebes, RD; Reynolds, CF; Boada, F; Meltzer, CC; Fukui, MB; Saxton, J; Halligan, EM; DeKosky, ST. Longitudinal increase in the volume of white matter Hyperintensities in late-onset depression. *Int. J. Geriatr. Psychiatry*, 2002, 17, 526-530.

[82] Nebes, RD; Butters, MA; Mulsant, BH; Nebes, RD; Butters, MA; Mulsant, BH; Pollock, BG; Zmuda, MD; Houck, PR; Reynolds, CF 3rd. Decreased working memory and processing speed mediate cognitive impairment in geriatric depression. *Psychol. Med.*, 2000, 30, 679-691.

[83] Olin, JT; Schneider, LS; Katz, IR; Alexopoulos, GS; Breitner, JC; Bruce, ML; Caine, ED; Cummings, JL; Devanand, DP; Krishnan, KR; Lyketsos, CG; Lyness, JM; Rabins, PV; Reynolds, CF III; Rovner, BW; Steffens, DC; Tariot, PN; Lebowitz, BD. Provisional diagnostic criteria for depression of Alzheimer's disease. *Am. J. Geriatr. Psychiatry*, 2002, 10, 125-128.

[84] Palsson, S; Skoog, I. The epidemiology of affective disorders in the elderly: a review. *Int. Clin. Psychopharmacol.*, 1997, 12(suppl 2), S3-S13.

[85] Pugh, KG; Lipsitz, LA. The microvascular frontal-subcortical syndrome of aging. *Neurobiol. Aging*, 2002, 23, 421-31.

[86] Rabins, PV; Pearlson, GD; Aylward, E; et al. Cortical magnetic resonance imaging changes in elderly inpatients with major depression. *Am. J. Psychiatry*, 1991, 148, 617-620.

[87] Rao, R. Cerebrovascular disease and late life depression: an age old association revisited. *Int. J. Geriatr. Psychiatry*, 2000, 15, 419-433.

[88] Rapp, MA; Dahlman, K; Sano, M; Grossman, HT; Haroutunian, V; Gorman, JM. Neuropsychological differences between late-onset and recurrent geriatric major depression. *Am. J. Psychiatry*, 2005, 162, 691-698.

[89] Reid, LM; Maclullich, AM. Subjective memory complaints and cognitive impairment in older people. *Dement Geriatr. Cogn. Disord*, 2006, 22, 471-85.

[90] Ritchie, K; Gilham, C; Ledésert, B; et al. Depressive illness, depressive symptomatology and regional cerebral blood flow in elderly people with sub-clinical cognitive impairment. *Age and Ageing*, 1999, 28, 385-391.

[91] Rockwell, E; Choure, J; Galasko, DR; Olichney, J; Jeste, DV. Psychopathology at initial diagnosis in dementia with Lewy bodies versus Alzheimer disease: comparison of matched groups with autopsy-confi rmed diagnoses. *Int. J. Geriatr. Psychiatry*, 2000, 15, 819-823.

[92] Robert, PH; Berr, C; Volteau, M; et al. Apathy in patients with mild cognitive impairment and the risk of developing dementia of Alzheimer's disease: a one-year follow-up study. *Clin. Neurol. Neurosurg*, 2006, 108,733-736.

[93] Robinson, RG. Poststroke depression: prevalence, diagnosis, treatment, and disease progression. *Biol. Psychiatry*, 2003, 54, 376-387.

[94] Roriz-Cruz, M; Rosset, I; Wada, T; Sakagami, T; Ishine, M; De Sá Roriz-Filho, J; Cruz, TR; Hosseinkhani, M; Rodrigues, RP; Sudoh, S; Arai, H; Wakatsuki, Y; Souza, AC; Nakagawa, M; Kita, T; Matsubayashi, K. Cognitive impairment and frontal-subcortical geriatric syndrome are associated with metabolic syndrome in a stroke-free population. *Neurobiol of Aging*, 2007, 28, 1723-1736.

[95] Roriz-Cruz, M; Rosset, I; Matsubayashi, K; et al. Association Between Cognitive Impairment and Depression in late-Life is partially attributable to Metabolic Syndrome. Alzheimer's and Dementia, 2008, 4(S2), T 269.

[96] Rubinow, D; Post, RM; Savard, R; Gold, PW. Cortisol hypersecretion and cognitive impairment in depression. *Arch. Gen. Psychiatry*, 1984, 41, 279-283.

[97] Salloway, S; Malloy, P; Kohn, R; Gillard, E; Duffy, J; Rogg, J; Tung, G; Richardson, E; Thomas, C; Westlake, R. MRI and neuropsychological differences in early- and late-life-onset geriatric depression. *Neurology*, 1996, 46, 1567-1574.

[98] Sheline, Y; Gado, M; Price, J. Amygdala core nuclei volumes are decreased in recurrent major depression. *Neuroreport*, 1998, 9, 2023-2028.

[99] Snowden, JS; Neary, D; Mann, DM. Frontotemporal dementia. *British J. Psychiatry*, 2002, 180, 140-143.

[100] Steffens, DC; Helms, MJ; Krishnan, KR; Burke, GL. Cerebrovascular disease and depression symptoms in the cardiovascular health study. *Stroke*, 1999, 30, 2159-2166.

[101] Steffens, D; Skoog, I; Norton, M; Hart, A; Tschanz, JA; Plassman, B; Wyse, B; Welsh-Bohmer, K; Breitner, JCS. Prevalence of Depression and Its Treatment in an Elderly Population: The Cache County Study. *Arch. Gen. Psychiatry*, 2000, 57, 601-607.

[102] Steffens, DC; Krishnan, KR; Crump, C; Burke GL. Cerebrovascular disease and evolution of depressive symptoms in the Cardiovascular Health Study. *Stroke*, 2002, 33, 1636-1644.

[103] Steffens, DC; Otey, E; Alexopoulos, GS; Butters, MA; Cuthbert, B; Ganguli, M; Geda, YE; Hendrie, HC; Krishnan, RR; Kumar, A; Lopez, OL; Lyketsos, CG; Mast, BT; Morris, JC; Norton, MC; Peavy, GM; Petersen, RC; Reynolds, CF; Salloway, S; Welsh-Bohmer, KA; Yesavage, J. Perspectives on Depression, Mild Cognitive Impairment, and Cognitive Decline. *Arch. Gen. Psychiatry*, 2006, 63, 130-138.

[104] Sultzer, DL; Mahler, ME; Cummings, J; et al. Cortical abnormalities associated with subcortical lesions in vascular dementia: clinical and positron emission tomographic findings. *Arch. Neurol.*, 1995, 52, 773-780.

[105] Thomas, AJ; Perry, R; Barber, R; Kalaria, RN; O'Brien, JT. Pathologies and pathological mechanisms for white matter hyperintensities in depression. *Ann. N. Y. Acad. Sci.*, 2002, 977, 333-339.

[106] Thomas, AJ; O'Brien, JT. Depression and cogntion in older adults. *Current Opinion Psychiatry*, 2008, 21, 8-13.

[107] Verkaik, R; Nuyen, J; Schellevis, F; Francke A. The relationship between severity of Alzheimer's disease and prevalence of comorbid depressive symptoms and depression: a systematic review. *Int. J. Geriatr. Psychiatry*, 2007, 22, 1063-1086.

[108] Vermeer, SE; Prins, ND; den Heijer, T; Hofman, A; Koudstaal, PJ; Breteler, MM. Silent brain infarcts and the risk of dementia and cognitive decline. *N. Engl. J. Med.*, 2003, 348, 1215-1222.

[109] Vinkers, DJ; Gussekloo, J; Stek, ML; Westendorp, RG; van der Mast, RC. Temporal relation between depression and cognitive impairment in old age: prospective population based study. *BMJ*, 2004 329-881.

[110] Wilson, RS; Barnes, LL; Mendes de Leon, CF; Aggarwal, NT; Schneider, JS; Bach, J; Pilat, J; Beckett, LA; Arnold, SE; Evans, DA; Bennett, DA. Depressive symptoms, cognitive decline, and risk of AD in older persons. *Neurology*, 2002, 59, 364-370.

[111] Wilson, RS; Mendes De Leon, CF; Bennett, DA; Bienias, JL; Evans, DA. Depressive symptoms and cognitive decline in a community population of older persons. *J. Neurol. Neurosurg. Psychiatry*, 2004, 75, 126-129.

[112] Wright, SL; Persad, C. Distinguishing Between Depression and Dementia in Older Persons: Neuropsychological and Neuropathological Correlates. *J. Geriatr. Psychiatry Neurol.*, 2007, 20, 189-198.

[113] Yaffe, K; Blackwell, T; Gore, R; Sands, L; Reus, V; Browner, WS. Depressive symptoms and cognitive decline in nondemented elderly women: a prospective study. *Arch. Gen. Psychiatry*, 1999, 56, 425-430.

INDEX

B

C

D

E

M

N

Q

R

S

W

Y